CREATING IN-HOUSE SALES TRAINING AND DEVELOPMENT PROGRAMS

CREATING IN-HOUSE SALES TRAINING AND DEVELOPMENT PROGRAMS

A Competency-Based Approach to Building Sales Ability

William J. Rothwell,
Wesley E. Donahue,
and John E. Park

Q

QUORUM BOOKS
Westport, Connecticut • London

Library of Congress Cataloging-in-Publication Data

Rothwell, William J., 1951–
    Creating in-house sales training and development programs : a competency-based
approach to building sales ability / William J. Rothwell, Wesley E. Donahue, and John E. Park.
        p.   cm.
    Includes bibliographical references and index.
    ISBN 1–56720–465–1 (alk. paper)
    1.   Sales personnel—Training of.   2. Sales management.   3. Employees—Training of. I.
Donahue, Wesley E., 1950–   II. Park, John E., 1956–   III. Title.
    HF5439.8 .R68   2002
    658.3′1245—dc21   2002067913

British Library Cataloguing in Publication Data is available.

Library of Congress Catalog Card Number: 2002067913
ISBN: 1–56720–465–1

First published in 2002

Quorum Books, 88 Post Road West, Westport, CT 06881
An imprint of Greenwood Publishing Group, Inc.
www.quorumbooks.com

Printed in the United States of America

The paper used in this book complies with the
Permanent Paper Standard issued by the National
Information Standards Organization (Z39.48–1984).

P

Copyright Acknowledgments

The authors and publisher gratefully acknowledge permisson for use of the following material:

SALES & MARKETING MANAGEMENT by HARRIS, E. Copyright 2000 by V N U BUS
PUBNS USA. Reproduced with permission of V N U BUS PUBNS USA in the format Other
Book via Copyright Clearance Center.

SALES & MARKETING MANAGEMENT by KAHN, R. Copyright 1997 by V N U BUS
PUBNS USA. Reproduced with permission of V N U BUS PUBNS USA in the format Other
Book via Copyright Clearance Center.

SALES & MARKETING MANAGEMENT by MENDOZA, R. Copyright 1995 by V N U
BUS PUBNS USA. Reproduced with permission of V N U BUS PUBNS USA in the format
Other Book via Copyright Clearance Center.

William J. Rothwell dedicates this book to his wife Marcelina Rothwell and his daughter Candice Rothwell. Without their loving support, this book would never have been written.

Wesley E. Donahue dedicates this book to his family. Heartfelt appreciation goes to his loving and supportive wife Lisa, their son Marc, and twins Alex and Alyssa. Their patience, encouragement, and insights made this book possible.
To sales professionals everywhere, this book is the result of contributions from numerous experts in the field of sales, however your family is your best source of guidance, inspiration, and the true key to success.

John E. Park would like to thank his wife Valerie and their children Amie, Sarah, and Stephen, for their support, patience, and encouragement during the early morning and late night writing sessions they had to endure as this book went through its many changes and revisions.

Contents

Figures

Preface

Sales professionals play a key role in generating revenue for their organizations, and without that revenue their organizations would soon be out of business. Sales professionals dramatically affect the lives of everyone in their organizations and provide a key link between their organizations and clients. Recognizing their importance, forward-thinking decision makers sponsor planned, in-house training and development efforts for sales professionals in their organizations to maximize sales effectiveness and thereby increase sales revenue. And, indeed, "training has been cited as the most often used intervention to improve sales productivity" (Erffmeyer, Russ & Hair, 1991, p. 17). And yet several authors have decried the generally poor quality of sales training programs sponsored by organizations (see Erffmeyer, Russ, & Hair, 1991; Kerr & Burzynski, 1988).

There is a shortage of trained sales professionals and practical training and development programs that are intended to help them. Many sales professionals are ill-equipped to represent their organizations in a world that is increasingly characterized by e-commerce. New sales professionals need training and development in both the basic fundamentals of sales and the realities of the new world that is dominated by e-commerce.

Globalization . . . constant organizational change, mergers and realignment . . . cost containment and limited resources . . . employee turnover and retention issues . . . information technology revolution. . . . These words and phrases, like magical incantations, present potentially awesome challenges to anyone who contemplates enacting a sales leadership role. By examining the sales essentials and the lessons learned from experience by other sales professionals in the field, those who assume sales management responsibilities can better prepare for their organizational roles and avoid the pitfalls others have experienced. What is needed is an examination of the core competency dimensions of effective sales professionals and a collection of experiences from which the lessons learned from other sales professionals may be extracted and anchored to a framework for the systematic training and development of sales professionals. Such a competency-based framework can serve as a roadmap for creating in-house sales training and development programs for business owners, sales managers, or human resource professionals who are charged with the responsibility for building in-house sales capabilities.

THE PURPOSE OF THIS BOOK

How should organizations manage the training and development of their sales professionals? This book is intended to answer this question. It is intended to furnish sales managers with ideas to build the competencies of sales professionals at all levels. It is also intended to shed light on how diverse organizations are addressing this important issue.

Numerous books have been written about selling and sales. But little detailed research has been conducted on sales training practices (however, see Fresina & Associates, 1988; also Coker, Del Gaizo, Murray, & Edwards, 2000). Nor do many recent books offer detailed guidance on how to design, deliver, and evaluate in-house training and development programs for sales professionals, although some books have been written over the years to do just that (see Asherman & Asherman, 1992; Blake & McKee, 1994; Craig & Kelly, 1989; Higgins, 1993; McLaughlin, 1982; Magee, 2001; "Sales training basics," 1993; Salisbury, 1998; Stolz, Majors, & Soares, 1994; Zoltners, Sinha, & Zoltners, 2001). Yet not one of these books focuses on building *competencies*, understood to mean the characteristics linked to successful performers (Rothwell & Lindholm, 1999), by describing real-world sales experiences and offering action-oriented sales tips. But this book does that. Consequently, this book should prove to be useful to sales managers, human resource professionals, business owners, and educational providers who are responsible for the orientation, training, and continuing education of sales professionals.

DEFINITIONS OF IMPORTANT TERMS

Since people can become confused by terms, allow us to spend a moment on that. For purposes of this book, a sales professional is anyone who provides direct service to the organization's clients. Hence, sales professionals may include sales, customer service, and client relationship professionals and may also include (in small organizations) business owners and (in government agencies) relationship managers. According to the U.S. Bureau of Labor Statistics (see http://ftp.bls.gov/pub/special.requests/ep/indp-occ.matrix/MLRTabs2.tx), marketing and sales occupations include the following:

- Cashiers
- Counter and retail clerks
- Insurance sales agents
- Marketing and sales worker supervisors
- Models, demonstrators, and product promoters
- Parts salespersons
- Real estate agents and brokers
- Retail salespersons
- Sales engineers
- Securities, commodities, and financial service sales agents
- Travel agents
- All other sales and related workers

About 15,341,000 people were employed in these categories of the U.S. workforce in 1998, and about 17,627,000 people are expected to be employed in these categories by 2008. That means the expected increase is approximately 10.9 percent (http://ftp.bls.gov/pub/special.requests/ep/indp-occ.matrix/MLRTabs2.tx).

Sales training is the process of providing useful information and building essential skills necessary to help clients and increase sales. Sales development is the process of helping sales professionals maintain their skills as conditions change in a dynamic business environment. The client is the individual or organization who benefits from the services of sales professionals.

SOURCES OF INFORMATION FOR THIS BOOK

As we began to write this book, we decided to base it on practical research about the best sales-training practices. To that end, we consulted several major sources of information:

1. *A customized survey.* As an initial step in researching this book, the authors surveyed sales professionals in year 2001 about training and development practices in their organizations. The survey results are published in this book for the first time.

2. *Personal interviews.* To provide a richer description of the challenges faced by sales professionals and those who manage them, we conducted many personal interviews. The information we gained from those interviews has been distilled and is reported throughout the book in examples and critical situations. The criti-

cal situations in the book are often told in the exact words of the respondents who agreed to be interviewed.

3. *Focus groups.* To reach a deeper understanding of the coaching and mentoring challenges faced by those who supervise sales professionals and to find out how those challenges are met, we conducted a series of focus groups. The results of these focus groups appear throughout this book.

4. *A literature search.* We conducted a literature search on sales training and development practices over the last twenty years. We provide key references to those sources so you can delve deeper into issues of special interest to you.

5. *Personal experience.* The authors of this book have extensive sales and consulting experience in diverse industries and cultures. Many of our personal experiences are reflected in this book.

ABOUT THE SURVEY AND ITS RESULTS APPEARING IN THIS BOOK

How are organizations handling the in-house training and development of their sales professionals? To answer that question, the authors prepared a survey and mailed it to 350 sales professionals selected from listed members of a sales and marketing organization. Sixty-six sales professionals responded to the survey, making for a 19-percent response rate to the survey. Although this response rate was disappointing, the authors supplemented the results with personal interviews and focus groups. Taken together, the results of the survey, interviews, and focus groups provide useful information about sales training and development practices. The findings and conclusions should furnish new ideas about ways to build the competencies of sales professionals.

The survey respondents represented a cross section of different industries. They also represented organizations that ranged in size from large to small. Figure P.1 summarizes the industries represented by the respondents to our survey. Figure P.2 summarizes the size of the organizations employing our survey respondents. Note that the category "Other Services," shown in the figures, included such diverse respondents as those from chemical distribution, technology sales, and medical sales.

Most survey respondents reported their job titles as sales executive or manager, as indicated in the breakdown of survey respondent job titles shown in Figure P.3. Other titles most often reported included president, owner, CEO, COO, vice president, and sales training executive.

THE AUDIENCE FOR THIS BOOK

This book is designed to meet the needs of sales executives, sales managers, sales leaders, human resource professionals, business owners, and others who wish to build the competencies of sales professionals in their organiza-

Figure P.1
Percentage of Survey Respondents by Industry Classifications

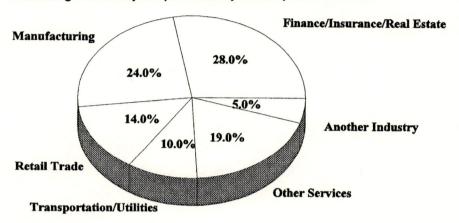

Source: From *A Survey about Sales Training Programs* by W. Rothwell, W. Donahue, and J. Park, 2001 (unpublished survey results), University Park, PA: Pennsylvania State University. Copyright 2001 by W. Rothwell, W. Donahue, and J. Park.

Figure P.2
Percentage of Survey Respondents by Organization Size

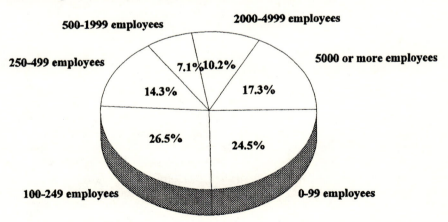

Source: From *A Survey about Sales Training Programs* by W. Rothwell, W. Donahue, and J. Park, 2001 (unpublished survey results), University Park, PA: Pennsylvania State University. Copyright 2001 by W. Rothwell, W. Donahue, and J. Park.

Figure P.3
Percentage of Survey Respondents by Job Title*

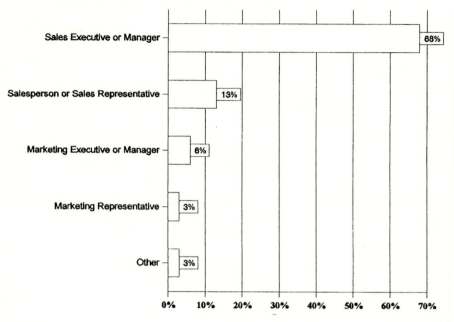

Source: From *A Survey about Sales Training Programs* by W. Rothwell, W. Donahue, and J. Park, 2001 (unpublished survey results), University Park, PA: Pennsylvania State University. Copyright 2001 by W. Rothwell, W. Donahue, and J. Park.

*Title not specified in 7 percent of cases.

tions using a systematic approach. However, as we wrote this book, we kept front-line sales managers foremost in mind, since they are often the people who oversee the training and development of sales professionals on a daily basis. This book is meant to be a valuable resource to them and to others, such as human resource management and human resource development professionals, who are looking for a resource to help them establish a planned, systematic approach to in-house sales training and development programs. This book may also be useful as a supplementary text to bridge theory and practice for faculty members teaching in university and community college-based sales development programs.

THE ORGANIZATIONAL SCHEME OF THIS BOOK

The book is divided into four parts, and each part consists of four chapters (see Figure P.4). Part I examines ways of creating in-house sales training and development programs. Chapter 1 focuses on defining sales staff roles and

Figure P.4
Process Map: Creating In-House Sales Training and Development Programs

I. ⋅ **Essentials of Creating In-House Sales Training and Development Programs**

1. Defining Sales Staff Roles and Functions	2. Identifying Staff Training Needs and Designing Curricula	3. Planning Learning and Development Opportunities	4. Leading and Evaluating an In-House Sales Training and Development Program

Competency Development Framework for Sales Professionals

II. **Knowledge of Self**

5. Enhancing Interpersonal Selling Skills and Self-Development	6. Managing Client Communications	7. Enhancing Negotiation and Influencing Skills	8. Resolving Sales and Interpersonal Conflicts and Coping with Change

III. **Knowledge of Products and Services**

9. Establishing Ongoing Client and Stakeholder Information Processes	10. Identifying and Communicating Product Features and Benefits	11. Establishing and Maintaining a Competitive Analysis Process	12. Linking Sales and Marketing Strategies

IV. **Knowledge of Clients and Business**

13. Forecasting, Planning, and Prospecting for Clients	14. Managing Calls, Time, and Sales Territory	15. Providing Service and Managing Client Relationships	16. Developing New Products and Services and Managing Projects

functions, an essential starting point for establishing an effective in-house sales training and development program. Chapter 2 explains how to identify staff training needs and design curricula. Chapter 3 summarizes ways of planning learning and development opportunities, and Chapter 4 reviews key success factors that are essential to leading and evaluating an in-house sales training and development program.

Part II focuses on the core competency of Knowledge of Self. Each chapter in Parts II, III, and IV has a parallel organizational scheme. Each chapter opens with a description of a competency that is essential to successful sales. Then, readers are invited to self-assess their organizations against key questions that are related to those competencies. The chapter is then organized around those key questions.

Chapter 5, the first in Part II, explains how to demonstrate and build the competency of enhancing interpersonal selling skills and self-development. Chapter 6 explains how to demonstrate and build the competency of managing client communications. Chapter 7 explains the competency of enhancing negotiating and influencing skills, and Chapter 8 explains the competency of resolving sales and interpersonal conflicts and coping with change.

Part III focuses on the core competency of Knowledge of Products and Services. Chapter 9 explains the competency of establishing ongoing client and stakeholder informational processes, while Chapter 10 explains how to demonstrate and build the competency of identifying and communicating product features and benefits. Chapters 11 and 12 provide details on how to demonstrate and build the competencies of establishing and maintaining a competitive analysis process, and linking sales and marketing strategies, respectively.

Part IV focuses on the core competency of Knowledge of Clients and Business. Chapter 13 covers the competency of forecasting, planning, and prospecting for clients. Chapter 14 focuses on the competency of managing calls, time, and sales territory. Chapter 15 explains how to demonstrate and build the competency of providing service and managing client relationships. And Chapter 16—the final chapter in the book—explains the competency of developing new products and services and managing projects.

There are three Appendixes at the back of the book. Appendix A supplies an example of a customized job profile of a client development manager. Appendix B supplies a written questionnaire that may be of use in assessing sales training needs. Finally, Appendix C consolidates all the action tips found throughout the book, and it is a useful job aid to supplement the hands-on training of sales professionals.

If you are just now beginning to think about establishing an in-house sales training and development program, the task may seem to be daunting. Moreover, dealing with the development of your sales organization may be a key part of your job if you are to be successful in achieving an enviable track record of sales in your organization. Consider such important questions as these: Are your sales professionals serving your clients in the most effective ways? Are they producing needed business results? Are they prepared for the challenges ahead?

To help you organize your thinking, begin by completing the sixteen-item self-assessment that appears in Figure P.5. Each item corresponds to a chapter in this book. By pinpointing your areas of greatest need, you may be able to focus your attention directly on the most relevant chapters. Alternatively, you may wish to read the entire book to provide a framework for designing and delivering competency-based sales training programs in your organization that get results.

As you begin your efforts, allow us to take this opportunity to wish you success in your venture.

Figure P.5
Self-Assessment: Program Development Needs of Sales Professionals

Directions: Read each question carefully. With your sales organization in mind, please rate your level of agreement with each of the sixteen statements. Assume for purposes of this survey that the definition of sales professional includes all sales, customer service and client relationship related personnel. Each statement of this self-assessment relates and corresponds to a chapter of this book. **Use the scale from 1 to 5, where 1 = Disagree; to 5 = Agree.**

Disagree 1	2	3	4	Agree 5		Statements
Essentials of Creating In-House Sales Training and Development Programs						
1	2	3	4	5	1	The roles and functions of all of our sales professionals are well defined.
1	2	3	4	5	2	The training and development needs of our sales professionals have been identified.
1	2	3	4	5	3	Learning and development opportunities for our sales professionals have been identified.
1	2	3	4	5	4	We evaluate the effectiveness of our in-house sales development efforts.
Knowledge of Self						
1	2	3	4	5	5	Individuals in our sales organization possess excellent personal selling skills.
1	2	3	4	5	6	Our organization effectively plans and manages client communications.
1	2	3	4	5	7	Our sales professionals know how to effectively negotiate and influence others.
1	2	3	4	5	8	Everyone in our sales organization attempts to resolve conflicts in a constructive manner.
Knowledge of Products and Services						
1	2	3	4	5	9	Individuals in our sales organization understand our operational processes.
1	2	3	4	5	10	Individuals in our sales organization know the features and benefits of our products.
1	2	3	4	5	11	Our sales professionals know how to obtain competitor information.
1	2	3	4	5	12	Sales professionals in our organization know the best methods of promoting our products.

Figure P.5 (*continued*)

Knowledge of Clients and Business						
1	2	3	4	5	13	Individuals in our sales organization know how to prospect, network, and prioritize clients.
1	2	3	4	5	14	Individuals in our sales organization work toward goals and manage resources efficiently.
1	2	3	4	5	15	Sales professionals in our organization actively seek to improve our products.
1	2	3	4	5	16	Our sales professionals actively pursue innovative solutions for developing new business.
					☜ **Total Your Score**	

Scoring

How did you score? How did you rate the development efforts of sales professionals in your organization?

Score	Interpretation and Comments
71-80	Give your organization a big hand! Keep doing what you are doing.
61-70	By using some of the tips in this book, you will be on your way to the top.
51-60	A handshake will do, but there's room for improvement.
0 - 50	Your organization will benefit from reading and applying the tips in this book.

Acknowledgments

If we have learned nothing else in the process of writing this book, we have learned that writing any book is more difficult than it appears to be. To be effective in this process, teamwork is essential. That is especially true when three coauthors undertake the task.

But few people write a book alone. Help is always needed. This is our chance to offer thanks for those who contributed to this effort. Accordingly, we wish to express our thanks to the following: Ralph Oliva, director of the Institute for the Study of Business Markets, Smeal College of Business, Pennsylvania State University, University Park, Pennsylvania, for his willingness to review the manuscript and offer suggestions for improvements; Xeujun Qiao, research assistant of William Rothwell, who tracked down many articles, books, and other sources to add to the reference list of this book; and the many sales professionals who participated in our survey, our focus groups, and our interviews. Without the examples they provided, this book would suffer from less richness of real-world detail. To these people, we owe a debt of gratitude.

ESSENTIALS OF CREATING IN-HOUSE SALES TRAINING AND DEVELOPMENT PROGRAMS

The following four chapters describe a systematic process intended to guide the design and delivery of in-house sales training and development programs to build the competencies of sales professionals. These chapters introduce the critical success factors for a program, summarize the potential barriers to such a program, and offer suggestions for overcoming those barriers.

1

Defining Sales Staff Roles and Functions

The playing field for businesses is changing with blurring speed. Sales roles and responsibilities are taking on new shapes. However, few observers of the contemporary business scene dispute that the importance of sales is enormous. A key starting point for thinking about managing the sales function is to define sales staff roles and functions and align them with the organization's vision, mission, and goals.

Defining sales staff roles and functions means that sales professionals

- understand and establish the scope of sales activities, goals, policies, guidelines, plans, and priorities.
- define specific staff roles and functions.
- outline needed competencies of specific sales positions.

This chapter focuses on the process of defining sales staff roles and functions as a starting point for designing and delivering in-house sales training and development programs.

To organize your thinking, begin by rating your perceptions using the following self-assessment. As you rate each statement in the self-assessment, be sure to think about your organization as it exists today.

Self-Assessment: Defining Sales Staff Roles and Functions

Directions: Read each statement carefully. With your sales organization in mind, place the number in the left column that best fits with your level of agreement with each statement.

Disagree   Agree
1   2   3   4   5   6   7   8   9   10

____Your organization has established sales policies and guidelines aligned with your organization's overall vision, mission, and goals.

____Specific sales staff positions are adequately defined.

____The specific roles and functions are documented with written sales staff position descriptions.

____Your organization has adequately identified needed skills, behaviors, and competencies for each sales staff position.

____You are confident that your sales organization clearly understands the challenges facing today's sales professionals.

____You understand the depth and breadth of what is needed to develop a planned approach to develop sales professionals.

____Your organization's leadership has an appreciation for the reasons why organizations sponsor education and training.

____Your organization has identified major trends affecting the development of sales talent.

____Your organization has considered the types of activities that make up a planned in-house approach for sales training.

____You know who has the ultimate responsibility for establishing education and training policies for sales professionals in your organization.

____Total

How Did You Score?

Here is the key to defining sales staff roles and functions. Add up your responses to get your score.

91–100   Great job! Congratulations! Your organization is effectively working to define sales staff roles and functions.

81–90   Keep up the good work! You've probably had considerable success. But by using some of the tips in this chapter, you could improve your success.

71–80   Help is needed! There is room for improvement. You'll find this chapter helpful.

0–70   Warning! Your sales organization probably has some confusion. Read on!

Each statement appearing in the self-assessment will be addressed in a section of this chapter. This format will be used throughout the book to encourage you to think about ways to apply the information presented in this book in your organization. You may also want to use the open-ended worksheet to guide your thinking on the issue.

A Worksheet for Organizing Your Thoughts about Defining Sales Staff Roles and Functions

Directions: Use this worksheet to organize your thinking. Think about how to answer this question: What thoughts do you have about defining sales staff roles and functions in your organization? Use the space that follows to record your thoughts.

Notes:

Abraham Lincoln is reputed to have said that "I don't think much of a man who is not wiser today than he was yesterday." While the meaning of this quote still holds true today, many sales professionals will admit that finding the time to keep their knowledge and skills current is difficult. To do that, they must juggle such competing tasks as servicing their existing clients, cultivating new clients, staying on top of paperwork, and answering a daily avalanche of e-mails.

HAS YOUR ORGANIZATION ESTABLISHED SALES POLICIES AND GUIDELINES ALIGNED WITH ITS VISION, MISSION, AND GOALS?

Developing a selling system that provides a framework for how new sales professionals go about creating, developing, and managing client relationships can be a critical first step in building a successful sales development program. Empowering sales professionals to make decisions regarding pricing, financing, or product delivery, for example, within a set of guidelines aligned with your organization's vision, mission, and goals can enhance their position with clients and their sense of ownership in the success of the business. However, policies and procedures, if regarded as needless red tape, can quickly become an impediment or even a demotivator to sales professionals who in many organizations have historically been encouraged to be entrepreneurial and to push the limits. The following situation makes this point dramatically and illustrates some key points for the development of sales professionals.

Clarifying Policies and Procedures: "Sending Mixed Messages"

Situation: In my organization we send mixed messages. My primary responsibility as international client manager is to create consultative long-term relationships with clients, which means I need to spend face-to-face time with them. But on the other hand every time I fill out an expense account for a dinner with a client it seems they (the accounting office) require more documentation and evidence than the time before.

Now they want itemized food bills or they won't reimburse, and to complicate matters our organization has a policy of not paying for alcohol. Therefore, I end up eating hundreds of dollars per year out of my own pocket. Sometimes it just doesn't seem worth all the effort and administrative trivia to take someone out for lunch or dinner. On a number of occasions I've had heated discussions and had to spend days trying to get an itemized menu or bills from a restaurant, which in some cases don't issue them, or because I forgot to ask for one upon paying. To make things worse, my expense checks have at times been held up for weeks. Quite frankly, I'm ready to quit and go somewhere that values my sales abilities.

Development Issues: Obviously, in this organization the roles and functions of sales professionals need to be clarified. So, too, do the organization's policies and procedures. A balance between selling and administrative activities is a necessity. In this situation, the sales executive in charge must take action. Otherwise, the executive may lose a good client manager as well as create hostility with the organization's accountants, who are only trying to do their jobs by ensuring that employees follow the organization's policies.

Action Tips:

- Document and communicate the organization's sales vision, mission, and goals.
- Clarify and document the roles, responsibilities, and expectations of sales professionals.
- Ask your sales staff what organizational policies and procedures get in the way of serving their customers and clients and then set priorities.
- Review or flowchart business processes that are causing problems, and then consider how to streamline them.
- Hold annual training sessions with your sales staff conducted by appropriate members of your support functions—such as accounting, finance, operations—to discuss policies and clarify requirements.
- Document and communicate accepted methods and procedures.

When sales staff in your organization perceive that compliance with policies or procedures is more important than generating new revenue or making a profit, it is time to become concerned. These are symptoms of a potential problem. Policies and procedures provide structure to an organization, keep it in compliance with legal and accounting requirements, and eliminate the need for employees to go to their managers for every decision. However, when sales executives sense that sales professionals are conflicted between making sales and following policy, then it is time to investigate the causes of these problems.

ARE YOUR SALES POSITIONS ADEQUATELY DEFINED?

Role ambiguity can be a major source of stress in organizations. Unclear job assignments can lead to errors and poor customer service. Just like a great baseball or basketball team where every team member understands his or her role and the contribution he or she makes to the team, effective sales organizations create an organizational structure intended to support the sales team and allow them to focus on managing client relationships and generating sales.

Sales professionals can better manage their time and focus on new client development activities when they have a clear understanding of when a client should be handed off to a client support representative. For example, clear communication with client support on the status of the production and delivery of an order in a production environment can reduce or eliminate client calls. As a starting point, you should develop and communicate position descriptions for the sales roles and functions in your organization. A sample position description format is illustrated thus:

A Sample Position Description Format

Position	_____
Person	_____
Reporting Relationships	_____
Position Objectives	_____
Major Job Categories, Duties, Tasks, and Responsibilities	1 _____
	2 _____
	3 _____
	4 _____
	5 _____
Performance Standards	_____
Qualifications	_____
Frequency of Performance Review	_____

ARE THE SPECIFIC ROLES AND FUNCTIONS ADEQUATELY DOCUMENTED WITH WRITTEN SALES STAFF POSITION DESCRIPTIONS?

Position descriptions can play an essential role in hiring and placing sales professionals. They can also clarify how each position fits within a sales organization and what results are expected from each one. The following provides an example of a position description for a client manager that can help to clarify the requirements of that role in an organization.

A Sample Position Description of a Client Manager

Position	Client Manager
Person	John (Jane) Doe
Reporting Relationships	Regional Sales Manager
Position Objectives	• Increase sales 10% annually • Provide clients with professional service • Project a positive image in the community
Major Job Categories, Duties, Tasks and Responsibilities	• Self management: Proactively sell and market organization's services and products to achieve agreed upon revenue goals • Product and service management: Establish and maintain operational processes to expedite and communicate client needs and to ensure needs are met • Client management: Maintain and enhance relationships with current clients and actively identify and secure new clients for the organization • Business management: Monitor project accomplishment against plan by tracking procurement and budget expenditures as projects move through planning, design and production
Qualifications	• Bachelor's degree or equivalent • Two years of proven work experience in a sales, marketing, or customer service capacity • Self-motivated team player with excellent communication skills
Performance Standards	Outlined in the annual performance plan and budget
Frequency of Performance Reviews	Quarterly

DOES YOUR ORGANIZATION ADEQUATELY IDENTIFY NEEDED SKILLS, BEHAVIORS, AND COMPETENCIES FOR EACH SALES STAFF POSITION?

If you have clearly identified the skills, behaviors, and competencies needed for successful sales professionals in your organization, then you have the basis for preparing effective interview questions, sales scenarios, and assessment tools to identify potentially successful sales professionals. By clearly understanding what it takes to succeed in a sales position in your organization, you can also create results-oriented sales training and development programs.

Many competency models have been created to identify what it takes to be successful in organizational settings. Of course, competencies are characteristics that underlie successful performance (Dubois & Rothwell, 2000; Rothwell & Lindholm, 1999). Competency models are narrative descriptions of the competencies essential for success in a job category (such as supervisor), in a department (such as sales or marketing), or in an occupation (such as accountant or human resource management professional). The following checklist presents a competency model for sales.

A Checklist of Sample Competency Dimensions for Sales Professionals

Directions: Below are listed competency dimensions identified as important to sales professionals. Select a specific sales position and check those competency dimensions that you feel are important for individuals holding that position in your organization. If you desire to take your assessment one step further, please assign a "Developmental Need" rating to each competency dimension by assigning a rating from 1 to 5 with 1 = low need and 5 = high need. This checklist is intended to help you focus your developmental efforts for sales professionals in your organization in the future.

Position:
Competency Dimension
Check (✓) the box if important for the position

Knowledge of Self
☐ Enhancing interpersonal selling skills and self-development
☐ Managing client communications
☐ Enhancing negotiation and influencing skills
☐ Resolving sales and interpersonal conflicts and coping with change
☐ Other (please specify)

Knowledge of Products and Services
☐ Establishing ongoing client and stakeholder operational processes
☐ Identifying and communicating product features and benefits
☐ Establishing and maintaining a competitive analysis process
☐ Linking sales and market strategies
☐ Other (please specify)

Knowledge of Clients and Business
☐ Forecasting, planning, and prospecting for clients
☐ Managing calls, time, and sales territory
☐ Providing service and managing client relationships
☐ Developing new products, services, and managing projects
☐ Other (please specify)

Use this framework validated in our survey (described in the Preface) to clarify the competencies essential to success in your corporate culture. It can become the foundation for an effective in-house sales training and development program. To double check, compare how your ratings match up to those you identified in the Preface to this book (see Figure P.5).

ARE YOU CONFIDENT THAT YOUR ORGANIZATION CLEARLY UNDERSTANDS THE CHALLENGES FACING TODAY'S SALES PROFESSIONALS?

Client expectations are often influenced by the rapid changes occurring in the clients' organizations. In many organizations, the sales professional's role is sometimes perceived as that of "an order taker" (Segall, 1986). When a phone call comes in from an existing or potential client, the salesperson follows up with a sales call and closes the deal. While this may be a common stereotype of what salespeople do, those involved with sales know that sales are earned. With the advent of e-commerce, clients are not always required to speak to a sales professional to place an order. But most clients do wish to place their orders in a secure, user-friendly environment. When they speak to a sales professional, they expect polite and effective treatment. For that reason, the ability of sales professionals to establish and maintain effective client relationships is growing in importance. Client relationship management is growing more complex, requiring sales professionals to understand client needs even when they are not clearly articulated. Establishing and maintaining good client relationships now requires far more than a charge card to pay for lunch (Jolles, 1998).

Critical Situation: Changing Client Relationships

Situation: The conversion of the banking and insurance industries has created complex, multifaceted organizations that have forced sales professionals to broaden their perspectives and elevate the level of training required to effectively perform their jobs and manage client relationships. Clients are seeking consultative relationships with trusted professionals who can provide financial advice in a timely manner that is trustworthy and of value. But, does this mean sales professionals do not require the ability to ask for the order and close the sale? We found that was not the case. If we emphasize creating and maintaining long-term relationships and improved product knowledge to meet the broader needs of clients, then good things will happen.

Development Issues: It is not just a matter of asking for orders and closing deals to be an effective salesperson. There are strong regulatory and compliance issues that require attention and must always be in the back of your mind when you are trying to sell a product or service. This means with all of the industry changes and consolidations, the level of required knowledge about how business works has gone up; plus it must be continually updated. The expectation is that we should be trusted advisors who provide sound, logical advice.

Action Tips:

- The knowledge and skills needed continues to increase and it takes smart, motivated people to continue to learn and stay current.
- To stay current an organization must proactively research the impact of changing laws and regulations.
- An organization's planned training efforts can be a cheap investment compared to fines, lawsuits, or loss of a major client.

DO YOU UNDERSTAND THE DEPTH AND BREADTH OF WHAT'S NEEDED TO DEVELOP A PLANNED APPROACH TO DEVELOPING SALES PROFESSIONALS?

All too often the public's image of what it takes to be an effective sales professional is linked to the unfortunate stereotype of the fast-talking, flamboyantly dressed (and not always entirely honest) used-car salesperson. Hollywood productions have hardly been kind to the sales profession. But it goes without saying that this stereotype is far from the truth. Creating a continuing flow of successful sales professionals into an organization is a challenging task that requires careful thought and a systematic approach.

Critical Situation: Retaining Talent as a Reason for Development

Situation: We never had trouble hiring good salespeople. Over the past fifteen years we have had steady growth and have been able to hire people as we needed them with an occasional one leaving but it was no big deal. They weren't a great sales force but they did well enough to allow us to meet the goals we set for the business. Then about two years ago that pool of sales professionals seemed to dry up. Since then we've had problems and even had a couple of people work six weeks for us and just disappear. It is extremely frustrating and we are finally to the point where we are going to do something about it. Putting blind ads in our local newspaper for salespeople just isn't working.

Development Issues: Hiring and retaining a qualified sales force is a complex and difficult task. When you begin to quantify the cost of hiring and training sales professionals, the need for a planned and focused effort becomes very clear.

Action Tips:

- Inertia can be hard to overcome, and change can be slow, but change is a necessity and should be managed.
- Planned training efforts can be a significant part of a retention strategy.
- Sales professionals are not plentiful.

Much has been written on how to plan and carry out effective sales training (see, for instance, Boyan & Enright, 1992; Callahan, 1986; Eady, 1988; Falvey, 1988, 1990; Fox, 1992; Hahne & Schultze, 1996; Harris, 2001; Herr, 1992; Honeycutt, Harris, & Castleberry, 1987; Huckaba, 1999; Kerr & Burzynski,

1988; Kodiyalam, Segal, & Pathak, 1988; Marchetti, 1996; Mason, 1992; Parker, Pettijohn, & Carner, 1993; Peterson, 1990; Rosen, 1998a, 1998b, & 1998c; "Sales training: Keeping ahead of the pack," 1987; "Sales training: Programs for the next generation," 1989; "Sales training resources in print," 1992; Vaccaro, 1991). Less has been written about the unique competencies required of sales trainers (but see Evered, 1990; Kinney, 1990; Law, 1990; McGurer, 1990; Wenschlag, 1990), though that may be changing as in recent years more has been written for other business training professionals (see Rothwell, Sanders, & Soper, 1999). Of particular note are personal accounts, often written as case studies, about effective sales training efforts, since these descriptions contain important advice about what to do—and what to avoid (Cottrell, Davis, Detrick, & Raymond, 1992; "David Michael's," 2000; Ferguson, 1998; Ferrar, 1991; Fickel, 1998; Greer & McClure, 1996; "How Xerox Document," 1999; Kaeter, 1998; Lindheim, 1994; McNerney, 1994; Martin & Collins, 1991; Rasmusson, 1998; Richman, 1991; Singer & Lees, 1994; Stamps, 1997).

DOES YOUR ORGANIZATION HAVE AN APPRECIATION FOR THE REASONS WHY ORGANIZATIONS SPONSOR TRAINING?

Organizations sponsor sales training and development programs for many reasons. Figure 1.1, based on our survey of sales professionals, lists the most important reasons that organizations sponsor such programs in priority order.

Note that the top three reasons to sponsor planned sales training and development programs center around an organization's need to increase productivity and competitiveness. Will sales professionals be replaced by e-commerce and direct on-line sales? According to our research, that is not so much of a concern to sales practitioners as managing client relationships. To facilitate those relationships, sales managers should focus their attention on helping sales professionals understand the organizational culture of the sales organization and client needs and expectations. In the future, organizations that are not positioned to align with clients' product and information needs will cease to exist. The impact on supply chains and distribution channels is also one of those indirect factors that have the potential to negatively impact a sales professional's ability to succeed. What can be worse than those days when you close the biggest sale of your career only to discover that the production department does not possess sufficient capacity to fill the order on a timely basis? Finally, the playing field is changing. There are some obvious shifts in the demographics taking place in many areas of the United States and the world. All point to the need for organizations to increase their ability to customize products and services to meet clients' individualized needs.

We recently spoke to sales professionals in a property management and real estate organization. They discussed the growing need to manage multiple re-

Figure 1.1
Reasons for Sponsoring In-House Sales Training and Development
Programs According to Survey Respondents

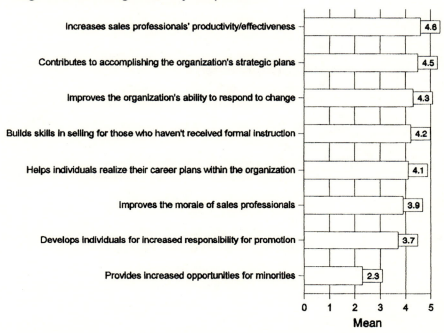

Source: From *A Survey about Sales Training Programs* by W. Rothwell, W. Donahue, and J. Park, 2001 (unpublished survey results), University Park, PA: Pennsylvania State University. Copyright 2001 by W. Rothwell, W. Donahue, and J. Park.

lationships in each client organization. That is important because their clients are experiencing high turnover, and under those conditions sales professionals must have many contacts if they are to maintain personal selling relationships with their clients. Sales professionals must think more strategically about their relationships with clients and how to create sustainable relationships that will produce profitable long-term business clients. Sales professionals that think strategically can spot broader sales opportunities in an organization. They can also make decisions according to the potential for long-term impact and also a return on investment in hard dollar resources, emotional energy, or the time required to build and maintain a relationship. Long-term success may have to be gained at the sacrifice of short-term results. The challenge is this: How do you train individuals to think strategically to manage client relationships and generate sales revenue? We will examine this issue in further detail in later chapters and provide you with questions designed to serve as a framework for creating this competency in your organization.

Critical Situation: The Necessity of Balancing Time and Training

Situation: In a discussion group we recently held with several financial services executives they focused in on how sales professionals and their managers need to be able to manage their time in a manner that allows them to focus on the high pay off activities. They found their sales staffs falling behind in the use of technology as again they struggled to take time away from the sales role to participate in training. They discussed in detail the conflicts that developed when sales professionals were forced to take time away from their clients to receive training that the sales professionals did not translate to increased sales and income.

Development Issues: How do we create balance between the need to produce and the need to be trained? Truly, what organization does not desire to have a cadre of high-performing sales professionals driven to generate revenue, but on the other hand what are the long-term implications if organizations do not continue to refresh and train their sales professionals? Will they become obsolete? Or will they burn out and become less productive or even leave the organization?

Action Tips:
- Ask your sales staff to describe how they currently manage their time.
- Ask your sales staff how much their time is worth in dollars per hour.

HAS YOUR ORGANIZATION IDENTIFIED MAJOR TRENDS AFFECTING THE DEVELOPMENT OF SALES TALENT?

Our survey research revealed that sales professionals feel the increasing pressure of both internal and external trends, which obviously influence their ability to succeed. These trends also affect an organization's ability to train and develop their sales talent. The following checklists outline the major trends reported by our survey respondents to affect their future efforts to train and develop their sales professionals.

Checklist of Major Internal Trends Affecting Sales Professionals as Reported by Survey Respondents

Directions: Outlined below are the consolidated internal trends affecting sales professionals as reported by survey respondents. Please check (✓) those items that you believe are most influential in their impact on your organization.

☐ Increasing use of computers and technology

☐ Turnover escalating; finding talented people and then trying to make them productive is a major challenge

☐ Retaining talent; salary expectations—best talent leaving for best offers

☐ Expect training; new hires increasingly recognize and expect to attend and receive training or they walk

☐ Level of professionalism and loyalty appears to be dropping

❏ Moving different people into different skill sets as they mature into salespeople is becoming more difficult

❏ Constant budget reductions; doing more (increased sales targets) with fewer people is increasing

❏ Sales executives and administrators are becoming increasingly responsible for major clients

❏ Realization of sales rep's importance to the bottom line and survival is increasing

Checklist of Major External Trends Affecting Sales Professionals as Reported by Survey Respondents

Directions: Outlined below are the consolidated external trends affecting sales professionals as reported by survey respondents. Please check (✓) those items that you believe are most influential in their impact on your organization.

❏ Being able to change and keep pace with the technology needs of our clients; larger clients outpace us in this area but increasingly expect us to keep up.

❏ Should we move completely to laptop environment? Use of technology to manage client relationships is becoming a necessity.

❏ Fewer people spread out geographically; the profession is consolidating and shrinking.

❏ Competitors are adding many supplemental products beyond traditional products and services that increasingly challenge the abilities of our salespeople to keep up and compete.

❏ Trend toward training efforts as a necessity will soon be a reality as the baby-boomers retire.

❏ The impact of Business to Business (B–B) models is increasingly creating stress among older professionals.

❏ Corporate takeovers and mergers; we don't have time to train; we have our hands full constantly trying to absorb, sort out, and streamline our sales organization.

❏ Corporate raiding of talent is escalating; rather than train, they raid.

In our discussion with the representatives of the financial services industry the ability to understand and adapt to internal and external trends and manage change surfaced as a strong challenge. The convergence of the banking and insurance industries has created complex organizations that force sales professionals to broaden their perspectives and increase the training needed to perform effectively. Clients now seek consultative relationships with trusted professionals who can provide professional financial advice in a trustworthy manner that adds value. But does this mean that sales professionals just require the ability to ask for the order and close the sale? We found that the answer was clearly "no." Sales professionals continue to be among the most accountable of employees in any organization.

Our research also surfaced another growing trend among sales professionals. That was a keen sense of being overwhelmed to the point of discouragement with how much information they must read and process every day. In one group, several sales professionals argued that over 75 percent of the e-mails they received on a daily basis did not relate to them or else had little or no impact on their ability to perform. This sense of being overwhelmed also directly related to struggles with time management. Several participants in a focus group we conducted talked about their struggle with staying informed about their organizations while they were also being pressured to achieve their measurable sales goals.

HAS YOUR ORGANIZATION CONSIDERED THE TYPES OF ACTIVITIES THAT MAKE UP A PLANNED IN-HOUSE APPROACH FOR SALES TRAINING?

Many activities can be instrumental in improving the effectiveness of sales professionals. The following provides a sample of the comments given by our survey respondents. These comments yield insights into their thoughts about planned sales training and development efforts.

- "We have a specific detailed program and course of instruction for all levels."
- "Each year, we send our salespeople to a designated location for customer-focused training. The topical areas include proper image; identifying needs; and needs, benefits, features."
- "We integrate sales training into each of our monthly sales meetings."
- "Formal training programs are conducted at our headquarters followed by local training in our regional offices."
- "Our development process consists entirely of working with other reps within our own organization."
- "We have formalized home-office training followed by regional sales seminars and annual sales conventions."

It stands to reason that most unplanned sales programs are driven by crisis rather than by opportunity. Sales training is too often handled in the same way. Training may be offered as a solution to a problem rather than as a continuing effort designed to improve performance in ways aligned with the organization's strategic direction. Training can also be an important component of a retention strategy that is intended to enhance the organization's image and show sales professionals how they may advance.

While many sales managers may feel that training is expensive, the cost of not training can be even greater. The demands on sales professionals continue to escalate. And the cost of replacing a client continues to exceed the cost of retaining a client. Relying on informal shadowing approaches to training may end up costing more in lost clients than they are worth.

DO YOU KNOW WHO ULTIMATELY HAS RESPONSIBILITY FOR ESTABLISHING EDUCATION AND TRAINING POLICIES FOR YOUR SALES PROFESSIONALS?

It is perhaps not too surprising that in most organizations the responsibility for establishing training policies rests with an organization's sales or corporate leadership. As Figure 1.2 illustrates, the respondents to our survey indicated that many decision makers have a say in establishing the organization's training policies. What may be surprising, in light of substantial research on training practice conducted by others, is that the human resource staff does not play much of a role in the respondents' organizations to establish sales training policies.

The responsibility for developing training policies resides with those responsible for sales staff performance. That underscores the key importance of the sales manager's leadership role in designing and delivering planned sales

Figure 1.2
Who Establishes Sales Training Policies?

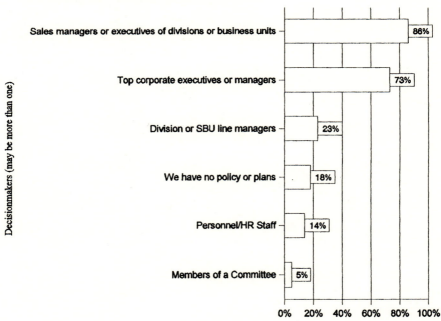

Source: From *A Survey about Sales Training Programs* by W. Rothwell, W. Donahue, and J. Park, 2001 (unpublished survey results), University Park, PA: Pennsylvania State University. Copyright 2001 by W. Rothwell, W. Donahue, and J. Park.

training. Sales training initiatives driven by the human resources or training department may encounter resistance, or meet with limited success, unless championed by top managers or the sales manager (Peterson, 1992). That raises one important question for you to consider: What actions can you take to define the roles and functions of your sales organization better? Use the following worksheet to organize your thoughts in response to that question.

A Worksheet for Action Planning

Directions: Use this worksheet to help you organize your thoughts in response to the following question: What actions can you take to define the roles and functions of your sales organization better?

Notes:

2

Identifying Staff Training Needs and Designing Curricula

You set the stage for designing and delivering a successful in-house sales training and development program by acknowledging the need for such a program and demonstrating that the top leaders of the organization support it. This chapter focuses on identifying staff training and development needs and designing an instructional plan for it called a "curriculum." *Curriculum* is a Latin word that means "to run a race," and it simply means having a plan for training (Rothwell & Sredl, 2000).

Identifying staff needs and designing curricula means that sales professionals do the following:

- Recognize the training needs of individuals.
- Identify performance gaps.
- Help set learning goals and objectives.
- Establish, document, and organize the required tasks, skills, behaviors, and activities needed to perform specific sales staff roles and functions in an exemplary manner.

As you begin thinking about how to identify staff training and development needs and carry out instructional planning, read over the following brief descriptions of best-in-class sales training.

The Best at Sales Training: Studies in Best Practices

If you want to find examples of superior sales training, look no further than the pharmaceutical industry, where giants Merck and Pfizer are known for their outstanding programs.

Last year, Scott-Levin, a market research firm in Newtown, Pennsylvania, surveyed salespeople and trainers in the health-care field to find out how they rated training programs at their companies and others. "Pfizer and Merck finished one and two. It wasn't just reps from Merck and Pfizer who rated them best, it was reps from 30 companies," says Bryna Elder, Scott-Levin's director of strategic studies.

Though both companies' training programs are successful, their approaches are quite different. Merck, headquartered in Whitehouse Station, New Jersey, "takes a highly scientific approach to the market, and trains reps to understand the science of the medicine so that they can maintain a peer-to-peer discussion with the physician," says Bob Holmes, vice president of client relations at the pharmaceutical relationship-management solution firm Strategic Technologies, a division of IMS Health in Atlanta.

Elder agrees. "Merck's main strategy of training is to focus more on classroom time," she says. Reps report that they spend 90 percent of their training time in the classroom.

While Merck's sales approach is generally described as scientific, Pfizer's is more aggressive, Holmes says. "They have legions of sales reps who are well-trained. Marketing messages are memorized and there's one unified voice." New York-based Pfizer also uses its training programs to evaluate salespeople, and it reportedly weeds out reps who don't perform well in the classes.

Of course, companies in other industries offer excellent training, too. One of them is financial services firm Charles Schwab, named for its chairman and co-CEO. Because Schwab offers customers financial advice, the company makes sure that its entire sales force is educated to give their clients unbiased information.

Schwab has an aggressive approach to education. Previously Schwab's computer-based tutorials for its salespeople, known as investment specialists, were largely text-based, difficult to update, and not Web accessible. Now, the tutorials are on-line, can be accessed through the Schwab intranet, are easier to update, feature improved graphics and user interaction, and serve as enhanced self-training tools.

Schwab's ongoing education program, called LEAP (Learning for Excellence in Advice and Professionalism), includes a curriculum of Web and classroom courses and a series of off-site workshops for salespeople and managers at different stages of their professional development.

There are also one- to two-week programs for new brokers with ten to thirty participants, all of whom are nominated by their managers. These programs are preceded by a series of sessions focusing on Schwab systems, products, and policies. Then the off-site sessions focus on learning that reinforces Schwab's needs-based client approach with an emphasis on the company's investment philosophy and methodology in giving advice. "We have a pledge to ongoing learning," says Andrew Salesky, senior vice president, retail sales and infrastructure. "The emphasis in the sales force is to deliver advice. Our customers want us to guide them."

IBM Global Services salespeople, who sell consulting and various information technology services, are challenged to call on high level executives and have an extensive knowledge of e-business. So each year IBM has them take at least two weeks of in-class and Web-based training on both consultative selling and the technical aspects of business (Harris, 2000, 68ff).

Then, with your sales organization in mind, complete this self-assessment by rating the ten statements.

Self-Assessment: Identifying Staff Needs and Designing Curricula

Directions: Read each statement carefully. With your sales organization in mind, place the number that fits with your level of agreement with each of the ten statements.

Disagree									Agree
1	2	3	4	5	6	7	8	9	10

_____You recognize the differing needs of your individual sales professionals.

_____Your organization has a process in place to identify specific performance gaps of your sales professionals.

_____Your organization sets learning goals and objectives for sales training and education efforts.

_____Your organization has established and documented specific required tasks critical to the success of your sales professionals.

_____You are aware of the sales professionals in your organization that are in most need of development.

_____You understand the important considerations for development of sales professionals.

_____You are aware of the appropriate methods for assessing development needs.

_____Your organization understands the most difficult challenges faced by sales professionals.

_____Your organization understands the typical challenges faced by sales professionals.

_____You are aware of other organizations that have planned training and education curricula for their sales professionals.

_____Total

How Did You Score?

Here is the key to identifying staff needs and designing curricula. Add up your responses to get your score.

91–100   Great job! Congratulations! Your organization is effectively working to define sales staff roles and functions.

81–90   Keep up the good work! You've probably had considerable success. But by using some of the tips in this chapter, you could improve your success.

71–80   Help is needed! There is room for improvement. You'll find this chapter helpful.

0–70   Warning! Your sales organization probably has some unmet development needs. Read on!

These statements provide the organizational scheme for this chapter. When you finish the self-assessment, do some open-ended brainstorming by completing the following worksheet.

A Worksheet for Organizing Your Thinking about Identifying Staff Needs and Designing Curricula

Directions: In your opinion, what problems or challenges does your sales organization face in identifying staff needs and designing curricula? Use this worksheet to organize your thinking in answering this question.

Notes:

DO YOU RECOGNIZE THE DIFFERING NEEDS OF INDIVIDUAL SALES PROFESSIONALS?

Many sales professionals share some common training needs. For example, new sales professionals usually require an orientation to the organization, its products or services, and its chief competitors. Sales professionals also share the need to listen carefully, plan effectively, and manage their time and territory. Common training needs of this kind are called *macrotraining needs* and are usually shared by all sales professionals.

However, individuals also have training needs that are unique to them or to the unique requirements of the organizations in which they function. These are called *microtraining needs*. These must usually be pinpointed as a result of experience with the organization. They can also be discovered through focus groups, interviews, performance appraisals, and surveys (Immel, 1990).

According to the anecdotal evidence collected by the authors in preparing this book, the most widely used form of training needs assessment is the answer to the simple litmus test question, "Do they sell, or don't they?" Review the following checklist and think about its implications.

❑ To determine training needs, we created a scorecard aligned with our organization's objectives. We then measure the outcomes of individuals and business units in all defined areas of activities as well as monitor productivity.

☐ We ask each salesperson to self-assess strengths and weaknesses and develop an action plan for the year and to outline development needs and desires. It is part of our senior executives' job to spend 20 percent of their time making joint calls, observing performance, and providing needed feedback.

☐ We compare sites and individuals on a monthly basis, then assess and review needs and actions using the highest performing sites and individuals as the benchmark. We ask our highest performing sites and individuals to share their success stories for the period and insights for success.

☐ Dollar sales per period and the number of add-on optional sales is a primary method of assessing preformance and determining training needs. We also track the number of referrals and repeat customers. Salespeople are trained to achieve target goals and provide customer service.

☐ Each quarter, all sales reps are evaluated using a standard form. Results against the budget are evaluated first. If a shortfall occurs, the rep is assessed as to how effectively he or she is conducting identified activities that have proven to lead to revenue generation. Training and follow-up occurs on those activities not being adequately performed.

☐ Reps are asked to submit a monthly self-assessment of their performance and needs which are supplemented by quarterly evaluations by sales managers. As a side note, the more we spend on a rep's salary, the greater our expectation that he or she has the full inventory of skill sets. For experienced salespeople, we conduct a 360-degree multirater assessment to help them recognize their needs.

☐ We focus assessment and training primarily on new people. We conduct weekly performance reviews and conduct planning sessions with new hires during the first three quarters to assess needs. Needs are addressed with individual instruction and drill. After they are experienced it is pretty straightforward; we assess or evaluate performance outcomes against sales goals. They either perform or they know the consequences.

DOES YOUR ORGANIZATION HAVE A PROCESS IN PLACE TO IDENTIFY SPECIFIC PERFORMANCE GAPS OF INDIVIDUALS AND THE ORGANIZATION?

The sales profession is greatly influenced by sales production figures. It is easy to see who is successful at selling and who is not. But the sales figures of individuals do not tell the whole story. Performance gaps are different from training needs. Training gives people the knowledge they need to perform. But performance gaps can stem from many causes, such as competitive conditions in the industry, national economic conditions, differences in individual ability, organizational barriers to performance, or motivation level (Rothwell, Hohne, & King, 2000).

It is important to identify baseline performance and then examine people who do not meet that performance. Some method should be devised to do just that. And, it is important to provide sales professionals with prompt, specific feedback on their performance. After all, providing feedback is a powerful improvement strategy in its own right.

Consider the following scenario. Note the developmental issues and action tips provided at the end of that situation as key points for helping sales professionals cultivate their talents.

Critical Situation: Conducting a Gap Analysis— Current Realities versus Desired Results

Situation: In Jennifer's region the demographics have shifted and the Spanish-speaking population has tripled. Jennifer speaks no Spanish. In research conducted throughout the region it is determined that having a minimal Spanish vocabulary improves Hispanic clients' comfort level with financial consultants and improves their ability to sell follow-up products.

Development Issues: For individuals it is often helpful to determine the gap between the current job realities and desired job realities as they relate to improving performance. In Jennifer's case, the current reality is that she can't speak Spanish and the desired reality is for her to have a conversational vocabulary in Spanish. Thus, a training gap and desired action should be obvious: Jennifer should learn conversational Spanish as part of her developmental plan. There are a number of different training methods that Jennifer could pursue to acquire the skills and knowledge needed to close the gap. These methods include classroom training, self-study courses, audiotapes, and so forth.

Action Tips:
- To conduct a gap analysis, ask yourself what skills and knowledge would the ideal sales professional have for a particular position. Compare the desired skills and knowledge to the current skills and knowledge of incumbent sales professionals to determine the performance gap.
- Identify selected training and development actions that close the gap.

DOES YOUR ORGANIZATION SET LEARNING GOALS AND OBJECTIVES FOR SALES TRAINING EFFORTS?

Top managers establish the strategic goals and objectives of the organization to provide direction. Sales managers establish sales goals and objectives for the same reason. It is thus not surprising that effective sales training programs should also possess goals and objectives.

Of course, a *goal* is a desirable result. When a goal is made time-specific and measurable, it is transformed into an *objective*. Effective training objectives clarify what participants should be able to do upon completion of the training. In other words, the objectives should be established and then sales trainers should work backward to identify the instructional methods and media by which to achieve those objectives.

Training objectives should clarify the behaviors that participants should be able to demonstrate, the resources (conditions) necessary for them to demonstrate their knowledge and skills, and measurable criteria by which to assess how well participants can perform. One way you can establish effective training objectives is to rely on the framework described by the acronym SMART. The acronym is formed from the first letters of the following words:

S = Objectives are *specific* enough that they can be understood by everyone involved.

M = Objectives are *measurable* and success can be easily determined.

A = Objectives are a stretch to achieve but realistically *attainable*.

R = Objectives are *relevant* to the situation.

T = The objectives have a *timeline* for their achievement.

A sample goals worksheet follows that may be customized for your organization. The authors have found it useful to have the worksheet printed as a three-part form which aids in the recording of trainee input and focusing efforts on those objectives that are essential to the learners and to a sales manager.

A Goal-Setting Worksheet

Directions: Agreeing upon and documenting goals is an important ingredient for success. The first step in the process is writing the goals down for review and discussion. Use this Worksheet for that purpose. Remember to set S.M.A.R.T. goals:
Specific **M**easurable **A**chievable **R**elevant **T**imely
Goal 1
Goal 2
Goal 3
Goal 4
Your Signature **Date** **Sales Manager's Signature**

Setting goals and objectives can be extremely valuable. But it will be a waste of time if sales professionals are not given measurable objectives for performance or if their achievement is not reviewed regularly. Factors that must be accomplished for the sales development program to be successful must be identified and the metrics should be created so progress toward their achievement can be monitored and tracked. Review this situation for a dramatic example of why this is important.

Critical Situation:
Designing a Training Curriculum for New Salespeople

Situation: We train twenty-five new sales professionals per year which meant that we needed to design a standard curriculum to make sure we were covering the basics in a consistent manner. Before we had this curriculum we had chaos. To start, we first developed some very clear goals and objectives for our sales development program that we integrated into a customized sixteen-hour basic course on the essentials of sales that is updated annually. In addition, we created over a dozen new job aids to support our training curriculum, and a resource reference manual supplemented with an on-line library of recommended learning resources. To add accountability we expect each of our salespeople to complete an annual self-development plan as part of our organization's performance management system.

Development Issues: Training new salespeople and creating a sustainable source of qualified sales professionals is not a luxury, it is essential. If you have standard methods and procedures you want employees to follow, there needs to be a plan for them to acquire the knowledge and skills. The secondary benefits are less obvious: less conflict, reduced errors, improved retention of sales professionals, higher productivity, and resultant profitability.

Action Tips:
- Segment sales professionals into logical groups to initiate planned development efforts such as new salespeople, telesales, customer service, and so on.
- Set goals and objectives for the selected group(s).
- Assemble exemplary performers for each group to brainstorm critical job related activities and actions needed to achieve desired performance.

HAS YOUR ORGANIZATION ESTABLISHED AND DOCUMENTED SPECIFIC REQUIRED TASKS CRITICAL TO THE SUCCESS OF YOUR SALES PROFESSIONALS?

A customized job profiling (CJP) process is a systematic review of a position that identifies the tasks involved in that position and the skills and knowledge necessary to succeed in it. The CJP process may also be used to review and document important work processes. The customized job profiling process usually involves bringing together the top performers of a particular position or process to identify, in detail, what they do. The information collected from a customized job profiling session can provide the framework for an effective sales training curriculum.

The CJP process is a simple, yet powerful, approach to job and task analysis. This proven methodology is a timely, cost-effective way to obtain a comprehensive analysis of a particular job, position or process. The main purpose of the CJP process is to develop a list of the work activities carried out by top performers in a job category, department, or occupation.

Documenting these activities and carefully organizing them into a customized job profile chart provides a useful framework for many subsequent organizational uses. For instance, it can be used to guide planned on-the-job training or coaching, preparing job-specific interview questions, establishing job-specific performance appraisals, and clarifying the career paths among and between positions. It can also provide a starting point for establishing measurable work standards, performance expectations, or performance objectives.

The CJP process is based on several key assumptions:

- Job incumbents are best able to identify the work activities associated with a given position or process.
- Top performers provide the best, most accurate, profile of job activities or process steps.
- The CJP process builds involvement and commitment in the results.
- There is a direct relationship between a worker's knowledge, skills, and attitudes and successful job performance.
- The result of a customized job profile process is a valid job model or job map that has many possible and practical organizational uses.

To carry out a CJP, choose about eight to twelve top sales performers, then lead them through a modified brainstorming technique. Ask them to describe what they do every day. Write this down on sheets of paper and post them on the wall in front of the performers for all to see. Continue this process until the performers cannot think of anything else they do. Then give them a break. While they are on break, take down the sheets of paper from the wall and organize them into categories based on the sales process or on categories that emerge from the topics on the sheets. Then bring the performers back and ask them to verify (or revise) the categories. When that step is completed, divide the group up into teams and ask each team to take a category or two and eliminate redundancies, add any forgotten activities, and combine related activities. Ask each team to sequence the activities based on what a newcomer to the position should be trained on first. Activities can be further assessed according to their frequency, criticality, and ease of learning. When these efforts are finished, adjourn for the day—but have the papers typed up into a chart and bring the performers back into a short meeting later just long enough to review the job profile and make any final changes. The CJP process can also be conducted electronically in a computer lab using one of the group decision-making software packages available.

A skilled CJP facilitator should guide the process as the CJP chart is developed. The facilitator keeps the group focused and manages group dynamics to help the CJP participants reach consensus. The result of a CJP session is a customized job profile. The CJP represents the collective expertise of the top performers and provides an excellent picture of the important activities associated with the position. An example of a CJP appears in Figure 2.1.

ARE YOU AWARE OF THE SALES PROFESSIONALS IN YOUR ORGANIZATION WHO ARE IN MOST NEED OF DEVELOPMENT?

Who or what groups should be the focus of training and development efforts among your sales force, and how are these priorities established? That is a key question for any sales manager to think about. Resources are limited. You cannot do everything for everyone at once. Consequently, you must set priorities. But how do you do that?

In our survey of sales managers (described in the Preface), we asked what groups are given special training consideration in the respondents' organizations. Figure 2.2 presents the results of our survey of sales professionals. Note that the highest priority is placed on recently promoted sales professionals. That might include individuals who are new to sales from other parts of the organization—or else it could include individuals who are promoted to supervise others in sales.

How you set priorities may have as much to do with the type of organization, and its industry, as it does the preferences of sales managers. Of course,

Figure 2.1
A Sample of a Simplified Customized Job Profile for a Client Development Manager

Job Categories and Duties	Competency Dimensions - Activities and Tasks			
Self Management	Enhance interpersonal selling skills and self development	Manage client communications	Enhance negotiation and influencing skills	Resolve sales and interpersonal conflicts
Product and Service Management	Establish ongoing informational processes	Identify and communicate product features and benefits	Establish and maintain a competitive analysis process	Link sales and marketing strategies
Client and Business Management	Forecast, plan, and prospect for clients	Manage calls, time, and sales territory	Provide service and manage client relationships	Develop new products, services, and manage projects

Figure 2.2
Groups Given Special Sales Training Consideration as Reported by Survey Respondents

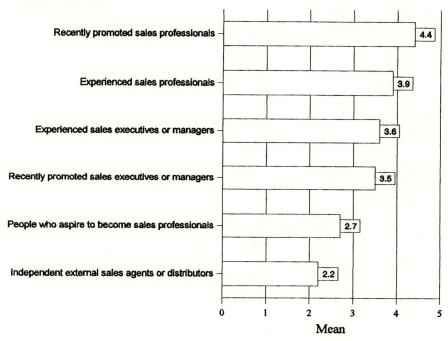

Source: From *A Survey about Sales Training Programs* by W. Rothwell, W. Donahue, and J. Park, 2001 (unpublished survey results), University Park, PA: Pennsylvania State University. Copyright 2001 by W. Rothwell, W. Donahue, and J. Park.

the priorities for sales training should match up to the organization's strategic objectives. At the same time, however, the industry of which your organization is a part should be a consideration. On the one hand, if your organization (or its industry) is experiencing rapid growth, you might find that the greatest return on sales training dollars is realized from focusing on new-hire training. Or, if your organization is in a stable low-growth market with low employee turnover, you may find the most value in updating the skills of veteran sales professionals while (at the same time) establishing a systematic succession planning program. These are two examples of focusing on a special group within your organization.

Organizations represented by independent sales professionals, such as manufacturing representatives or independent sales agents, encounter a different set of issues related to sales development. Issues such as loyalty and retention of clients frequently surface as factors that are important. Consequently, the highest priority may be placed on training that is intended to foster loyalty and retention.

In our discussions with sales managers around setting priorities for training, we heard them express much frustration about setting priorities. One sales manager, for instance, complained about the lack of a systematic process for setting priorities for training in her organization. She felt that decisions were not made based on objective issues about where the greatest return might be realized. Instead, she felt that decisions were made based on the notion that "the squeakiest wheel gets oiled." For a real example, consider the following situation.

Critical Situation:
Identifying Training Needs and Planning a Training Approach

Situation: In our firm we provide a ton of training but who gets the training changes from year to year and it just seems to me that there is no rhyme or reason to it. We have a lot of salespeople that are in their sixties and have been here for years. Every time one of them reads a new book or meets some consultant in an airport we end up with a training program at our next quarterly sales meeting. Then either the new people get invited as an afterthought if we are lucky, but lots of times they tell us it is over our heads, so why don't we just go play golf? This lack of any systematic approach for identifying needs just drives me crazy.

Development Issues: It is easy to focus training on the group that strategically may not give the best return to the organization. Without a systematic approach to identifying training and development needs, sales training can end up focusing around the latest flavor of the month. Too many sales professionals have historically looked for a quick fix. It is important to avoid jumping to conclusions—and to jumping on the latest bandwagon presented to solve a problem—but rather to take a logical planned approach to identifying sales training needs. One way to do that is to create a planned sales training curriculum for specific sales groups that is aligned with the organization's strategic goals and objectives.

Action Tips:
- Identify your long- and short-term organizational goals.
- Document critical skills and tasks needed to achieve the goals.
- Establish a cross-training or job rotation initiative and plan.
- Establish programs for your critical performance areas.
- Consider developing a succession plan for key leadership positions.

DO YOU UNDERSTAND THE IMPORTANT CONSIDERATIONS FOR THE DEVELOPMENT OF SALES PROFESSIONALS?

Creating a sales development program because it is the right thing to do, or because this book suggests you do it is a flawed perspective. For the successful creation of an effective and organizationally valued in-house sales development program there must be an alignment with the strategic direction of the organization. Investing in a sales development program can bring short-term results. However, the potential for long-term gains can be even more substantial. As the sales development program matures, it should evolve to become a part of the organization's culture that is recognized for its contributions to achieving the company's profitability goals. The following is a real-life example of how that can happen.

Critical Situation:
Meeting Changing Needs and Managing Client Relationships

Situation: In banks over the past ten years the word "sell" has gone from a four-letter word to an important part of the organizational culture. It is not even pure selling that is the issue for us but rather how we create a client-focused organization not only from a people perspective but also from a process perspective. We continue to be heavily regulated and as much as we talk about becoming more flexible and user-friendly we hide behind the idea that we have to do things a certain way because of government regulation. We are seeing changes in the organization as we hire new people and have included client relationship management in our new employee orientation.

Development Issues: The positive impact of a well-established sales development program can be seen beyond the sales professionals who are involved in the program. Cultural change does not happen overnight and takes time and support. All employees of an organization need to view client relationship management as part of their job.

Action Tips:

There are a number of suggestion actions taken by this organization to help establish a planned approach to training you might consider:

• Ask your front-line employees what support the organization can give them that will help them do better in meeting client needs.
• Organize a representative team to formulate recommended actions.
• Pilot recommendations on a small scale to gain insight and obtain enhanced credibility.

What are the most important issues for you to consider when establishing a sales training and development program? We asked this question in our survey (described in the Preface). The respondents rated the relative components of a planned sales training and development program. Their ratings appear in Figure 2.3. Note that the most important single characteristic of a successful sales training and development program is that it is aligned with the organization's strategic business objectives. Another way to say that is that all the training offered is perceived to meet real business needs—and not supply quick fixes or pursue flavors of the month.

The survey results support the value of taking a planned, deliberative, calculated, and long-term approach to meeting the macrotraining and microtraining needs of sales professionals (see McClung, 1990; Rothwell & Kazanas, 1998). On the other hand, if training is perceived to be something that is only "nice to have" or is "just a morale builder" it will not last long. When the company

Figure 2.3
Important Success Factors for Sales Training as Reported by Survey Respondents

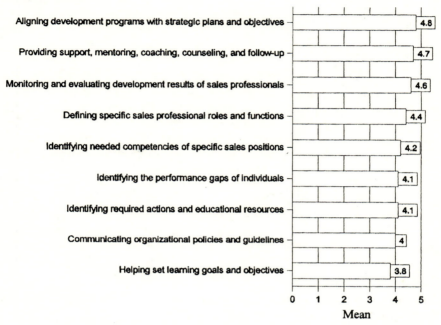

Source: From *A Survey about Sales Training Programs* by W. Rothwell, W. Donahue, and J. Park, 2001 (unpublished survey results), University Park, PA: Pennsylvania State University. Copyright 2001 by W. Rothwell, W. Donahue, and J. Park.

begins to experience a downturn, training will be the first thing that is cut back. But if training is perceived to be genuinely useful in achieving business goals, it will hold steady—or may even experience an increase—when times are bad.

ARE YOU AWARE OF THE APPROPRIATE METHODS FOR ASSESSING DEVELOPMENT NEEDS?

Many ways exist by which to assess the training and development needs of sales professionals. The choice of which approach to use will depend, in part, on how much access you can gain to the sales staff, what time constraints exist, how much the organization is willing to spend, and what previous experiences the organization has had to training. For instance, techniques for training-needs assessment may range from interviews with sales professionals to focus groups to written or e-mailed surveys. Sales supervisors and managers may also be polled about recent problems and successes and any trends that may be developing across performance appraisals. Care should also be taken to consider differences in individual learning styles among the sales staff, as the following situation illustrates.

Critical Situation: Managing Different Learning Styles

Situation: In a recent training program for a financial services organization there were several participants who were openly upset that they had to waste their time being there and that the facilitator could "tell them nothing they did not already know." There were three challenges for the facilitator. The first was to create credibility and to prove herself to the group. The second challenge was having the group recognize there was a need for the training. The third challenge was identifying preferred learning styles. The facilitator began this process by asking the group to discuss the most difficult challenge they faced on a daily basis. The participants worked in small groups and as each group presented the results of their discussions it became obvious that the issue of time and personal management cut across every group. From there the facilitator was able to begin her presentation that she had developed in collaboration with the sales manager addressing time management. However, by facilitating the discussion up front she had allowed the need for the training to bubble up from the group.

Development Issues: As adults we learn differently and at differing rates. It is important to recognize that as the sales development program is created, attention should be given first to identifying training needs, then focus on the creation of a diversified learning system that is not totally focused on any one delivery style or technique such as classroom training or self-study courses. As needs are identified alternative strategies for addressing the needs should be available via audiotapes, one-on-one coaching sessions, or classroom instruction.

Action Tips:
- Ask your sales staff what is the most critical sales situation they have experienced in their careers and then analyze for training needs.
- Ask your sales staff what are the typical challenges they face on a daily basis and then analyze them for training needs.
- Offer your sales group suggested training delivery options: classroom, self-paced audio, on-line, and so forth.

DOES YOUR ORGANIZATION UNDERSTAND THE MOST DIFFICULT CHALLENGES FACED BY SALES PROFESSIONALS?

The face of the sales profession is changing. Sales has always encouraged the lone-wolf mentality because each salesperson's productivity is usually analyzed. For that reason, salespeople are encouraged to work on their own. That tendency toward encouraging solitary action is further promoted by the advances in telecommunications that make virtual offices and e-mail contact more prevalent and socially acceptable. In fact, the impact of technology on the sales profession is creating new training needs for sales professionals.

When we asked sales professionals in our survey to describe the most difficult challenges they face in their careers as sales professionals, many respondents indicated that finding the true decision maker was a key challenge. The following provides a description of a situation that dramatically illustrates this point.

Critical Situation: Identifying Critical Needs— Who Makes the Buying Decision?

Situation: One time I flew in a person, had a limo pick her up, and put her in the presidential suite only to find out that her boss made the decisions. I should have better-qualified the account and found out who the decision maker really was. I'm still embarrassed.

Development Issues: Identifying the most difficult challenges leads to identifying critical training and development needs. Basic selling skills involves committing to memory a number of essential questions that should be asked of potential clients. Role playing can help and is an effective way of practicing your skills.

Action Tips:
- Practice identifying who makes the buying decision.
- Practice identifying who needs to authorize the purchase or sign the memo of agreement.

The following checklist summarizes the most difficult challenges faced by sales professionals as reported by our survey respondents, and these can be a useful starting point for you to consider in identifying sales training needs for sales professionals in your own organization. Think about how your salespeople might handle each issue.

- ☐ Instability of corporate management in our organization and at other organizations
- ☐ The rules change, corporate management keeps changing the sales compensation systems
- ☐ Initially dealing with rejection from customers
- ☐ Unrealistic sales goals
- ☐ Developing cost-effective advertisements and promotions
- ☐ Maintaining a continuous follow-up strategy
- ☐ Trying to push and position our company to build a better Web site
- ☐ Trying to differentiate our product variables (price, delivery, quality)
- ☐ Dealing with the issue of making that first cold call
- ☐ Recognizing that sales training is needed and should be conducted when growth is good, not when things turn downward

☐ Recognizing and acting on the "close"

☐ Determining and getting to the true decision maker

☐ Clients who lie and use you to get a lower price

☐ As a young sales rep, earning the respect and credibility of an older, more mature customer base

☐ Theft by deception: clients knowingly taking advantage of mistakes or errors, taking discounts when not entitled to them or withholding payment due to minor quality problems

DOES YOUR ORGANIZATION UNDERSTAND THE TYPICAL CHALLENGES FACED BY SALES PROFESSIONALS?

When we asked sales professionals in our survey to describe the typical challenges they face on a daily basis in their careers, survey respondents provided input in a variety of ways. Dealing with constant rejection emerged as perhaps the most significant challenge. As one respondent explained, "You can't make every sale. However, knowing how to turn rejection into future opportunity is a skill worth having."

The typical challenges identified by sales professionals in our survey can serve as a starting point for you to use in planning useful sales training for your own organization. Examine this checklist and consider which challenges you already provide training on.

☐ Dealing with constant rejection

☐ Getting clients to try the product

☐ Competing for internal sales support resources

☐ Turning bids, quotations, and prototypes in a timely fashion

☐ Keeping subcontractors focused, including key suppliers

☐ Getting products out of research and development faster

☐ Lack of support at times from corporate leadership who focus more on "bean counter" management versus strategic management

☐ Responding to competitive challenges from new business models; that is, on-line auctions to continued demands from large industrial markets for cost reductions of 5 percent per year

☐ Finding time to do all the paperwork and still meet goals

☐ Is our overall experience at our organization equal to or better than what our competitors provide? Is the grass greener on the other side or not?

☐ Keeping motivated in hard times

☐ Constantly servicing clients with delivery, pricing, and competitive issues

☐ Turnover of contacts at companies where you have invested a lot of time and effort to build a relationship

ARE YOU AWARE OF WHICH SALES GROUPS
IN OTHER ORGANIZATIONS
HAVE PLANNED TRAINING CURRICULA?

A curriculum is a long-term, standard series of planned learning experiences—such as training courses—for individuals, work units or departments, and job categories (Rothwell & Sredl, 2000). As indicated in Figure 2.4, most planned sales training efforts are targeted at new or recently promoted sales professionals.

Building a training curriculum that is aligned with and linked to the needs of the organization and specific sales professionals is critical for success. As the authors' survey for this book revealed, many organizations do not invest the time or resources to develop a planned sales training curriculum. It is important to note that the term *curriculum* does not mean that the sales training and development program should consist only of classroom lectures (Pike, 1990). Based on individual and organizational needs, training strategies may draw on a broad array of media including the Web, audio and video tapes, and on-the-job training (see Baker, 1990; Cataldo & Cooper, 1990; Kersen, 1990; Kotler, 1990; Lafferty & Range, 1990; Newman, 1990; Parry, 1990; Ward & Wolfson, 1990; Wills, 1990). The following provides a sample outline of a sales training program that may be integrated into an overall curriculum for new sales professionals.

A Sample Program Outline on Essentials of Sales for New Sales Professionals

Description: This program is for new or emerging sales professionals, small business owners, and other individuals who have little formal training in the sales process. Experienced sales professionals can also refresh and expand their skills by attending this interactive program focused on the essentials of sales.

Overview and Focus: Sales is one of the oldest professions in the world. The fact is, most of us engage in some act of selling every day; selling our ideas, getting others to help us, or selling our products and services. From all of our experiences, we can distill a selling process that enhances our chances of success in sales. These essentials are detailed in this program to assist participants to acquire a higher skill level in sales. This highly interactive workshop features case studies, a variety of planning exercises, and other activities designed with an action–learning focus.

Learning Objectives:
- Assess your current sales practices
- Determine the critical factors that contribute to higher sales performance
- Develop sales skills that will better enable you to cultivate and satisfy the needs of customers and prospects
- Prepare plans to increase your personal sales effectiveness

Figure 2.4
What Groups Are Targeted for a Planned Sales Training Curriculum as Reported by Survey Respondents?

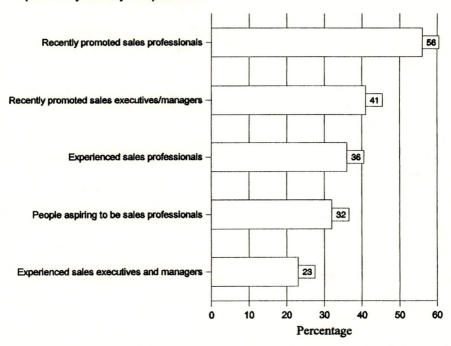

Source: From *A Survey about Sales Training Programs* by W. Rothwell, W. Donahue, and J. Park, 2001 (unpublished survey results), University Park, PA: Pennsylvania State University. Copyright 2001 by W. Rothwell, W. Donahue, and J. Park.

Program Contents:
- Introduction to the essentials of successful sales
- Presales skills and strategies
- Preplanning the sales call
- Developing effective listening skills
- Successful sales calling
- The written proposal: a tool for closing
- Keeping your customer satisfied

What actions can you take to better define the curricula for your sales organization? Use this worksheet to organize your thoughts about the answer to that question.

A Worksheet for Action Planning

Directions: Use this worksheet to organize your thinking. Make notes about the planned training curricula that should be sponsored by your organization. For each job title of a sales professional in your organization, note what incumbents of that job category should do to help them qualify for the job, keep their skills updated, and qualify for advancement.

Notes:

3

Planning Learning and Development Opportunities

In order to plan learning and development opportunities, sales professionals must do the following:

- Identify required actions and educational resources.
- Provide appropriate learning and development opportunities.
- Deliver them in ways appropriate to close performance gaps.

In this chapter, then, we will explain how to create a plan for designing and developing learning and development opportunities for sales professionals. The plan that is established should center around three key competency areas that sales professionals should possess:

- Knowledge of self
- Knowledge of products and services
- Knowledge of the clients and the business

These three key areas will also be the focus of the next three parts of the book and provide an anchor point for conceptualizing the essential competencies of sales professionals.

As you begin this chapter, complete the ten-item self-assessment. As you do that, be sure to note that each question is important for establishing a well-planned sales training and development program.

Self-Assessment:
Planning Learning and Development Opportunities

Directions: Read each statement carefully. With your sales organization in mind, place the number that fits with your level of agreement with each of the ten statements.

Disagree									Agree
1	2	3	4	5	6	7	8	9	10

_____Your sales organization requires individuals to prepare professional development plans for themselves at least annually.

_____Your organization has identified education and training resources available to your sales staff.

_____Your organization provides appropriate in-house learning and development opportunities.

_____You considered the pros and cons of different methods of education and training delivery.

_____You recognize the education, training, and development methods employed most frequently in other organizations.

_____Your organization plans on-the-job training opportunities for your sales professionals.

_____You recognize the usual types of in-house customized programs conducted by their sales organizations.

_____Your sales organization identifies and assigns responsibilities for in-house mentoring.

_____Your sales organization seeks proposals for customized services from education and training providers.

_____Your organization is effective at documenting education, training, and development best practices.

_____Total

How Did You Score?

Here is the key to planning learning and development opportunities. Add up your responses to get your score.

91–100 Great job! Congratulations! Your organization is effectively working to identify sales staff needs and designing an appropriate curricula.

81–90 Keep up the good work! You've probably had considerable success. But by using some of the tips in this chapter, you could improve your success.

71–80 Help is needed! There is room for improvement. You'll find this chapter helpful.

0–70 Warning! Your sales organization probably has some confusion. Read on!

By recognizing and addressing the real or perceived issues that influence the design and development of the training and development program in your organization, you can increase the chance of its success. If you wish, use the following worksheet to organize your thinking in a more open-ended way about how to plan learning and development opportunities that are uniquely suited to sales professionals in your organization.

Worksheet for Planning Learning and Development Opportunities

Directions: In your opinion, what problems or challenges do your sales professionals face in planning their learning and development opportunities? Use this worksheet to organize your thinking in answering this question.

Notes:

DOES YOUR ORGANIZATION REQUIRE INDIVIDUALS TO PREPARE PROFESSIONAL DEVELOPMENT PLANS AT LEAST ANNUALLY?

Ideas without actions are useless. That principle holds true for sales training and development programs. To be of greatest benefit, individuals must be matched up to the training needs identified through the needs assessment and curriculum design process described in Chapter 2.

An Individual Development Plan (IDP) is a way to do that. As its name implies, an IDP is a plan intended to guide the professional development of each person over some timespan, such as one year. An IDP should set forth who will be developed, what results are sought from those activities, when those activities will be undertaken, where the activities will be undertaken, why they are worth doing, how the developmental activities will be carried out, and how much they may cost. The goal of most IDPs is to narrow the gap between what the person knows or can do and what he or she should know or do to perform effectively. IDPs should be established for each sales professional at least annually (Dubois & Rothwell, 2000).

The IDP is essentially the action plan that is intended to activate the training curriculum for an individual. It provides sales managers with insight into a sales professional's commitment and motivation level and becomes a tool for tracking progress. When incorporated into the sales professional's performance review process, IDPs can become a means to the end of rectifying some performance deficiencies, planning refresher training when needed (Anderson, 1989), or preparing individuals to meet future challenges.

Sales professionals should reflect on important issues as they devise an IDP in cooperation with their managers. Many such issues are listed in the following checklist. Ask sales professionals in your organization to check the items that should be considered in your organization during the individual development planning process.

☐ Have I identified two or three key areas of improvement and created learning goals and objectives for each area?

☐ Is my plan created in a way that will force me to take action on a daily or weekly basis that will keep me engaged in my learning activities?

☐ Does my plan have a feedback or evaluation mechanism built in that will allow me to determine if I am learning and doing things differently?

☐ Is there someone I can go to if I am not succeeding and need help?

☐ Have I clearly defined what success is?

☐ Have I identified any potential roadblocks and the strategies I will use to overcome the barriers?

HAS YOUR ORGANIZATION IDENTIFIED EDUCATION AND TRAINING RESOURCES AVAILABLE TO YOUR SALES STAFF?

Many resources exist to support the development of sales professionals. Hundreds of books, tapes, and on-line resources are available to help meet many training needs (see Del Gazio & Fox, 1990). To narrow the number down, start by identifying the training needs listed on the sales training curriculum and then find the most effective resources to meet those needs. Then consider the learning style preferences of sales professionals in your organization to refine the list further. If you do not know the learning style preferences of your sales professionals, consider administering a learning style inventory.

Avoid the temptation to make training mandatory for everyone. Sales professionals understand that few customers believe that "one size fits all," and the same principle applies to training. A better approach is a targeted one focused on meeting individual needs. In that way, training is more likely to be time-efficient and cost-effective.

Training success is not the result of a one-shot event. Instead, it results from long-term effort. To make it most effective, try to find ways to integrate learning opportunities with the daily work activities of sales professionals. Transfer of learning can be enhanced by making learning part of a sales professional's daily work activity. Training should be a constant theme in all sales meetings.

Critical Situation:
Developing Annual Learning Plans for Sales Professionals

Situation: We spent thousands and thousands of dollars on all sorts of training stuff. But half the time no one even knew where it was and there seemed to be no rhyme or reason for what we bought. Some of the audiotapes were alright and I used to listen to them in the car when I was making company calls. But after I listened to one or two of them it all started to sound the same. Most of the books were so elementary that they weren't much use for anyone other than new people who didn't have a clue. I know there are areas where I could develop, but I don't have time to spend going to seminars, and when I do take off I end up worrying about stuff or even getting calls on my cell phone from clients looking for a late delivery.

Development Issues: Most sales professionals recognize the need for training. However, that competitive nature that helps to make them a successful salesperson also creates internal conflict when they are pulled away from their clients for training. Scheduling is an important challenge of a sales development program, as well as identifying effective training resources.

Action Tips:
- Establish a development plan format for sales professionals to input and submit annually.
- Ask sales professionals to identify education and training opportunities or other learning resources they believe might help them improve their performance.

Of course, everyone knows that finding time for training in today's fast-paced business environment can be difficult. With the advent of cell phones and e-mail, many clients expect immediate access to their sales representatives twenty-four hours per day, seven days a week. When your sales professionals are participating in training, some of them—and some clients—may expect that others are there to take over their accounts. Scheduling time for face-to-face training events can be difficult. Long-term planning is thus essential to have dates placed on calendars.

In addition, many sales managers may wonder how much training time is reasonable. While the answer to that question is rarely simple, many successful organizations ask their workers to set aside 5 percent of their annual work time for professional development. That translates to mean about 80–100 hours each year per worker. Of course, professional development efforts can also be undertaken individually through self-paced learning—such as books, audiotapes, videotapes, and Web-based instruction—as much as by classroom time.

What training opportunities are appropriate for your sales professionals? One place to start in answering that question is to ask your sales professionals to identify the learning resources that they have found most useful. That might include time spent with mentors, off-site courses, books, and many other materials or methods. Use the following checklist to help in this process of identifying preferred methods.

    ☐ Classroom training
    ☐ Independent study and/or correspondence course
    ☐ Web-based on-line training
    ☐ CD–computer-based training
    ☐ Simulations
    ☐ Role plays
    ☐ Videotapes
    ☐ Audiotapes
    ☐ Books and articles
    ☐ On-the-job training
    ☐ Job rotation
    ☐ Job aids
    ☐ Mentoring

Avoid purchasing training materials without careful review (McCullough, 1990). Hundreds or thousands of dollars can be wasted on ineffective videos or books. Worse yet, some training materials may be inappropriate for the clients with whom your sales professionals must interact or with the corporate culture in which they function. No single resource will work for all uses and individuals. Consequently, your sales professionals should have access to many training and development opportunities to reflect their unique learning needs.

DOES YOUR ORGANIZATION PROVIDE APPROPRIATE IN-HOUSE LEARNING AND DEVELOPMENT OPPORTUNITIES?

Self-development and guided professional development call for more than just access to learning resources. They also necessitate time, management support, and encouragement. They may also require a clear message that shows the link between the sales training and the organization's competitive challenges (Hessan & Keiser, 1990). Quick fixes such as one-time motivational speakers or junkets to luxurious locales do not create sustainable sales training and development programs that are aligned with the organization's strategic direction. Avoid confusing training as a means to build competencies with the mistaken use of training as a substitute for more tangible rewards for successful sales performance.

Effective professional development does not occur in isolation. It may require sales professionals to interact with others, discuss opportunities for improvement, and receive feedback from others. It may also require some trial-and-error learning in which mistakes are to be expected.

Informal training can also be very helpful. But do not expect it to happen on its own. Most people need some kind of structure in which to carry out interpersonal interactions that are intended to foster learning, as this situation illustrates.

Critical Situation: Customer Service in Review—Friday Mornings

Situation: In our manufacturing facility the supervisors hold brief informal "toolbox talks" on production and safety issues every Friday morning. The supervisor brings in doughnuts or something and the crew spends fifteen minutes reviewing some type of minisession on safety and debriefing on any problems that happened during the week. They are pretty informal and all of the supervisors think they really help. So we decided to try the same type of idea with our inside customer service people and any salespeople who are in the office on Friday mornings. I bring in doughnuts or bagels for the group, there are anywhere between ten and fifteen of us, and we review four key agenda items or questions:

1. What were the customer complaints for the week and how did we resolve them?
2. Were there any internal issues or problems we should be aware of?
3. What pieces of information have we heard about the competition?
4. What did you do that was exemplary this past week?

Development Issues: Learning new things or changing old ones can be a lot less threatening if they are introduced in smaller bite size chunks versus giving someone a drink out of a fire hose. Doing little things like buying doughnuts can go a long way in creating a sense of team and trust in an organization. Asking sales professionals what they did that was exemplary inspires discussion and validates what your organization really believes and stands for. Invariably, team members are doing numerous things that go unnoticed and often underappreciated by sales executives.

Action Tips:
- Consider weekly customer service review sessions.
- Ask your sales professionals each week what they have done that was exemplary.

According to the American Society for Training and Development (ASTD), citing previously conducted research, 73 percent of sales, clerical, and administrative support workers received formal (planned) training in 1995—the most recent year for which detailed information is available—while 98 percent of workers in the same group received informal (unplanned on-the-job) training in the same period. Workers in this group averaged twenty hours per employee per year of formal training and forty-six hours of informal training for a total of sixty-six hours of training per employee per year (see http://www.astd.org/members/data_book/chapter_4/chapter4_q8.htm). This represented less training than that received by other groups. According to ASTD, "examination of the data by occupation reveals that professional and technical workers, and managers, are most likely to receive training."

HAVE YOU CONSIDERED THE PROS AND CONS OF DIFFERENT METHODS OF EDUCATION AND TRAINING DELIVERY?

Individuals differ in how they learn. And some information is more appropriately distributed in one way rather than others. Likewise, not all ways of delivering training are equally effective to facilitate learning, provide information, or build skills.

In recent years, much attention has focused on Web-based training (Bersani, 1999). Nearly everyone has jumped on this bandwagon. And, to be sure, on-line learning—which is sometimes called e-learning or Web-based training—is viable for many learning experiences. Compared to classroom delivery, for instance, on-line learning provides opportunities for learners to be more thoughtful in framing their responses to questions, access voluminous amounts of information, and receive the benefits of instructor-guided delivery without the costs or dangers of travel. Much has been written about on-line learning and other high-tech training methods (see, for instance, Atkinson, 1989; Eline, 1997; Force, 1990; Kerwin, 1994; Moxley, 1993; "Retooling sales training," 1999; Rogers, 1994; Rottenberg, 1990; Russ, Heir, Erffmeyer, & Easterling, 1989; Schriver & Giles, 1998; "Technology," 1994).

However, on-line learning is no panacea. When the learners lack computer skills (Campbell, 1998), lack the technology savvy, or use outmoded technology, the focus of an on-line learning experience can quickly shift from learning to managing the technology. Furthermore, on-line learning—perhaps more than classroom-based instruction—may require individuals to take more initiative and demonstrate greater motivation. Review the special focus article on this topic.

Special Focus: Sales E-Learning

It's already happening. Reps are being trained over the Internet, intranets, and CD-ROMs. Could classrooms become extinct?

Sales training is gearing up for a wired future. During the past eighteen months, big and small businesses alike have been trading classroom training for technology-based programs that are available over the Internet, corporate intranets, or on CD-ROMs. The trend is sure to continue into the next century. Not because wired training is slicker or jazzier, but because it's cheaper, say users and program developers.

One company estimates that it typically costs $8,000 to train one salesperson at a three-day, instructor-led course. That's $1,500 for an instructor, plus airfare, hotel, and a per diem for trainees. Then there's overhead associated with the venue. What's more, if a salesperson is out of the field, there's a large opportunity cost—reps make money when they're in front of customers, not sitting in a classroom.

Says one marketing manager: "It's not cost effective to bring salespeople together at a meeting all the time. If you can train using technology, you can recognize big benefits."

Increasingly, companies are providing sales skills training over the Internet. Businesses that want training available in a Web format can set up programs on their own internal intranets, which allow access only to the companies' reps and distributors. Whether located on the World Wide Web or an intranet, these programs are accessed via a central server. Users study text on screen and often participate in interactive assessment tests. Other companies have opted to use CD-ROM technology for training, bypassing the slow speeds and lack of video associated with Net-based tools.

So far, video-friendly CD-ROM is the more practical vehicle for technology-based training, but over the long term, the Internet and intranets will take over, says Tom Minero, president of Training Resources Inc., a Clifton, New Jersey-based company specializing in sales automation training. "I think what most people are realizing is that the training has always been a crafted product where you brought twenty-five people into a room," he says. "But of course that wasn't very cost-effective. Now, for the first time, people have found a technology that actually works. What it does is allow us to take training and turn it into a commodity."

Intranet Savings

Salespeople at Sun Microsystems Computer Company in Mountain View, California, are already learning that firsthand. Lifecycle Selling Inc., a sales training firm in Foster City, California, recently developed an intranet version of its training program for Sun. Users log onto a centralized server and call up a browser that steps them through the Lifecycle Selling application. "What we've done with Sun is put together an intranet-based course that provides classroom training outside the classroom, so their sales reps can now spend more time in the field," says Rick Brown, Lifecycle's president.

Those time savings can add up. For example, Sun just launched a new set of enterprise servers (a huge server with mainframe capability). In a typical training class, the optimum size of a classroom is about 25 to 30 trainees. In the case of Sun, which has 5,000 distributors and 2,000 direct salespeople, it could take more than a year to effectively train all the direct and alternate sales channels. "If you can offer training over an intranet or the Internet, you can shorten the sales training time by probably seventy-five percent," Brown says. "You have now recouped a tremendous time-to-market advantage in that you have adequately trained both your direct and alternate channels to effectively sell a new product line within three months instead of more than a year."

Sun has started the Lifecycle program on its own intranet and CD-ROMs, and plans to eventually make it available on the Internet. The company has reported that it expects to cut its sales training costs by as much as 50 percent with these techniques.

"It's an expansion to our sales methodology," explains Kate Barclay, director of worldwide field training for Sun. "This is a sales tool that can be used if you've got an account call the next morning. It can refresh your memory before your call."

Barclay asked Lifecycle to develop Sun's intranet program because she needed something that would enhance the other sales courses that are taken in the field. She looked for a program that could be written into a Web-based format. "We did it, and it worked," she says.

Barclay estimates that 500 Sun field reps currently use the system. Eventually, Sun's resellers will be able to access the same types of training courses via the Internet.

Billion-Dollar Business

The enthusiasm for computer-aided training has led many companies to place their bets on the World Wide Web. The U.S. Internet-based training market, estimated to be worth $19 million in 1995, will grow to $1.7 billion by the end of the century, according to Ellen Julian, research manager for International Data Corporation in Framingham, Massachusetts.

Some of the products on—or preparing to enter—the Internet-based training market (the trendy will call it IBT) include Lifecycle, ToolBook II, and LearnItOnline, and Seattle-based Asymetrix provides on-line training via its ToolBook II product line. The programs let users convert applications directly into HTML and Java, the industry standards for Internet content. That means anyone with a Web browser can access training material created with software like ToolBook II Instructor and ToolBook II Assistant, authoring tools for professional course developers.

Asymetrix supports both intranets and the Internet, but Marketing Manager David Burke sees an advantage to offering training over an intranet. "In all networks, you're limited to your lowest common denominator," he says. "With the Internet, that's a telephone line. With an intranet, you can have video and audio, because an intranet is usually based on an internal network."

Burke adds that the tools his company offers are flexible, so users can choose how sophisticated a program they want to develop. "If it's for the Internet, we help them understand they should use text or simple graphics," he says. "But if you're developing a corporate intranet, we tell them to take advantage of the capabilities that let you add audio, video, and animation."

Logical Operations' LearnItOnline provides on-line software training for people who are learning how to use a word processor, a spreadsheet, or a contact manager like ACT. If your sales force was upgrading from Windows 3.1 applications to Office 97, you could send reps to specific company modules on the Internet for at-their-desk training. The company offers training on all the popular application software from Corel, Microsoft, Lotus, and Novell.

Like other programs of its ilk, the system has three major features: It is transportable; it has a centralized administration, so if you're in charge of a sales force automation rollout you can see who is logged in and what kind of training they've taken; and it has an assessment feature—take a test and it will point you to the tutorials you need to improve your skills.

Prices are based on the library of courses a company purchases, the number of users, plus the length of time for which the programs are ordered—in this case, a three-, six-, or twelve-month period. When you get up into the thousands of people, the training runs about $20 to $30 per head. At the first entry point, fifty people, it's less than $100 per person per year. The pricing model was devised to compete against a day of classroom training, which typically costs $150 per person just for the training, before travel, lodging, and meal expenses are factored in.

KN Energy, a Lakewood, Colorado, natural gas company, currently uses the Internet-based product for training remote users on an array of Microsoft programs, including Windows 95, Word, Excel, and PowerPoint. The firm is expanding into rural parts of western America, like Gillette, Wyoming, and has satellite offices in Montana, Kansas, Texas, and Nebraska—but has the services of just two training professionals who can't possibly work with all the KN Energy employees throughout the country.

Sharon Pike, KN's training manager, gave out ten LearnItOnline subscriptions to employees in Wyoming last March to see how the service would be received. Although instructor-led classes are still the most ideal method of training, Pike feels LearnItOnline will save money in the long run. "The feedback we've gotten from the Wyoming location is that this is really going to add value," Pike says. "To go to some of our remote locations, to send an instructor, airfare is at least $1,000, plus there's an overnight hotel stay. So we're promoting this internally as one of the first choices to use."

Another recent entry to the market is Network Publishing's ABLE training infrastructure. Like other programs, ABLE purports to reduce the amount of training time learners spend by tailoring the curriculum to their particular needs. Participants are profiled and tested to assess experience, knowledge, and skills. The program then directs them to the appropriate learning materials.

Herd Mentality

Not everybody is sold on the virtues of Internet–intranet training. Some argue that there are better multimedia training alternatives. For instance, CD-ROMs lend themselves to extensive video and graphics-heavy displays. Minneapolis-based Wilson Learning Corporation, one of the nation's oldest sales training firms, with clients as diverse as Norstar Steel, NationsBank, and IBM, distributes a series of about a dozen CD-ROM programs that help train people in live video simulations relative to sales and management.

"I'm certainly a supporter of the Internet and intranets, but in the herd mentality toward them, we're not discussing enough about CD-ROMs," says Steve Bainbridge, Wilson's director of interactive media. "The hardware and software people have brainwashed everyone with talk about 'the next big thing.' You get these wild things like, 'Everything needs to be on the Internet.' Why? Did we close down radio because now we have TV? CD-ROM is a capability that allows you to handle 'fat' media. The Internet can handle 'thin' media—text, some graphics, voice—but anything else is excruciatingly slow. CD-ROM is highly portable—I can take it on an airplane and I don't need to dial in to a service provider to get in."

Wilson's CD-ROM titles include "Sell to Needs: A Consultative Program"; "No Trust, No Sale!" which focuses on building relationships; and "Start to Sell," which addresses introductory issues of selling. "We can present these ideas, and the neat thing CD-ROM does is we can then take you into a real-life situation, have you practice those skills, and have a client in your face yelling at you."

Wilson's customers enjoy the flexibility their CD-ROMs provide. "We use their interactive product to support their seminar programs," says Dan Shirk, vice president of sales for Minneapolis-based Walman Optical, an optical-supply wholesaler. "We use it to reinforce the sales staff and as a coaching tool."

In fact, Walman now has more than one-third of its sixty-five-member sales team using the programs on a regular basis. "If they feel they're missing something in their presentation, this gives them the opportunity to revisit their training in a safe environment," Shirk says. "It allows them to practice it and get their skills back to speed."

Even Logical Operations, while doing a full-court press for LearnItOnline, realized there is a market for CD-ROM training, prompting them to release the Custom Classroom Library, training vignettes similar to those available on their Web site. "There's a happy medium," says Jerry Weissberg, vice president and general manager of Logical Operations. "We take the same training and make it available on CD-ROM because some people just aren't using the Internet."

"A good sales training program makes use of at least two—and preferably three—types of media," adds Sun's Barclay. "There are places in the world where we don't have telecommunications as well as we do in the United States, so we have it on CD."

Like Internet-based programs, the CD-ROMs can be applied to extend into audiences that won't be given the budget to go to a seminar, such as large telemarketing departments. Says Bainbridge, "Sales training is still done in groups of fifteen or twenty, but the CD-ROMs are provided as 'prework.' The idea is to get as much content done out in the field on a CD-ROM and then, when you get together as a group, where you've spent money on airplanes and hotels, to actually solve the business problem at hand—namely, 'How are we going to sell this to our client base when we go back to work Monday morning" (Kahn, 1997, pp. 81–88).

The debate rages on as to the effectiveness of on-line learning. But the authors suggest, based on their experience, that you do the following:

- Focus on course content before selecting a delivery method.
- Direct your attention to finding ways to increase student interaction no matter what delivery method you use.
- Ensure learner interaction with the instructor and try to provide as much of a personal touch as you can. Suppot the creation of learning communities.
- Think about what rewards the learners will receive as a result of their participation in the learning experience, since participation (and learning commitment) is influenced by how much and what kind of reward the participants will receive upon completion.

Consider the following situation as a starting point if you contemplate using on-line delivery for training.

Critical Situation: On-Line Learning— Check Out the Technology Needs

Situation: We have been providing an on-line customer service course to employees in our regional sales offices for about a year. The content is solid and we like the fact that everyone is getting the same message. We put them through the class in groups so they can discuss some of the little case studies that are included and help each other out with the assignments. When we decided to go with this idea it made sense because we have people all over the country working different shifts and pulling people together at the same time is difficult. What we didn't count on is problems with getting people access to the Web. Some of our regional offices have gotten real strict about who can access the Web after they caught a couple of people playing the stock market and doing on-line gambling during work hours. In fact for many departments they have blocked access or limited it to only certain sites so people can track packages or get information on production. We also thought this way those individuals that were really interested could do the course at home in the evenings on their own computers. What we found out was that a lot of the people we hire in customer service don't have a computer at home with access to the Web or if they do it is running a modem so slow the course wouldn't perform the way it was supposed to. So, we are considering buying laptops that can be distributed to people to use during the course and if they go on to get involved in additional training we may sell them to the students at a reduced cost.

Development Issues: As much as we look to technology as the magic bullet, rarely is it that simple. Planning for multiple deliveries and anticipating where problems can arise can enhance the effectiveness of a sales-development effort.

Action Tips:

- Take an inventory of your sales team's technology needs before implementing on-line learning activities.
- Ask your on-line learning provider if the company has a twenty-four-hour help desk, and check out their reputation.

Keep in mind that learning styles differ. Some people learn most effectively by reading a book. Others learn best by watching someone. Still others have to have a hands-on experience to learn. And some must listen to explanations or directions. Often the best approach is to combine all of these requirements so that all learning styles are accommodated.

Learning also takes place formally (through planned training), informally (through listening to stories told by others or watching someone carry out an activity), and incidentally (through trial-and-error experience or even by accident). If sales professionals understand that, they can take advantage of almost anything to learn. For example, when reading a book, they can review the table of contents before they start to focus on chapters to help them solve the immediate problems they face. They can write down key points from everything they read to increase what they remember. They can also go beyond what they read to brainstorm on how a new idea might be applied creatively.

DO YOU RECOGNIZE THE TRAINING AND DEVELOPMENT METHODS EMPLOYED MOST BY OTHER ORGANIZATIONS?

Benchmarking, which involves examining what other organizations do, has gained widespread attention in recent years as a tool for continuous improvement. Deciding how to deliver sales training and development programs is an issue that is well-suited to it. Benchmarking can be carried out deliberately, or it can be done less informally by reading about practices in other organizations. You can find out how other organizations deliver training by attending professional training conferences or reading magazines written for trainers.

In our survey of sales professionals, we asked them how they deliver sales training. You may find the results useful, and interesting, for purposes of benchmarking. Examine Figure 3.1 and consider why some delivery methods may be preferred to others.

DOES YOUR ORGANIZATION PLAN ON-THE-JOB TRAINING OPPORTUNITIES FOR YOUR SALES PROFESSIONALS?

On-the-job training (OJT) surfaced as the most popular delivery method for sales training for our survey respondents. When planned, OJT is a most effective method for enhancing the performance of new sales professionals. But, unfortunately, much OJT is not planned. Giving someone OJT has too often meant "send the rookie out with one of the experienced salespersons to tag along on a couple of sales calls and then turn that person loose." Unplanned OJT is frequently not effective and can even create problems of inconsistent (or even unknown) training among new hires. If new hires are not trained in ways that align with the organization's preferred approach, then the new hire can be set up to fail.

In contrast, a planned approach to OJT is guided by checklists based on work requirements. Trainers are given job aids to use in the training process. Learners are also evaluated for what they have learned.

If managed, OJT can give trainees powerful experiences to learn and is a powerful approach to training (see Rothwell & Kazanas, 1994). Spending one-on-one time in a car with an experienced trainer can give new sales professionals unique insight about client expectations and shed light on "tricks of the trade" learned by top performers. It also facilitates the socialization of the new hire which can be so important to retention.

Think about the following situation. What does this situation dramatize about OJT?

Critical Situation: On-the-Job Training—Selecting Assignments

Situation: Twenty years ago when I started with the organization I spent my first two weeks riding around with Bill as he called on clients. That was it for my sales training until a few years ago. Those were the days when smoking was much more acceptable and Bill would chain smoke and drink coffee all day long as we drove for hours at a

Figure 3.1
Sales Training Delivery Methods Used by Organizations as Reported by Survey Respondents

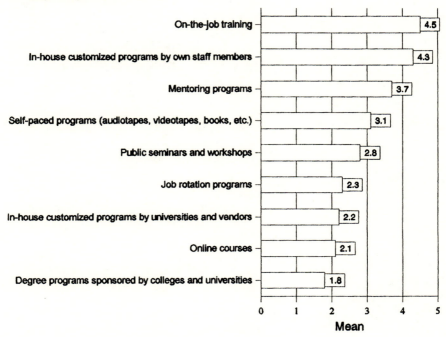

Source: From *A Survey about Sales Training Programs* by W. Rothwell, W. Donahue, and J. Park, 2001 (unpublished survey results), University Park, PA: Pennsylvania State University. Copyright 2001 by W. Rothwell, W. Donahue, and J. Park.

time. I think I sampled every greasy-spoon within two-hundred miles. Bill shared lots of war stories about his big sales, and he certainly had an opinion on everything about the organization. It was interesting because when I tried to talk to him about what made him successful he never really answered my questions. He just wanted to tell me more stories about the big account he sold ten years ago. One thing he did share with me was the importance of closing a deal and making sure you ask for the order. That is one lesson I learned and still remember today.

Development Issues: It is easy for a sales manager to assume that if you send a new person out with a seasoned person that the new person will gain a wealth of knowledge and an understanding of what it takes to be a successful salesperson. The new person can also pick up a lot of bad habits. The seasoned or most successful salesperson does not necessarily make the best sales trainer or mentor.

Action Tips:
• For on-the-job training select seasoned sales professionals who have the skills and patience to explain the tricks of the trade to new salespeople.

- Expose new sales professionals to a variety of your exemplary performers and highlight what it is about those professionals that makes them exemplary and potentially good role models.

DO YOU RECOGNIZE THE TYPICAL TYPES OF IN-HOUSE CUSTOMIZED PROGRAMS CONDUCTED BY ORGANIZATIONS?

Review the description of the typical in-house learning events reported by respondents to a recent survey.

Course or Program	Conducted by	What Made It Effective
Customer-focused selling priorities	Vice President of sales and marketing	Communicated priorities Outlined expectations Good overview and summary
Customer service	Internal staff	Job specific Practical Outlined responsibilities
Annual convention	Internal symposium	Shared best practices

The survey respondents were asked what training courses would contribute most to the organization's bottom line. Notable in these survey results was the emphasis on customer service. In addition, what is deemed as needed most by internal sales professionals is the sharing of best practices and a venue for communication about expectations. Trends change. But the basics are still regarded as critical to success.

DOES YOUR ORGANIZATION IDENTIFY AND ASSIGN RESPONSIBILITIES FOR IN-HOUSE MENTORING?

Mentoring ranked near the top of the list of sales training methods revealed in our recent survey. Mentoring means more than on-the-job training (Ward & Wolfson, 1990). Mentoring refers to a relationship between an individual and his or her trusted counselor, guide, or coach.

Mentoring can play a significant role in the professional development of new sales professionals. However, effective mentoring programs can be time consuming. Although, from a sales manager's perspective, mentoring can be a cost-effective strategy to improve how well sales professionals understand the corporate culture of their organizations and their responsibilities.

On the surface, mentoring appears to be easy to implement. However, mentoring programs do not always succeed. One reason for failure is that sustaining relationships between mentors and mentees can be difficult. In many cases, the natural candidates to be mentors are sales managers or outstanding, experienced sales professionals.

However, the characteristics that make them successful in their sales positions may also inhibit their ability to be effective as mentors. Effective mentors must be willing to take the time to play the role. But many successful sales professionals would prefer to devote their time to cultivating new clients or enhancing relationships with existing clients. While mentors may initially voice interest and support in the role, they may find it difficult to sustain that interest without a reward or recognition system for mentors. The following situation dramatizes this point.

Critical Situation: Mentoring—Rewarding and Cost-Effective

Situation: We continue to pair up our new salespeople with an experienced rep. What we are trying to do is match up our successful salespeople with the new ones. When we first started this process we really just did it haphazardly and didn't worry too much about it. It was a combination of on-the-job training and mentoring. But in the last few years we have begun to approach it in a systematic way and have learned that if our new salespeople have some friends around the company they trust and can count on they are much happier and for the most part stay longer and are more productive. Part of this process of creating this network is working with a mentor to help establish this network of friends and colleagues. There is no doubt in my mind that a good mentor can definitely help to improve the productivity and satisfaction of our sales staff. But the problem is getting the good ones to do it. We are experimenting with a reward and recognition system for our mentors. We are scheduling time at the end of our quarterly sales meetings for the mentors to meet with the sales professionals they are mentoring and just send the mentors all $100 gift certificates as a token of appreciation.

Development Issues: Effective mentoring programs start with having a plan for the mentoring process and a set of goals to guide, not direct, the relationship. Mentors must be carefully selected, recognized, and rewarded for their efforts. Mentoring is not managing, and mixed messages can be sent to new sales professionals when their mentor also evaluates their performance.

Action Tips:
- Ask your sales professionals who they believe would make good sales mentors or sounding boards.
- Assemble a list of possible mentors and ask if they would serve in that capacity.
- Match mentors with mentees.

DOES YOUR ORGANIZATION SEEK CUSTOMIZED SERVICES FROM EDUCATION AND TRAINING PROVIDERS?

Selecting a vendor to create customized on-site sales training is a challenging task (Whitcup, 1992). The training can end up being less than effective unless the vendor is examined carefully beforehand and the outcomes of the training are clarified. If properly organized and facilitated, customized on-site training can be valuable. Proper organization should include individualized assessments, relevant case studies, and sales simulations or role plays tailored to the specific needs and performance gaps in your organization (Costa, 1989; "Games trainers play," 1990; Robinson, 1987). When selecting a facilitator, consider these criteria.

A Checklist for Evaluating a Training Provider's Qualifications

Yes	No	Does the proposed training provider or vendor possess the following:
____	____	Experience in teaching the subject areas and with similar groups?
____	____	Experience within your industry and culture?
____	____	The ability to create activities that are geared to the audience?
____	____	Experience in teaching adults?
____	____	Content grounded in a competency model that is aligned with your organization's needs?
____	____	The ability to deliver training in a flexible format that meets your needs?
____	____	The ability to deliver programs that meet your daily time schedule?
____	____	The ability to provide you with examples of long-term clients and references or testimonies from them?
____	____	Financial stability to ensure that the training provider or vendor will be around long-term?

What are the types of training courses or programs your local college, university, or respected private vendors could conduct on-site at your location that would contribute to your organization's bottom line (Husted, 1990; Schrello, 1990)? What would make them effective? The following provides a sample of typical sales courses indicated by our survey respondents that they have subcontracted to educational providers:

Course or Program	What Made It Effective
Basic selling skills	Experience of the presenters Practical tools and tips
One- to three-day public workshops	Stimulation of thinking Networking with local professionals
In-house customized programs	Tailored relevant examples

IS YOUR ORGANIZATION EFFECTIVE AT DOCUMENTING TRAINING AND DEVELOPMENT BEST PRACTICES?

Few small to medium-size organizations effectively identify and document their own internal best practices. Many larger organizations are forming knowledge management departments focused on sorting and cataloging best practice information. The process of creating a database-driven knowledge repository that is accessible from the Web can help sales professionals learn from each other. This strategy can add value to the organization and create an institutional memory that can outlive the departure of any sales professional.

With the overwhelming amount of knowledge and information available to all of us through television and the Internet there remain few secrets in business and manufacturing. In many businesses there is very little differentiation among competitors, especially in fields such as insurance or financial services. One way organizations continue to set themselves apart from the competition is how they add value for their customers and clients. This value is determined by the client perceptions. By sharing best practices with clients, an organization can add value for clients, as this critical situation dramatizes.

Critical Situation: Database-Driven Knowledge Management

Situation: As a provider of financial services we have a large geographically dispersed sales force that must comply with licensing and professional education requirements as well as constantly be involved in all types of training to improve skills and product knowledge. One of the best practices in our organization has been our knowledge-management system. It allows us to monitor and track all of the training requirements and the training completed for each employee. We have also linked it with several on-line learning activities and programs so we can utilize a variety of delivery mechanisms to meet the needs of our sales staff. Initially it was a huge undertaking to get the templates created and the data entered but after about eighteen months we are starting to see the real pay off on this investment as we can have up-to-date information on each of our sales professionals. They also can use the templates we provided to create their own annual learning plan which they discuss with their manager and is included as part of their performance evaluation. We haven't gotten to the point where we use the development plan as a factor in considering raises, but if someone is on the border line it can come in to play.

Development Issues: Organizations lacking a formal system for managing their knowledge are missing tremendous opportunities to add value to their own organization and to clients. This also fits into the need to look at management strength and to plan for succession.

Action Tips:
- Proactively identify potential education and training providers in your industry and area and create a database of learning resources.
- Establish an individual development plan template for your sales professionals to input and track.

What actions can you take to improve the planning for learning in your sales organization? Use the worksheet to capture your ideas about how to answer that question.

Worksheet for Action Planning

Directions: Use this worksheet to help you identify and document your thinking about ways to plan learning and development opportunities.

Notes:

4

Leading and Evaluating an In-House Sales Training and Development Program

A successful in-house sales training and development program consists of a systematic approach to developing the capabilities of an organization's sale professionals. Creating a sustainable sales organization begins with planning how to recruit, select, orient, and train sales professionals in line with the individual's sales competencies that are, in turn, linked to the organization's sales success. That individually focused development effort is also carried out in a corporate culture that encourages and rewards high performance in sales (Coker, Del Gazio, Murray, & Edwards, 2000).

This chapter focuses on the key success factors essential to leading and evaluating the in-house sales training and development program. To be effective in leading and evaluating such a program, a sales manager or other sales trainer must demonstrate and encourage high standards of performance, plan and evaluate outcomes, provide support, mentoring, coaching, counseling and follow-up, and monitor and evaluate sales training and development results to ensure that they are aligned with the organization's strategic business plan, objectives, and measures of success (Marx, 1990).

To be sure, evaluating the results of sales training can prove to be a daunting task (Currie, 1990; Hahne, Lefton, & Buzzotta, 1990). Much has been written about it (see Basarab, 1991; Bragg, 1989; Erffmeyer, Russ, & Hair, 1991; Evered, 1988; Faloon, 2000; Foshay, 1988; Honeycutt & Stevenson,

1989; Keenan, 1990; McMaster, 2001; Mendosa, 1995; Moses, 1992; Rackham, 1997; Rapp, 1990; Rojas, 1988; "Sales managers as trainers," 1995; Stolz, Majors, & Soares, 1994; "Web sales training," 1999). But this task is also an important one, since decision makers expect results—and not just the uplifting, albeit temporary, effects of motivational speakers, weekend retreats at elegant resorts, or inspiring cruise experiences. And, indeed, training evaluation has emerged as a key focus of attention in sales training.

Is There a Payoff to Sales Training?

Every year it's the same nightmare: Corporate wants your sales budget for the coming year and you're struggling over one line item—training for your salespeople. You projected travel and entertainment costs with no problem. Same with promotion, trade shows, computer equipment, and everybody's favorite—miscellaneous.

But that dreaded sales training. You spent several thousand dollars on it this year, and you're still trying to figure out what good it did, if any. Need some consolation? You're not alone in wanting to measure the return on investment for training. If sales managers and trainers agree on anything, it's that measuring the contribution of training to a company's bottom line is both important and difficult. Some even say it's impossible.

The trends are contradictory. On one hand, companies are becoming more concerned with evaluating their sales training programs, says Robert VeVerka, president of Professional Learning Systems in Cincinnati. On the other hand, he says, there are not as many evaluations of results being conducted as there were a few years ago. The reasons: cost, time, and proof that the evaluations are truly meaningful.

The dilemma for trainers is that management demands proof that training works, but refuses to budget the dollars for such evaluating. "Sales training managers are in a quandary," VeVerka says.

Need some inspiration? Trainers at such companies as Microsoft, R. R Donnelley, and AT&T have developed criteria—based on a model now almost forty years old—that they say provide enough benchmarks to judge the success of their sales training programs. They've avoided relying on the simple assumption that an increase in sales is the result of better training. Instead they have chosen to look at the behavioral development of salespeople both during and after a training program to analyze what good such education is doing.

Getting Reps up to Speed

"Management at Microsoft is data driven," says Mark Faber, research and measurement manager sales planning for Microsoft Corporation in Redmond, Washington. "If I were to attribute increased sales solely on increased sales training, they would take that apart and throw me out in five seconds. There are always so many other factors involved."

Microsoft offers nearly 100 training courses each year, but until 1992 never had a course specifically for the 120 new salespeople it hires annually. "I've heard horror stories about that," Faber shudders. "Salespeople would get up to speed eventually if they survived on the job."

Faber can use that legacy in his favor, though, when evaluating the effectiveness of the company's new-hire training program. He compares how fast new hires become proficient at doing their jobs versus those who did not receive training when first hired.

To evaluate new-hire trainees, Faber follows "The Four Levels of Valuation" model originally developed in 1959 by Donald Kirkpatrick, a former marketing professor at the University of Wisconsin. (The four levels are reaction, learning, behavior, and results.) He can easily measure the first two levels—reaction and learning—right in the classroom. For example, in a test for product knowledge, trainees are given a time limit to create an Excel worksheet. Further evaluation comes from managers, acting as customers, who score reps on their presentation skills, sales skills, and product knowledge. For level three—measuring the behavior of reps by how they applied their new attitudes, knowledge, and skills on the job—Faber conducts follow-up interviews with groups of 20 who had attended training sessions. "By identifying specific behaviors and having reps describe how these behaviors were used on sales calls, we determined how skills that were taught in the class were being applied," Faber says.

At the fourth level of evaluation—an actual measurement of the effect the training has on the company (such as increased sales, better quality, or reduced costs)—Faber and his staff conduct focus groups of Microsoft's sales managers who have new hires working for them. Even though the interviews produce evidence that is more anecdotal than scientific, past results have convinced management of the value of the training.

"We asked the managers to estimate how long it took the people who didn't attend the training [when hired] to get up to speed compared with those who did," he says. "In the past, managers estimated that for what it had taken new hires a year to ramp up on now took three months."

A Controlling Effect

In essence, though unintentionally, Microsoft used control groups (new hires with training versus those without) to test its training value. It's rare that companies purposely set out to separate reps into control groups or deprive one set of salespeople with tools simply to make a point. After all, who wants to go into the field with a disadvantage?

"In the businesses I've been in, nobody, especially in sales, wants to volunteer to be in the control group," Faber says. "The military has no trouble getting control groups: 'You guys go out with guns and you other guys go out without them.' Nobody in sales wants to go out without guns."

Plus, setting up control groups can be difficult, if not impossible. "Salespeople move from company to company, so your control group doesn't stay put," says Jane Holcomb of On-Target Training in Playa del Rey, California. "Even with a few people leaving the group, statistics change, so your level of significance isn't valid."

As Faber and other trainers have shown, there are ways of achieving the ends of a control method without actually using the means. One such way is to phase in a training program with one group of reps or in one region of the country at different time intervals. "You can implement [training] in one site and see a change," suggests Dan Baitch, research project manager for Learning International in Stanford, Connecticut. "Then you implement it in another site and see another change.

Meanwhile, nothing is changing in the other sites, so each acts as a control group for the one before it."

Maureen Haga is applying this staggered training approach at R. R. Donnelley and Sons Company in Chicago. As manager of sales performance development for the world's largest commercial printer, she is midway through a training program designed to develop the personal-computer skills of its sales force.

Between June and November of last year, 91 sales professionals (including sales assistants and senior vice presidents) in the company's international book publishing services division received training in using computers. This year another R. R. Donnelley merchandise media unit is receiving similar training, Haga says. By training the two groups in similar methods but at different intervals, Haga will have different benchmarks to measure the training's effectiveness.

For instance, in pretests given in January and March 1994, the company evaluated the computer knowledge of all 91 salespeople. At the time, 70 percent of the sales force was computer illiterate. Many people didn't even know how to type "win" to activate Windows or do a copy and paste function, she says. A post-test conducted last January showed how salespeople's on-the-job behaviors changed. "We found that eighty-eight demonstrated computer mastery," Haga states. "It's an extreme behavior change."

In addition to such statistical data, Haga can see the practical effects of the training. For example, the sales force is turning out quotes much faster and with less overhead. "Before computers were implemented in the sales force, it would take a sales rep anywhere from eight to sixteen hours to get a quote typed," she recalls. "Then, it had to be edited two or three times and put in the mail to the customer. If it takes two days for a customer to get a quote, you're giving your competitors more opportunity to capitalize on that small window. We've taken a two- to four-day quotation process and brought it down to twenty-five minutes."

The training is also reducing R. R. Donnelley's cost of doing business by eliminating word processors. "We had two or three people in the word processing room of each sales office, and all they did all day long was crank out quotes," Haga says. "That's why there was such a long lead time to get a quote out the door. We eliminated all those positions and the equipment, which are also areas of cost reductions that we're tracking. We even cut down on the volume of paper we had to order."

Planning for Results

Trainers such as Haga demonstrate how critical planning for an evaluation of training is often just as important as its implementation. Too often, evaluation is viewed as secondary, thus not enabling it to be conducted thoroughly throughout the process. "You have to know what your training goals are," says Haga, "and then establish your data collection mechanisms, such as revenue targets, profitability of sales, additional closed sales, and sales closure ratio."

Trude Fawson never intends to prove that the training programs she develops at the AT&T School of Business in Somerset, New Jersey, will produce verifiable evidence of success or failure. But she does set targets.

As product line manager she is planning an evaluation of a program that currently is being given to more than 400 people in AT&T's sales organization in China. Before the training even started, Fawson says that goals were established that the education should help achieve, such as personal sales quotas and number of contacts. Such evaluation measures were not in place just a few years ago. "We looked at training differently [years ago] than we do today, just like we looked at quality differently," says Fawson. "It used to be a checker at the end of the assembly line looked for rejects. Likewise, follow-up evaluation was the last step in training. Now, we build in evaluation from the day we conceive the training."

The emphasis at the Information Services Division of TRW Inc. in Orange, California, is to bring customers' input into the evaluation of training. Dwight Lambert, manager of national sales training and development, says the company's training program generally involves two days in class, 60 days in the field, and then back to the classroom for one day of presentations. "This 'action learning project' was a prototype with sixty people," Lambert says. "This year we will roll it out to our entire field sales organization of two hundred and thirty people."

In evaluating the training, TRW uses what evidence it can find. From interviews and focus groups with both customers and the salespeople, TRW is convinced that its reps are managing information significantly better. "Based on the anecdotal evidence that our salespeople have given us, we've seen a direct revenue result from our training programs," says Lambert. "For example, in the last two years we beat our profit plan by twelve to fifteen percent each year."

Evaluating Results

The problem, though, with equating sales increases with successful training is this: too many other variables—the effect of a new product, the failure of a competitor, a revamped pricing structure—aren't being considered for such revenue growth. "We've come to the conclusion that [evaluating results] can't be done," says John Myers, senior vice president, sales and marketing for TracomCorporation in Denver. "Not to the extent that you can say that training created the difference."

Yet while shortsighted, trainers admit pointing to revenue increases is often an easy way to justify training expenditure. When they feel the pressure from upper management to show dollar-for-dollar proof of training's payoff, the temptation to cite growing profit margins grows as well.

Jeff Pingrey, senior consultant for the Kodak Education and Development Center in Rochester, New York, says he refuses to buckle under such pressure, but can feel for trainers who are put in that position that do. Management wants the training staff to prove that their training is actually producing results, but doesn't provide the time or resources to do that, Pingrey laments. He calls it "an ethical issue" where some trainers "may be drawing conclusions that are one hundred eighty degrees from what they should be."

Pingrey and Robert VeVerka of Professional Learning Systems agree that it's better to be happy with a well constructed evaluation of how people apply the skills that they have learned from training on the job.

"The difference between an evaluation of behavior change and results in time and complexity may not be worth the effort," VeVerka says. While no study of behavior change will show the return on investment, it will show whether the sales staff is applying the training on the job. VeVerka concludes, "That's the proof of any good sales training program, as far as I'm concerned" (Mendosa, 1995, p. 64).

As a sales executive, sales manager, or other leader, you are positioned as a role model. The sales professionals who report to you watch how you act. In most cases, you work hard to project a positive image and establish yourself as a leader who cares about the development of his or her staff. Rate yourself and your sales organization by completing the self-assessment. Then organize your thinking on this issue by brainstorming about it on the following worksheet.

Self-Assessment:
Leading and Evaluating an In-House Development Program

Directions: With your sales organization in mind, place a number in the left column below that matches your level of agreement with each statemens. Then score your assessment.

Disagree									Agree
1	2	3	4	5	6	7	8	9	10

____Your organization aligns individual sales development plans with the organization's strategic business objectives incorporating an effective sales performance scorecard.

____Your organization has communicated the importance and need for everyone in your organization to contribute to achieving sales results.

____You routinely evaluate individual and organizational development improvement against expected performance outcomes.

____Your organization demonstrates high standards of sales performance and professionalism.

____Your organization supports planned efforts to develop the talent of sales professionals.

____Everyone in your organization understands and realizes the key benefits from developing the talent of sales professionals.

____You take actions to overcome barriers to developing sales talent.

____You actively oversee and coordinate efforts to improve sales talent.

____Your organization and individual sales professionals look for industry role models to benchmark against.

____Your salespeople assume ownership for their individual development.

____Total

How Did You Score?

Here is the key to Leading and Evaluating an In-House Development Program. Add up your responses to get your score.

91–100 Great job! Congratulations! Your organization is effectively working to lead and evaluate an in-house development program.

81–90 Keep up the good work! You've probably had considerable success. But by using some of the tips in this chapter, you could improve your success.

71–80 Help is needed! There's room for improvement. You'll find this chapter helpful.

0–70 Warning! Your sales organization probably has some confusion. Read on!

A Worksheet for Leading and Evaluating an In-House Sales Training and Development Program

Directions: In your opinion, what problems or challenges does your sales organization face in leading and evaluating an in-house development program for sales professionals? Use this worksheet to organize your thinking about how to answer this question.

Notes:

DOES YOUR ORGANIZATION ALIGN INDIVIDUAL SALES DEVELOPMENT PLANS WITH THE ORGANIZATION'S STRATEGIC BUSINESS OBJECTIVES INCORPORATING AN EFFECTIVE SALES PERFORMANCE SCORECARD?

Creating a sales scorecard for your organization can provide a blueprint to guide decision making and analyze organizational gaps. Many organizations are using a scorecard approach to evaluate performance. A scorecard communicates the factors critical to the organization's success and how they relate to individual performance.

Organizational scorecards usually focus on such issues as profitability, client satisfaction, and new product development. These factors should be aligned with the goals identified in the organization's strategic business plan or operational budget. Scorecards serve as planning and reporting tools. The frequency of reporting can vary, though many organizations report on a monthly or quarterly basis.

A sample scorecard format is shown in Figure 4.1.

Figure 4.1
A Sample of a Sales Performance Scorecard

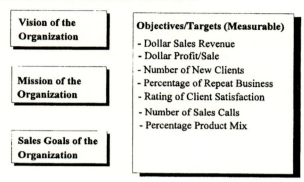

Critical Situation: The Sales Performance Scorecard as a Performance Management Tool

Situation: In several in-depth interviews with sales managers the conversation eventually returned to the ultimate litmus test of success for any sales professional. What total sales revenue did they generate and how profitable were the products or services they sold to their organization? In particular one sales executive from a mid-sized transportation organization discussed the challenges he faced in managing a group of sales professionals distributed across the country such that he had little control of where they focused their time and efforts. In fact one of the largest challenges he faced was getting the sales professionals to sell a broader set of products and services beyond what they had traditionally sold and been very successful with. The challenge he faced was educating them in the fact that the percentage of profit on the services they provided had changed and services that once maintained a reasonable margin had slipped and were no longer profitable. However, the high-volume business service continued to command the most attention from the organization's sales professionals. The challenge he faced was how to get them to focus on smaller volume services that generated twice as much profit margin as the less productive high-volume business that they had historically sold. He was finding this a difficult challenge because the sales staff was very competitive and had measured their effectiveness by the total volume of their sales, not the profitability of those sales. They were all on a salary with a modest bonus system.

Development Issues: Sales professionals must see the relationship between their performance evaluation system and their reward system. It is difficult to communicate important issues when you are separated by distance and time. By developing a written plan that is understood and accepted by the sales professional and the sales manager miscommunication on goals and targets can be avoided or reduced.

Action Tips:
- Align performance management and reward structure with organizational goals and objectives.
- Establish a sales scorecard to communicate results.

HAS YOUR ORGANIZATION COMMUNICATED THE IMPORTANCE OF AND NEED FOR EVERYONE IN YOUR ORGANIZATION TO CONTRIBUTE TO ACHIEVING SALES RESULTS?

As you know, sales and customer service are key to the organization's success. An effective sales effort is not an isolated activity. For each successful sales department there is usually an equally effective operations or production department, a logistics department that supports product distribution, a marketing and advertising department that provides effective promotional materials, and a customer service department that follows-up on sales and preserves customers.

A seamless public image is critical to the success of every sales organization. A flowchart can graphically depict how many and what kind of people are involved in the sales process and how they influence client relationship management and thereby contribute to organizational success. Think about the sales process in the organization and try to flowchart the steps in your organization's sales process from first client contact through first sale through first client delivery. If you have no experience with flowcharting, ask questions like those appearing in the following checklist to gain a better understanding of the sales process in your organization:

☐ Where does the process begin?

☐ Who must touch the product or service before it reaches the client?

☐ What value does each person bring to the process?

☐ What impact does your part of the process have on meeting client needs?

☐ Where are the bottlenecks in the process that are slowing down our ability to meet the needs of our clients?

☐ Where are the delays in the process where nothing happens?

☐ What are the clients' most frequent complaints?

If you have never seen a flowchart, then consider the example appearing in Figure 4.2.

Figure 4.2
A Simple Flowchart of the Famous Edward Deming Chain Reaction

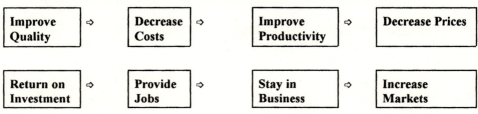

Improve Quality	⇨	Decrease Costs	⇨	Improve Productivity	⇨	Decrease Prices
Return on Investment	⇨	Provide Jobs	⇨	Stay in Business	⇨	Increase Markets

DO YOU ROUTINELY EVALUATE INDIVIDUAL AND ORGANIZATION DEVELOPMENT IMPROVEMENT AGAINST EXPECTED PERFORMANCE OUTCOMES?

Sales scorecards can encourage planning and the application of measurement to sales. Successful organizations measure organizational and individual performance. Many organizations promote the view that is perhaps best summarized by the phrase, "If it is not measured, then it must not be important." By pinpointing organizational performance gaps and thereby routinely evaluating individual and organizational performance, you can discover the need for strategic initiatives. By pinpointing individual performance gaps, you can help each sales professional create his or her own individual development plan to foster learning and development.

How do we gain knowledge of self? In a simple sense, that refers to each sales professional's understanding of his or her self, their capabilities and how they interact with others. That is the starting point for professional development. Knowledge of self can be gained in many ways, ranging from the informal to formal. An informal way is to encourage self-reflection about strengths and weaknesses. A formal way is to use personality inventories. Self-assessment instruments designed to identify personality or behavioral types are useful because they can help individuals reach their own conclusions about why they work better with some people than others.

A full-circle, multirater assessment—sometimes called a *360-degree assessment*—is also valuable in self-analysis. The 360-degree assessment provides an opportunity for the target person to receive anonymous feedback from a variety of sources on items such as performance, relationships, decision making, and leadership.

However, the 360-degree assessment is not without drawbacks. It can sometimes do more harm than good, especially if the feedback is directly tied to an individual's performance rating and continued employment. In small firms or departments, where only a few individuals can carry out a 360-degree assessment, the danger always exists that people will receive retribution from their managers for rating the managers negatively. Ideally, of course, a 360-degree assessment can enhance a sales professional's knowledge of self and provide meaningful clues to development. However, a 360-degree assessment must be managed cautiously. The feedback is only as good as the people who provide it, and it is only as useful as the raters' honesty and objectivity make it.

DOES YOUR ORGANIZATION DEMONSTRATE HIGH STANDARDS OF SALES PERFORMANCE AND PROFESSIONALISM?

Professionalism and performance are often closely related. The image projected by your sales team reflects on the professionalism of your organization. That image can help to establish and maintain a positive brand image. Projecting a professional image and demonstrating business acumen cannot be easily taught from a book. However, as we examined this competency area, we noticed that the essence of professionalism can be distilled in a few key points. Use the following checklist to check how well a professional image is projected by the sales professionals of your organization.

Assessment of Professional Appearance

Yes	No	Is the sales professional
☐	☐	1. Wearing clothing and accessories aligned with the culture of his or her clients?
☐	☐	2. Dressed to show neatness, quality, and a style of clothing that projects professionalism?
☐	☐	3. Groomed in a way that is appropriate?
☐	☐	4. Corresponding with clients in a professional manner?
☐	☐	5. Able to use grammar appropriately in conversations at all times?

Of course, job knowledge and product knowledge are also part of professionalism. While appearance can help a salesperson get in the door for a first appointment, more than that is needed to build client loyalty. Indeed, clients demand that sales professionals today add value, and doing that requires more than interpersonal skills or good looks.

DOES YOUR ORGANIZATION SUPPORT PLANNED EFFORTS TO DEVELOP THE TALENT OF SALES PROFESSIONALS?

For an in-house sales training and development program to be successful, it must enjoy the support of top managers in the organization. They must, after all, approve expenses for such programs. Without that support, a sales training program cannot be successful for long because it will be starved for resources, and participants will ultimately ask, "Why should we care if the top managers do not?"

Think about your own organization. How would you characterize top management opinions about efforts to train and develop sales professionals in your organization? As you think about how to answer that question, examine the results of our survey of sales managers in Figure 4.3. Note how much top management support they perceived existed in their organizations. The percentage opposite each category indicates what percentage of respondents marked "agree" to that opinion, and the total adds up to more than 100 percent because respondents were permitted to check more than one opinion if they believed it accurately reflected the opinions of top managers in their organizations.

Figure 4.3
Survey Respondents' Perceptions of Top Management Views about Sales Training in Their Organizations

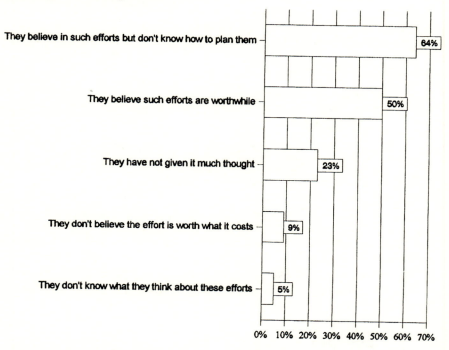

Source: From *A Survey about Sales Training Programs* by W. Rothwell, W. Donahue, and J. Park, 2001 (unpublished survey results), University Park, PA: Pennsylvania State University. Copyright 2001 by W. Rothwell, W. Donahue, and J. Park.

If you believe that top managers do not support sales training and development in your organization, then you as the sales manager need to begin by showing why it is useful and how it can influence sales results. Begin by championing the effort. Explain why such a program is needed and how it will contribute to achieving the organization's strategic objectives and sales targets.

DOES EVERYONE IN YOUR ORGANIZATION UNDERSTAND AND REALIZE THE KEY BENEFITS FROM DEVELOPING THE TALENT OF SALES PROFESSIONALS?

Sales drive most businesses. But it may be necessary to show others in the organization the value of investing in a planned sales training and development effort. If they do not see that value on their own, then they must be convinced. Doing that requires the same persuasive skills often necessary to make a sale. Just presenting the idea may not suffice. The benefits may have to be made explicit. Consider the benefits in the following checklist. Select those that you believe will exist for your organization if a sales training and development program is implemented in your organization. Use the benefits you selected to build a compelling case for a sales training and development program in your organization.

☐ Enhance business reputation as an organization that invests in its employees
☐ Bring sales professionals up to speed faster and increase their ability to produce sales revenue
☐ Improve ability to retain people because they are more effective, happier, and satisfied with their jobs
☐ Better understand the impact of their position and their impact on the overall performance of the organization
☐ More comfortable in working with clients and understand how to ask for the order and close a sale
☐ Able to manage time and territory more effectively to increase efficiency and reduce expenses
☐ Able to understand how to prioritize clients and recognize which clients can be the most profitable

As you begin to build the case for a sales training program, recognize that decision makers are often swayed to use training to solve problems. Examine the following problems. Check the problems that may apply to your organization, then invite decision makers to do so. Compare notes and then discuss the similarities and differences in your answers.

☐ Decreasing performance of current staff
☐ Recognition that existing staff are unable to meet the changing demands of the marketplace
☐ A poor pool of internal candidates for open sales positions pointing to their inability to step into open positions
☐ A poor or inadequate pool of external candidates for positions
☐ Retention problems that are recurrent and of a serious nature
☐ Poor morale or feelings of inadequacy in existing sales staff
☐ Poor communications between sales staff and other internal departments
☐ Poor results from current providers of sales training
☐ Lack of access to qualified providers of training

DO YOU TAKE ACTIONS TO OVERCOME THE BARRIERS TO LEADING EFFORTS OF DEVELOPING SALES TALENT?

Making changes in any organization can lead to resistance. Introducing a sales training and development program is a change. Consequently, it can lead to resistance. Consider the barriers that may exist to establishing a planned sales training and development program in your organization. Consult the following list that was compiled from the respondents' answers to our survey about sales training (Rothwell, Donahue, & Park, 2001). Check the items you expect will serve as barriers to implementing such a program in your organization as a starting point for thinking about how to overcome those barriers.

Individual Barriers

☐ Difficult to determine the needs of individual reps with different experience levels

☐ Salespeople sometimes fail to recognize their weaknesses

☐ Difficult to teach old dogs new tricks

☐ Salespeople don't want to take time to train

☐ Extensive travel and personal sacrifice

☐ Selfish pursuit of self-interests by salespeople

☐ Separating development versus personalized sales skills

Organizational Barriers

☐ No formalized process in place

☐ The capacity to develop programs doesn't exist in our organization

☐ Understanding key elements and follow-up

☐ Developing consistency throughout the organization

☐ Determining best person to administer programs

☐ Poor managers managing programs

☐ Logistics, geographical location, we are scattered

☐ With small staff our biggest problem is meeting for development

☐ Cost versus benefit sometimes hard to sell

☐ Commission structure can be an impediment to collaboration

☐ Silos without a good reward system to change

External Barriers

☐ Headhunters raid talent and salespeople are quick to change jobs for more money

☐ The culture never changes; sometimes we need to shake up the organization with outside help

☐ Sometimes new life is needed and a "hired gun" or top salesperson needs to be brought in

☐ Can't find good people to start with

☐ Difficult to recruit those who can and will do the job

☐ No local programs, must travel considerable distance for good programs

DO YOU ACTIVELY OVERSEE AND COORDINATE EFFORTS TO IMPROVE SALES TALENT?

To gain support for a planned sales training and development program, consider establishing a committee, team, or council to guide the effort. The purpose of this group is to launch the sales training and development program with active support. It is usually important to have at least one member of the organization's top-level executive team on the committee. In larger organizations that member may be the vice president of sales, and in smaller organizations that could be the company president or owner. The presence of this key person on the committee emphasizes its importance and can help to lay the groundwork for positive change.

Other members of this committee—which may take the name of a training council, training committee, or training advisory board—should consist of individuals representing groups that can influence program success. Try to limit the size of the council to no more than twelve, and usually about eight. Be sure that the individuals selected or nominated to serve are willing to do so, believe in the importance of training, and are perceived as good (if not first-rate) performers. Examine this list using the criteria listed to consider who should be invited to serve on such a committee.

☐ Do the individuals have specific knowledge of the sales function in your organization or in other organizations where they were employed?

☐ Have they been successful in their position, whether it be sales or a related field? It is critical that the members of the team are trusted and respected throughout the organization. This may exist either because of the position they hold in the company or based on their performance with the organization. Are they someone whose opinion is valued and listened to?

☐ Are they positive about the creation of a sales development program and are they willing to visibly communicate this support to others in the organization? However, it is important not to create a group that will not question issues and rubber-stamp everything.

☐ Do they understand the big picture and the strategic direction of the organization? Will they step forward and facilitate the making of good decisions and recommendations on actions that should be taken in a thoughtful and professional manner?

☐ Specify other criteria as appropriate for your organization.

DO YOUR ORGANIZATION AND ITS INDIVIDUAL SALES PROFESSIONALS LOOK FOR INDUSTRY ROLE MODELS TO BENCHMARK AGAINST?

The early focus of a training council can be on benchmarking sales training practices in other organizations. Benchmarking can be defined as the process of formally comparing a process or activity in one organization with a similar process or activity in other organizations. It is carried out to find ways of improving an organization's practices.

To that end, it may be important to have a thorough grasp of how sales training and development is carried out in the organization that seeks information. Flowcharting the process can be a helpful starting point for a training council. You may wish to direct the council members to direct their initial efforts to flowcharting how sales professionals are presently trained in your organization. That process should pinpoint specific areas for comparison with other organizations, which can then become the focus of benchmarking efforts.

As training council members set out to flowchart the organization's sales training process and benchmark other organizations' processes, be sure to let them know that they are not limited to the industry of which your organization is part. Effective benchmarking partners do not need to come from similar organizations, such as a glass manufacturer benchmarking with other glass manufacturers or a bank benchmarking with other banks. In fact, best practices may actually be found in other industries. Use this checklist to think about the questions to be asked in a benchmarking effort:

- ❐ Who are the exemplary sales organizations that you might learn from?
- ❐ What individuals in your organization who could be impacted by the study need to be involved in the process?
- ❐ What two or three processes or improvement areas in your organization might benefit most from a benchmarking study?
- ❐ What visits would be appropriate to gather firsthand information?
- ❐ Who should lead your benchmarking activities?

Of course, before any benchmarking effort begins, the council members should prepare a plan to guide their efforts. Benchmarking is not a fishing expedition. It is, instead, a focused effort to compare the practices of one organization to others to reveal areas for improvement. The focus should be kept tight. If not properly planned, benchmarking sessions can turn into unproductive social visits.

After the benchmarking trip, training committee members should provide a summary of what they learned. That can be prepared as a report that is delivered to others. At the same time, the organizations that participated should also receive a summary to increase the value of their participation.

DO SALES PROFESSIONALS IN YOUR ORGANIZATION ASSUME OWNERSHIP FOR THEIR INDIVIDUAL GROWTH AND DEVELOPMENT?

Professional development is not magic. It requires hard work. It begins with the recognition that sales professionals must continue to learn if they are to keep their skills up-to-date. All development begins with the recognition that it all boils down to self-development.

Critical Situation: Development Ownership—No Spoon Feeding

Situation: In a recent conversation with a large logistics organization the sales manager talked about the need for development and the need to present training options to her staff. However, she also emphasized the importance of the sales professionals needing to be motivated to participate in the training and to take ownership of their own development. They were evaluating an on-line training solution for their sales professionals and searching for ways to sustain the motivation level of the sales staff. From her organization's perspective they wanted to provide a smorgasbord of training opportunities that were convenient and easily accessible to their employees. But they were also interested in who was serious about taking responsibility for their own learning as they perceived this as an indicator of their seriousness and commitment to the position and the organization. Their position was that they wanted sales professionals who did not have to be "spoon fed" training. Their performance evaluation system included a factor for annual training and it was a weighted part of annual performance. If they weren't willing to take personal responsibility for personal improvement then they were not sure if that person had a long-term future with them.

Development Issues: Training for the sake of training is pointless. The challenge is placing the ultimate responsibility for improvement on the shoulders of individual sales professionals and aligning it with organizational goals and objectives.

Action Tips:
- Ask individual sales professionals to set realistic goals, targets aligned with organizational objectives, as well as develop their plan for individual improvement.
- Transform individual development plans into learning contracts signed by both you and the individual to instill ownership.

But sales managers also have some responsibility to demonstrate leadership and evaluate the sales training sponsored by their organizations. Use the worksheet to capture your ideas about how such leadership may be demonstrated.

A Worksheet for Action Planning

Directions: Use this worksheet space to organize your thinking about ways to plan for using what you learned in this chapter in your organization. Write your comments in the space below.

Notes:

II

KNOWLEDGE OF SELF

Part II focuses on four core competency dimensions related to knowledge of self. Each competency dimension is treated in a chapter that explains what the competency means for today's sales professional. Each chapter opens with a summary of the research results from our survey of sales professionals regarding the importance of skills linked to each competency dimension. That summary is followed by a self-assessment to allow you to think about key issues associated with the competency dimension.

—————————————5

Enhancing Interpersonal Selling Skills and Self-Development

Building relationships is fundamental to successful sales. This chapter focuses on the importance of interpersonal selling skills and building relationships. To demonstrate this competency, sales professionals should be able to do the following:

- Consult with, and respond appropriately to, the needs, feelings, capabilities, and interests of clients and workers
- Support organizational values, diversity plans, and vision
- Provide internal and external feedback
- Close sales and provide follow up
- Realistically assess their own strengths, weaknesses, and impact on others
- Invest in self-development

This chapter examines different interpersonal styles and their impact on personal selling. It provides examples, drawn from real life, to emphasize how important it is to select the appropriate sales techniques to use with different styles. The chapter also discusses the importance of self-development and of projecting a trustworthy professional image.

How important are the behaviors associated with interpersonal selling skills and building relationships? To answer that question, we posed it to our survey respondents. Examine Figure 5.1 to see how the respondents to our survey rated the relative importance of the behaviors linked to this competency. Then reflect how you would rate sales professionals in your organization.

Figure 5.1
Selling Behaviors as Rated by Survey Respondents

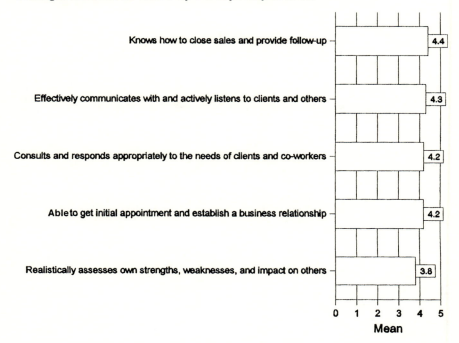

Source: From *A Survey about Sales Training Programs* by W. Rothwell, W. Donahue, and J. Park, 2001 (unpublished survey results), University Park, PA: Pennsylvania State University. Copyright 2001 by W. Rothwell, W. Donahue, and J. Park.

When you finish looking at Figure 5.1, complete the self-assessment as it applies to you and your organization. Each statement listed in the self-assessment is, of course, important to establishing and maintaining an effective sales training and development program in your organization. This chapter is organized around addressing the issues covered in these statements, which are related to enhancing the interpersonal selling skills of your sales professionals and promoting their self-development. Then use the worksheet to organize your thinking about ways of building this competency among sales professionals in your organization.

Self-Assessment:
Enhancing Interpersonal Selling Skills and Self-Development

Directions: With your sales organization in mind, place a number on the line in the left column following that matches your level of agreement with each statement. Then add up the numbers and score your assessment.

Disagree   Agree
1   2   3   4   5   6   7   8   9   10

____Your sales professionals have an understanding of different interpersonal styles and how to effectively communicate one-on-one.

____All of your sales professionals realistically assess their own strengths, weaknesses, and impact on others.

____Your sales professionals accept job ambiguity and establish positive techniques for handling rejection.

____All of your sales professionals are sensitive to cultural differences and act appropriately.

____Your sales professionals are skilled at planning, scripting, and calling potential new clients.

____Your sales professionals are able to get the initial appointment and establish business relationships.

____All of your sales professionals make clear and effective oral presentations to groups.

____Your sales professionals actively listen and appropriately respond to the needs of clients and coworkers.

____All of your sales professionals know how to close sales and provide follow-up.

____Your organization sponsors programs to enhance interpersonal selling skills and self-development.

____Total

How Did You Score?

Here is the key to enhancing interpersonal selling skills and self-development. Add up your responses to get your score.

91–100   Great job! Congratulations! Your organization is effectively working to enhance interpersonal selling skills and self-development.

81–90   Keep up the good work! You've probably had considerable success. But by using some of the tips in this chapter, you could improve your success.

71–80   Help is needed! There's room for improvement. You'll find this chapter helpful.

0–70   Warning! Your sales organization may have difficulty closing the sale. Read on!

A Worksheet to Organize Your Thinking for Enhancing Interpersonal Selling Skills and Self-Development

Directions: In your opinion, what problems or challenges does your sales organization face in enhancing interpersonal selling skills and self-development? Use this worksheet to organize your thinking about how to answer this question.

Notes:

DO YOUR SALES PROFESSIONALS HAVE AN UNDERSTANDING OF DIFFERENT INTERPERSONAL STYLES AND HOW TO EFFECTIVELY COMMUNICATE ONE-ON-ONE?

Effective sales professionals are proactive and adapt their communication styles to others. Clients respond more favorably to sales professionals who are likeable and professional. Some behaviors associated with such characteristics as likeability and professionalism can be learned and then improved with practice. Others are probably hardwired to our personality style.

Many assessment tools exist that can help you understand your own personality style and how you interact with others. Most noteworthy is probably the Myers-Briggs Type Indicator (MBTI). Based on the work of renowned psychologist Carl Rogers, the MBTI requires people to select a response to a series of situations. You determine your personality type through the scoring process once you have completed the inventory. That type provides valuable clues about your interactions with others.

Effective communicators know how to adjust their communication style to match up to others. Establishing rapport with clients involves relating to them in ways aligned with their own preferred communication styles. Interpersonal styles are the consistent actions people take in their interactions with others.

How sales professionals behave toward clients will frequently influence whether they make the sale or solve a client's problem. While stressful situations can lead to defensive behaviors or to emotional outbursts, successful sales professionals understand how their behaviors may be interpreted by others. By developing self-awareness of their own styles, sales professionals can begin to see how their own behaviors influence others. Effective sales professioals can step back and objectively ask if this is the most effective approach to dealing with this situation.

Here is an example of a typical four-quadrant model for interpersonal styles: analytical style, driver style, harmonizer style, and energizer style.

Analytical Style

- Facts and detail oriented
- Numbers oriented—bottom line
- Calculated risk taker
- Requires timelines
- Asks lots of questions during a sales call

Famous analyticals: Albert Einstein, Bill Gates, Thomas Jefferson, Colin Powell, Sherlock Holmes, Thomas Edison, Alan Greenspan, Benjamin Franklin.

Driver Style

- Focused on time right to the point

- Constant motion, always busy
- Results oriented
- Risk taker
- Interested in doing the talking during a sales call

Famous drivers: General George Patton, John Wayne, Hillary Clinton, Lee Iacocca, Donald Trump, Larry King, Scarlett O'Hara.

Harmonizer Style

- People oriented
- Friendly and likable
- Needs support of others
- Makes careful decisions
- Interested in learning about you and needs your help in decision making

Famous harmonizers: June Cleaver, Jimmy Carter, Mr. Rogers, Oprah Winfrey, Barbara Walters, Gandhi, Abraham Lincoln.

Energizer Style

- Makes decisions based on hunches and feelings
- Needs to be with people
- Less time oriented
- Focuses on generalities
- Interested in the big picture and the emotional benefits of the product or service

Famous energizers: Bill Cosby, Rosie O'Donnell, Bill Clinton, Robin Williams, Mohammed Ali, Johnny Carson, Lucille Ball, Richard Simmons.

Many instruments to assess individual personality style are commercially available. Most are based in some way on the work of Carl Jung. It is important for sales professionals to understand their own interpersonal style preferences and recognize that each person is unique. A "one-size-fits-all" approach will enjoy limited success. Sales professionals should adapt their communication style to fit client needs.

DO YOUR SALES PROFESSIONALS REALISTICALLY ASSESS THEIR OWN STRENGTHS, WEAKNESSES, AND IMPACT ON OTHERS?

The value of assessing personality types is that it can help sales professionals reach a deeper understanding of their strengths and weaknesses in communicating with clients. They can also gain a deeper understanding through the employee-performance review process, their interactions with coworkers, and their performance in client meetings and presentations. By reflecting on these strengths and weaknesses on their own or with others, sales professionals can begin to use this information to plan for their own development to improve the way they interact with others.

It is not difficult to point to areas where most people can improve. Listening skills are not a strength for most people, who range from fair to poor in their ability to listen and understand messages. Listening skills can be improved through training and other planned developmental efforts. Likewise, public speaking skills do not come naturally. If sales professionals need to improve their public speaking skills, they can participate in such groups as Toastmasters.

Finding other ways to discover individual strengths and weaknesses is not difficult. For instance, sales professionals can videotape their conversations or demonstration sales calls. Also, 360-degree assessments may also be revealing. Many 360-degree assessment instruments are on the market today. To help people gain experience with using them, try out a simple example like the one appearing in Figure 5.2.

DO YOUR SALES PROFESSIONALS ACCEPT JOB AMBIGUITY AND ESTABLISH POSITIVE TECHNIQUES FOR HANDLING REJECTION?

What happens when every call a sales professional makes turns into a "no"? New sales professionals can quickly begin to have second thoughts about themselves—and the products or services they are trying to sell—when they make calls and run into a streak of turndowns. Developing realistic expectations is a critical first step to avoid the "I can't sell anything" blues. It is to be expected, especially in telemarketing, that a new sales professional will experience a rejection rate of nine out of ten in their early attempts to make first contact with prospective first-time clients.

Resiliency, which means the ability to bounce back, is a crucial factor for success in sales. To maintain it in the face of possible failure, sales professionals need a support network that will give them feedback, insight, and encouragement when they encounter difficult times. They may also frequently need to revisit the principles, values, and goals that guide their lives. By constantly going back and reconfirming what is important in life, sales professionals can leap over the hurdles they encounter.

Sales professionals, to be successful, must eventually learn that success or failure in a sales call is not a reflection on their lives or their value as human beings. That is important to avoid the inflated self-confidence that can come from several repeated successes. Alternatively, repeated rejections can quickly snowball into a self-fulfilling prophecy that have sales professionals defeated before they make the calls. Review the situation described in the following situation and note the issues to be learned from it.

Figure 5.2
Sample Communication Activity: Obtaining Multirater Feedback

Directions: Ask each of your sales professionals to make 5 copies of the form below. Then on a scale from 1 to 5 with 1= Poor and 5= Excellent, ask each sales professional to complete one self-assessment of himself or herself, give one copy to three friends or associates to anonymously rate the sales professional, and also give one copy to you to complete. Ask that all copies be returned to the sales professional so that they may be compared.

Scale for Assessing Sales Professional					Rate on this issue:	
Poor				Excellent		
1	2	3	4	5	1	Do I actively listen and respond appropriately?
1	2	3	4	5	2	Are my non-verbals consistent with my verbal message?
1	2	3	4	5	3	Do I use proper grammar?
1	2	3	4	5	4	Do I take the time needed to make co-workers feel I value what they have to say?
1	2	3	4	5	5	Do I take notes and keep records as appropriate?
1	2	3	4	5	6	Do I make appropriate eye contact?
1	2	3	4	5	7	Do I avoid jargon and overly technical terms when not appropriate?
1	2	3	4	5	8	Do I select the right method for communicating my message?
1	2	3	4	5	9	Do I provide feedback and clarify important points?
1	2	3	4	5	10	Do I project a positive friendly image?

Critical Situation: Sales Rejection—
Try 100 Calls per Hour, Depressing

Situation: How would you like to make over 100 calls per hour? In our organization we do telemarketing and our 300 customer service representatives, as we call them, are on automatic dialers and assigned to teams of about twenty callers. It is typical that each representative will make over 100 calls per hour to some pretty nasty and irate people on the other end of the line without a single sale. Our callers' daily performance is judged in two ways: first, against historical success rates; and second, against their team members' performance that day with compensation, a combination of a small hourly base and generous performance bonus. As you can imagine, the internal competition is extreme as is the stress level from constant rejection.

Development Issues: A number of training issues are present ranging from performance management to team dynamics. However the immediate focus is how to help sales professionals deal with sales rejection. If not handled properly sales rejection can lead to depression, alcoholism, and even suicide. The authors have seen it all happen. Sales managers must establish programs for their sales professionals to handle rejection.

Action Tips:

- Have all of your sales professionals complete an interpersonal styles inventory to make them aware of their preferences and others.
- Commission a psychologist to conduct periodic sessions on rejection and stress management.
- Train and assign coaches to help with daily rejection.
- Offer free assistance and counseling to your sales professionals as they will un-doubtedly hit a slump at various times throughout the year.

ARE YOUR SALES PROFESSIONALS SENSITIVE TO CULTURAL DIFFERENCES, AND DO THEY ACT APPROPRIATELY?

The increasing globalization of business has intensified the need for sales professionals to be sensitive to cultural differences (Burgas, 1989; Corcoran, Petersen, Baitch, & Tarharr, 1989; Koslow, 1996; Schrage & Jedlicka, 1999; Sohmer, 2000; Urbanski, 1987). They must appreciate what those differences mean as they approach present or prospective clients. If the impact of globalization seems to be remote, think again: The number of Spanish-speaking individuals has risen significantly in the United States over the past ten years. In many parts of the United States now, proficiency in Spanish is essential to be successful in making sales. As just one practical tip, sales professionals should be cautioned that the use of stories or examples that are specific to U.S. culture, if used to build rapport with international clients, can confuse or dismay them. They may not understand the context.

Ignorance of culture is sometimes regarded as a sign of disrespect. Even worse, it may be regarded as an indication that sales professionals have not taken the time to do their homework for the client meeting. Issues as simple as how you greet a potential client on the first meeting can be complicated. For instance, a handshake is not recognized as a universal greeting around the world.

Understanding cultural differences is also important in interactions with coworkers. Effective sales professionals know that it is essential to build an open, trusting environment. For instance, how do people from different cultures feel about receiving positive or negative feedback? Positive feedback given to a customer-support representative about outstanding work that he or she performed can be misinterpreted or taken out of context. In some cultures feedback is given through a third party rather than directly. Problems can be avoided or minimized if care is taken to research what is appropriate in dealing with people—or if they are asked what is appropriate.

English continues to be the international language of choice. But sales professionals who work internationally realize that facility in two or even three languages is becoming a necessity rather than a luxury.

ARE YOUR SALES PROFESSIONALS SKILLED AT PLANNING, SCRIPTING, AND CALLING POTENTIAL NEW CLIENTS?

A call list is an important tool. It allows sales professionals to manage their time and ensure a systematic approach to identify potential clients and schedule appointments. Determining what potential and current clients will be contacted each day or week is critical to successful sales. Investigating who makes the decision to buy can also be a time-consuming process that may necessitate multiple calls.

If you, the sales manager, provide new sales professionals with the tools they need to be successful, you can reduce their learning curve and make them productive faster. Researching who should be on a daily call list is time consuming. But it is an investment that can pay off because it can keep track of potential clients who, in the end, admit they buy your product or service from their brother or sister-in-law.

Client research is a key component of preparing to make a sales call. A good place to start with is the Web site of many organizations. The Web site may provide important information about the organization's vision, mission, products or services, key personnel, financial status, organization history, and client base. This information can shed light on how a prospective client may have need for the products or services to be sold. Other sources of information about prospective clients could include common clients, suppliers, internal company contacts outside the purchasing function, trade or industry journals carrying articles on the organization or advertisements about the products or services they provide, or the sales manager or coworkers. It is important to collect as much information as possible about the products or services the potential clients provide, what purchases they have made in the past, who services the account, and who may have more information.

Sales professionals should plan their script to have appropriate questions prepared for the initial discussion with the potential client (Leigh, 1987). They should write out, and rehearse, the script while avoiding any appearance of a canned approach. Sales professionals may find it useful to record the message on a minirecorder and listen to it to detect flaws. Also useful is having a friend or associate listen to the tape and provide feedback.

As part of the relationship-building process sales professionals will find it useful to pose open-ended questions. That will prompt the client to explain potential opportunities and will give sales professionals opportunities to collect information on clients' needs. Examples of open-ended questions might include any of the following:

- What problems have you had with this equipment in the past?
- How do you feel about changing vendors?
- How reasonable is our price?

Closed questions prompt short answers only. They can be useful when asking such questions as "Will you be getting bids from other vendors?" The following checklist may give sales professionals precall ideas for scripting sales calls:

☐ Make sure you clearly introduce yourself and the company you represent.

☐ Have an introduction prepared and rehearsed.

☐ Start on the right foot and be positive and enthusiastic.

☐ Clearly state the purpose of your call, don't mislead the person.

☐ Ask a question(s) that requires the client to participate in the conversation and reveals important information.

☐ Focus on getting to the next step, which is scheduling an appointment.

☐ Close by confirming the action that you want the client to take.

☐ If the answer is no, be prepared to reply with a statement that leaves the door open for the future.

During sales meetings, sales professionals may also be asked to prepare a phone script for a sales call. They can then record and document scripts and vote on which one they feel is best. That script can then be added to your organization's sales resource guide.

Sales professionals should be prepared for those occasions when the client does not take the call and they are routed into voice mail. Sales professionals should be prepared to leave clear, succinct messages that explain why the potential client needs to speak with them and the value they can bring to the client's organization. Sales professionals can rehearse leaving messages by calling themselves and then asking others to evaluate their calls. Use this checklist to consider how effectively sales professionals can leave voice mail messages:

☐ Voice tone is critical; smiling while leaving the message comes across even if the person at the other end can't see you.

☐ Always begin with a greeting.

☐ Clearly introduce yourself and what organization you are from.

☐ State the purpose of the phone call.

☐ Clearly spell out what actions you hope the person at the other end will take.

☐ Conclude with your phone number and repeat it again slowly.

☐ Close on a positive note and reinforce the action you would like the client to take.

Review the example about the phone script to learn how someone actually handled this issue.

Critical Situation: Phone Scripts—Learn from the Best

Situation: In the past when we brought in green peas to the organization we said "welcome to the sales business and now get out there and start selling." Well it was not a surprise that less than half of them even made it through the first year. It took us a long time to figure it out, but this philosophy was costing us millions each year and we were developing a bad reputation as a place that ate up salespeople. One of the best things we ever did was take the time to look at how our top performers were able to pick up the phone and get appointments with potential clients. When we started to track this we found out that they weren't as successful as we thought, but what they did do was keep right on picking up the phone and making the next call. It was a numbers game to them. They didn't take it personally and they didn't get discouraged. They were organized and had their message well honed so they could quickly make a bunch of calls, and guess what? The more calls they made the more appointments they got. So, we work with our new sales professionals to develop their own script that they can use. We provide them with several good examples and then we let them develop their own to reflect their personality and style. But, before we turn them loose they must do several taped calls with people from our training department and the tapes are reviewed and suggestions made. After that, one of the managers periodically sits with them during a call and provides feedback and coaching.

Development Issues: By having a script and a plan it becomes much easier for new sales professionals to get comfortable using the phone. By giving them some flexibility they own the script and if it doesn't work it is not as easy to blame the script developed by someone else.

Action Tips:
- Ask sales professionals to prepare scripts of typical calls and ask them to compare with other sales staff.
- It is important to develop realistic expectations in your sales staff that are specific to your business and not based on broad general information.
- Record and document those scripts that are deemed the best.
- Develop a laminated card listing successful selling phrases and tips for your sales organization.
- Develop a listing of successful closing techniques and document.
- Develop customizable telephone scripts for sales professionals to use to convey consistent messages and uncover needs.
- Make sure that your call or presentations ends on a strong, positive note.

You can help to prepare your new hires by collecting information on the most frequently asked questions (FAQs) about the organization, its products or services, and related issues that are likely to come up during first contacts with potential clients. FAQs should be collected and distributed to all sales and customer service professionals regularly. Many organizations create databases of information to use as part of the client management process.

ARE YOUR SALES PROFESSIONALS ABLE TO GET THE INITIAL APPOINTMENT AND ESTABLISH A BUSINESS RELATIONSHIP?

Guidelines and job aids can be immensely useful to new sales professionals. They can ease the stress of a new position while encouraging consistency across the sales department. It is dangerous to make assumptions about what new sales professionals know. New sales professionals may experience problems with otherwise unremarkable tasks such as getting the appointment, arriving early yet on a timely basis for a sales meeting, asking for a facility tour at the appropriate time, and having company giveaway items ready for the client. The following checklist can serve as a reference for new sales professionals making those first few appointments or face-to-face calls:

❏ Appointment time and location confirmed

❏ Directions to location and approximate travel time determined

❏ Product information ready

❏ Client research done (Web search, brochures, annual report)

❏ Introduction and opening prepared and practiced

❏ FAQ list prepared and reviewed

❏ Take time to meet and speak with receptionist or other gatekeepers

❏ Organization tour requested when appropriate after initial discussions

❏ Open-ended questions used to understand client needs

❏ All support materials ready (if a group presentation: computer, projector, extension cord, batteries, and so forth)

DO YOUR SALES PROFESSIONALS MAKE CLEAR AND EFFECTIVE ORAL PRESENTATIONS TO GROUPS?

Making group presentations can be challenging for even the most experienced sales professionals. Communication techniques that work in one-on-one settings may not work in large group settings. Sales professionals should therefore receive training and coaching on how to plan and prepare presentations, field questions, use visual aids, and involve the audience.

Presentations can be made interesting when they contain stories of exceptional service, show why clients should do business with your organization, and weave in testimonials from satisfied clients. Providing the audience opportunities to ask follow-up questions and helping them identify potential solutions to their problems is a strategy that is effective. Sales professionals may also need advice on where to stand, how to present, and what habits to avoid when making presentations.

Visual support for presentations is critical. Traditional staples for presentations, such as flipcharts or traditional overheads, are quickly being replaced by electronic presentations with color graphics, video clips, and even soundtracks. Laptop computers and projectors have been dropping steadily in size and cost.

Consider two key issues when purchasing projectors. One is the compatibility with computers used by the sales professionals. The other is the brightness of the projector. Projectors in the 1,000 to 1,200 lumens range work well in lit or unlit rooms. Most sales professionals advise against using font sizes smaller than twenty-four. Consult this checklist of presentation tips.

☐ *Overprepare.* Plan the flow of your presentation and know everything you can about the products or services your organization provides. Master your content.

☐ *Rehearse.* Don't just think through your presentation, do a real live walk through. If possible do it in front of a friend or coworker.

☐ *Use your audio-visual support appropriately.* Don't just read your slides and narrate.

☐ *Know your audience.* Why were you invited to do the presentation? Who will be in the audience? Who are the potential clients?

☐ *Greet participants.* As participants enter the room try to shake hands and introduce yourself personally to as many as you can.

☐ *Involve your audience.* Don't talk at people; involve them in the presentation. Seek out opportunities for interaction using questions.

☐ *Share your enthusiasm and passion for what you do.* If you can't get excited about your presentation then you can't expect your audience to.

☐ *Have fun and use humor as appropriate.* If you tell jokes be careful. Less than 5 percent of speakers tell jokes effectively. Be sensitive to your audience and how they could be hurt or offended.

☐ *Begin and end on time.* Don't wait for latecomers unless your host requests that you do so and then alert the audience to the delay.

☐ *Summarize.* Provide a summary of the key points in your presentation. Make sure your key message points are repeated at least twice and if possible three times.

☐ *Identify potential questions.* Create a list of frequently asked questions and prepare responses in advance.

Critical Situation: Presentation Skills—Handling Hostile Audiences

Situation: I was asked to give a presentation in front of the local chamber on the services our organization offered to clients. I had belonged to the organization for about five years and attended most meetings. Everyone was friendly and even though public speaking is not one of my strong points I agreed to do the presentation. Well, to tell the truth, I put it on my calendar and forgot about it. Luckily, I check my calendar regularly and had two days to prepare. What I wasn't prepared for was a hostile guy who was sitting in the back row. I had barely started my presentation when he raised his hand and asked me point blank if several problems we had a few years ago with our tracking system had been corrected. He proceeded to start talking about the inefficiency in our company. I was shell-shocked and really didn't know what to say. I started again with my speech and he interrupted again. By this time I was totally out of sync and ready to pack it in. But, I didn't. I stopped for a minute, collected my thoughts and moved on as calmly and professionally as I could. I noticed a couple of people sitting next to the guy told him to lighten up and that seemed to calm him down as he didn't ask any more questions. After the presentation one of the people from the back of the room came up to me and apologized for the problem person's behavior. She explained to me that the guy used to work for our company in customer service and had been left go after several confrontations with his boss. This explained some of his behavior.

Development Issues: It is important to be prepared for difficult people and to not take it personally. By being prepared and pulling the attention back to you the hostile audience member can be diffused or at least controlled until you can complete your presentation.

Action Tips:
- Make a list of possible questions from the audience before your presentation and ask associates for their input.
- Prepare answers to questions you do not wish to answer at that time, such as "I'll be happy to address that issue after I'm done"; or "I'll be happy to discuss that issue with you in private after I'm done."

DO YOUR SALES PROFESSIONALS ACTIVELY LISTEN AND APPROPRIATELY RESPOND TO THE NEEDS OF CLIENTS AND COWORKERS?

Active listening, which means listening to the content of the message as well as the underlying feelings, takes time and energy. Active listening requires focus and concentration. Sales professionals must work to understand the content as well as the feeling underlying the client's message. Active listening is a skill that must be developed through practice. By focusing on understanding the message, sales professionals can identify multiple opportunities to provide clients with solutions.

There are two key components to the communication process, the *sender* (the person delivering the message) and the *receiver* (the person to whom the message is directed). Most people regard the communication process as a shared, and joint, responsibility. But, when communicating with clients, sales professionals should strive to assume all the responsibility for the process by constantly checking to ensure that clients understand the message.

Distractions and barriers can create breakdowns in the communication process. Some distractions can be minimized if a quiet area is chosen. However, this may not be possible when meeting in the client's office. To avoid further distractions, sales professionals should turn off their cell phones or beepers.

Some distractions are internal. To avoid those, sales professionals must learn to concentrate. They should avoid the temptation to allow their minds to wander. The listening effectiveness of sales professionals will decrease if they are worried about making the next sales call, managing a customer complaint, meeting the sales goal for the month, or even wondering what they will have for dinner. Everyone listens faster than others talk. As a result, concentration is necessary to avoid filling the gap with unrelated thoughts.

Train sales professionals to be more effective active listeners by coaching them on how to maintain the focus on the client. There are many tips that can help maintain focus. One is to restate key points made by the client. A second is to restate your key points, which gives clients the chance to elaborate on what they said to emphasize important points. A third is to ask follow-up questions. A fourth is to focus attention on body language to ensure that clients are being sent appropriate body language and nonverbals to confirm that they are being heard.

Effective note taking is also helpful in focusing attention on clients. It has other uses as well. For instance, note taking provides valuable information for the account files and is useful for future cross-selling or reference if sales professionals should leave the organization.

It is easy to enter a sales meeting with a predetermined plan of action, focusing only on message delivery. That can work at times. But the preferable approach is to encourage a long-term client relationship by showing that client needs are being thoughtfully considered. To that end, sales professionals should plan a sales meeting by creating a list of questions for the client. That gives the client an opportunity to talk about their needs. A good rule of thumb is the 80/20 rule, where the client is encouraged to talk 80 percent of the time and sales professionals only 20 percent. By preparing questions before the meeting, sales professionals channel their enthusiasm and avoid steamrolling the client.

As we discussed previously, using open-ended questions brings clients into the conversation. One technique is to ask clients to describe the most frequent challenges they face in their organization or to share their thoughts on a product or service. A second technique is to guide clients to discuss a topic by opening with the question "Could you tell me about . . . ?"

Be sure to give the client time to respond once a question is posed. New sales professionals often cannot resist a temptation to answer their own questions because they have not learned to allow silence to work for them. Apply the AWL strategy—that is, *Ask, Wait*, and *Listen*—when learning more about a client. Give the client at least five to ten seconds to respond to a question. By doing that, sales professionals show that they value the response. Encourage your sales professionals to improve their listening by following these tips.

❑ Make appropriate eye contact with the person they are speaking to.

❑ Show interest by asking clarifying questions and take notes when appropriate.

☐ Stay focused and allow the people speaking to complete their thoughts.

☐ Provide appropriate nonverbal supports—that is, eye contact, head nods, and smiles as appropriate.

☐ Do not interrupt or allow others to interrupt.

☐ Use appropriate verbal responses to encourage the speaker.

☐ Use open-ended questions to engage the client in the discussion.

☐ Paraphrase and provide feedback for clarification.

DO YOUR SALES PROFESSIONALS KNOW HOW TO CLOSE SALES AND PROVIDE FOLLOW-UP?

The close is to sales what the home run is to baseball. By *the close*, of course, we mean the time when sales professionals prompt their clients to sign a contract, provide a down payment, or otherwise show that they want to purchase the product or service.

Rarely is there one close. The sales profession today often requires many closes. And clients may require repeated coaxing and encouragement along the way, even before the product or service is delivered to them.

A close should take place each time a client objection is overcome and an agreement is reached. Clients rely on sales professionals to supply them with solutions to their problems. As they see a resolution, they experience the satisfaction of a need and then feel a new need surface.

Much has been written on the art and science of closing the sale. Most traditional sales books apply appealing names to the time in the selling relationship when sales professionals move from collecting information to guiding a transaction. Effective sales professionals make this transition seamlessly. They leave clients feeling that they have been treated fairly and that their needs will be met.

Refer to the following checklist for sample closes.

☐ *The facts close.* In this close the client is given a variety of supporting facts, including those that answer potential objections. Then the client is to understand and agree with the logic for buying your product or service. For example, "This pencil is perfect for you. It features the largest eraser in the industry and a self-sharpening point with a protective cover. It's also foldable and will fit into any pocket and is virtually indestructible." This close focuses on the salient features and benefits of your products and services.

☐ *The choices close.* In this close the client is asked to select the product they prefer from multiple choices. For example, "Which color do you prefer?" or "We could deliver this on July 15 or the 25th." This close does not force the issue and allows the client to say no without closing the door.

☐ *The "take it home and try it" close.* This close allows the customer to use the product or service for a short time period before they make their final decision. For example, once a new color printer or copier is placed in an office the old single color one just doesn't make it any more, or once that new convertible is sitting in the driveway the old sedan just doesn't fit.

☐ *The fear close.* This closing technique is from a traditional hard-sell type of approach in which the client is warned of the potential dangerous effects of not making the purchase. For example, security or emergency alert systems or a product that could be in short supply like power generators during the Y2K scare.

☐ *The just ask close.* For some professionals ultimately it just gets down to asking for the order. When other options have not met with success and prior to leaving it can come down to a straightforward question of the client "Would you like to purchase this product from our organization?"

Now give it to your new sales professionals. Use the list to encourage your sales professionals to share any special tips or approaches they use in making successful closes. Record and document their closes. Incorporate them into your own sales resource guide.

DOES YOUR ORGANIZATION SPONSOR PROGRAMS TO ENHANCE INTERPERSONAL SELLING SKILLS AND SELF-DEVELOPMENT?

Where should you start in your quest to enhance the interpersonal selling skills of your sales staff? Use this checklist for that purpose:

☐ Determine client needs by using active listening techniques and responding positively.

☐ Ask others to evaluate your listening skills and suggest ways to improve them.

☐ Practice listening skills by listening to other sales professionals or a news broadcast and testing yourself on what points you remember and can paraphrase.

☐ Consider having all members of your sales unit take an interpersonal style inventory so that everyone understands and develops a healthy respect for style differences within the group as well as an appreciation of their communication strengths and areas for improvement.

☐ Enjoy and utilize the opinions and capabilities in your sales unit, capitalize on the diversity by thinking or brainstorming ways in which each individual's unique talents and preferences can be drawn into the selling process.

☐ Hold brainstorming sessions and record ideas on techniques for closing sales and providing follow-up. Document the best practices.

☐ Role play successful closing techniques and practices.

☐ Encourage sales professionals to reach out and assist a peer if the work calls for it.

Ask the members of your sales staff to check as many activities above as they believe would be useful to help enhance their self-development and their interpersonal selling skills. Then, for your own purposes in training new sales professionals, refer to the following sample program outline.

A Sample Program Outline to Guide Enhancing Interpersonal Selling Skills and Self-Development

Title: Knowledge of Self

Competency Dimension: Enhancing interpersonal selling skills and self-development

Learning Objectives:
- Able to consult and respond appropriately to the needs, feelings, capabilities, and interests of clients and coworkers
- Demonstrates ability to provide internal and external feedback
- Demonstrates techniques for closing sales
- Able to realistically assess own strengths, weaknesses, and impact on others
- Can develop and execute a plan for self-development

Potential Content Topics:
- Communication skills for verifying needs, problems, and opportunities
- Understanding your special skills and gifts in dealing with others
- Developing ways to improve the quality of your sales relationships
- Developing strategies and tactics for handling objections
- Assessing current sales and client development practices
- Techniques for closing sales
- Customer service—it's everyone's job
- Providing superior customer service and follow-up
- Cultural diversity

6

Managing Client Communications

Much of a sales professional's time is spent communicating in such venues as one-on-one phone meetings, face-to-face meetings, virtual e-meetings with potential or current clients, or group sales presentations. Successful sales professionals understand that people buy, and organizations do not. Therefore, managing client communications is a highly important competency.

To demonstrate this competency effectively, sales professionals should be able to

- listen to clients and others
- make clear and effective oral presentations to groups
- manage telephone and e-mail communication
- develop appropriate proposals
- communicate effectively in writing
- plan and execute appropriate follow-up

Developing competence in communication cannot easily be learned from a book. For many people the ability to communicate effectively is a talent. However, other people must improve their communication skills over time.

This chapter examines the communication process, provides tips on how to prepare for communication opportunities, identifies potential communication pitfalls that sales professionals may encounter, and offers advice about how to avoid those pitfalls.

What are the development needs of your sales professionals in managing client communications? Consult Figure 6.1 to see how the respondents to our survey rated the relative importance of the behaviors associated with this competency. Then reflect on how you would rate sales professionals in your organization.

When you finish looking at Figure 6.1, complete the self-assessment as it applies to you and your organization. Each statement listed in this self-assessment is, of course, important. This chapter is organized around addressing the issues covered in these statements. Once you have completed the self-assessment, use the worksheet to organize your thinking about ways of building this competency among sales professionals in your organization.

Self-Assessment: Managing Client Communications

Directions: With your sales organization in mind, place a number on the line in the left column below that matches your level of agreement with each statement. Then add up the numbers and score your assessment.

Disagree									Agree
1	2	3	4	5	6	7	8	9	10

_____Your organization adequately maintains regular and ongoing planned client communication.

_____Individual sales professionals maintain client data profiles, follow-up logs, and input critical client data into a central database repository.

_____Individual sales professionals respond to client requests in a timely manner and provide appropriate follow-up.

_____Your organization provides internal and external product and service updates on a regularly scheduled basis.

_____Your organization has a planned strategy for participation in tradeshows.

_____Your sales professionals routinely interact with potential clients and other stakeholders.

_____Sales professionals in your organization plan and utilize specific social activities and events to enhance relationships.

_____Your sales professionals use your Web site as a source of information for your organization.

_____Your sales professionals are e-commerce literate.

_____Your organization sponsors programs to enhance managing client communication.

_____Total

How Did You Score?

Add up your responses to get your score on the self-assessment above.

91–100 Great job! Congratulations! Your organization is effectively working to manage client communications.

81–90 Keep up the good work! You've probably had considerable success. But by using some of the tips in this chapter, you could improve your success.

71–80 Help is needed! There's room for improvement. You'll find this chapter helpful.

Figure 6.1
Behaviors Related to the Competency of Communication as Rated by Survey Respondents

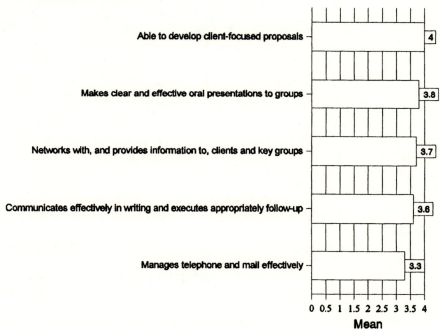

Source: From *A Survey about Sales Training Programs* by W. Rothwell, W. Donahue, and J. Park, 2001 (unpublished survey results), University Park, PA: Pennsylvania State University. Copyright 2001 by W. Rothwell, W. Donahue, and J. Park.

0–70   Warning! Your sales organization probably has some challenges managing client communications. Read on!

A Worksheet to Organize Your Thinking about Managing Client Communications

Directions: In your opinion, what problems or challenges does your sales organization face in managing client communications? Use this worksheet to organize your thinking about how to answer this question.

Notes:

DOES YOUR ORGANIZATION ADEQUATELY MAINTAIN REGULAR AND ONGOING PLANNED CLIENT COMMUNICATION?

To be most effective in client interactions, sales professionals should establish a routine to guide what they do and how much they do. You might think of that as a communication framework, which addresses the type and frequency of communication based on the client's status and needs. A communication framework of this kind also improves the time and territory management of sales professionals.

Large clients usually warrant regular, face-to-face contact. Smaller clients may warrant regular phone contacts and an annual or semiannual sales call. How much and what kind of contact should be made with clients is usually a result of the unique corporate culture of the sales organization. Of course, the nature and frequency of contact with clients can also be influenced by industry trends and clients' needs and expectations.

The ultimate goal of a communication plan is to build loyalty to your sales organization. By staying connected to clients, your organization remains visible. That builds an image of professionalism, leaving clients feeling positive about your organization's contacts with them.

Sales professionals who establish themselves as credible information sources can use that image to stay connected to their clients. One way to do that is to clip relevant articles and send them to clients. That shows the sales professional is staying current—and cares enough about the client to take time to forward information that might be useful. Of course, care should be taken to avoid overwhelming clients with information, or doing it so often that clients begin to feel that it is part of the service they are receiving. Article clipping can also be done electronically by forwarding relevant electronic news or Web site links.

Newsletters can serve a purpose similar to the article-clipping strategy. Of course, newsletters may be distributed in print or on-line. Newsletters are usually helpful to distribute information about new product development, large purchases by other clients, or showcases on high-performing sales professionals. They can be immensely helpful in training new sales professionals (Recchio, 1989).

To be most effective, newsletters should be produced professionally. They provide a means by which client stories can be spotlighted. That creates a win/win situation in which the client receives free publicity while the sales organization showcases successful product or service use.

Tools that allow sales professionals to track contacts and remind them when to contact clients are essential (Christeson, 1992). While software applications can be useful for that purpose, the traditional tickler file is still effective. It works!

DO INDIVIDUAL SALES PROFESSIONALS MAINTAIN CLIENT DATA PROFILES, FOLLOW-UP LOGS, AND INPUT CRITICAL CLIENT DATA INTO A CENTRAL DATABASE REPOSITORY?

Collecting and maintaining information is critical but presents a huge challenge. Maintaining a client database is key to managing client relationships, and it is part of the sales professional's role in successful sales force automation (Rasmusson, 1999). Client databases that can be accessed by intranets or the World Wide Web are available from many suppliers.

Client database systems track important contact information about clients. Such information might include addresses, phone numbers, e-mail addresses, Web site information, and key contact people with background information on each person. Each contact should be tracked and documented for reference by other client stakeholders. That includes face-to-face interactions, telephone contact, and mail, fax, or e-mail transmissions. That should also include pending client proposals, client usage history, and buying patterns. Other information can also be significant, such as personal data about the hobbies, family members' names, and personal interests of the clients' decision makers. That can be useful if, for instance, the sales organization sends out greeting cards for birthdays, anniversaries, or other special occasions as a polite and personal way to maintain client contact.

Client databases are only as good as the data entered in to them. Information must be inputted to them regularly if they are to be useful. Accurate, timely completion of client contact forms is often a category included on sales representatives' performance evaluation forms. Unfortunately, there is a tendency for the completion of these forms to slip during busy times. Sales professionals should therefore be encouraged to understand the importance of striking a balance between meeting pressing client needs and regularly recording client information.

It is also important that sales professionals understand the importance of living up to the commitments they make to clients and communicating those commitments to others in the organization. Sales professionals must act as a client advocate from the time a product or service is sold until it is delivered and used. Hence, sales professionals serve a key role in supporting and maintaining outstanding customer service.

DO INDIVIDUAL SALES PROFESSIONALS RESPOND TO CLIENT REQUESTS IN A TIMELY MANNER AND PROVIDE APPROPRIATE FOLLOW-UP?

Does your organization have a framework to guide customer service? How sales professionals respond to client requests is key to that. However, expectations should be developed, defined, and communicated clearly.

Some organizations create written policies and procedures about how they will respond to clients. But those are not always necessary. It may be sufficient to define expectations less formally. Corporate culture can serve to guide customer service expectations. Stories often embody the values of the corporate culture, dramatizing the importance of excellent customer service and the consequences of poor customer service.

Are sales professionals and others in the organization clear about their customer service goals? Do established guidelines exist for the response time on phone or e-mail messages? If decision makers in organizations cannot answer these questions, then they may be lax in their approach to customer service and may not have taken sufficient time and effort to establish and communicate their expectations to sales and customer service personnel.

Postsale follow-up is a critical factor in establishing long-term client relationships and repeat sales opportunities. It is easy for sales professionals to close a deal and move on to the next sales challenge. But that leaves the postsale follow-up to others. A better approach is to create a systematic process that clearly spells out expectations for postsale follow-up efforts. Formalizing the process emphasizes the importance of postsales follow-up to new sales professionals.

DOES YOUR ORGANIZATION PROVIDE INTERNAL AND EXTERNAL PRODUCT AND SERVICE UPDATES ON A REGULARLY SCHEDULED BASIS?

An effective sales program has one or more means by which to update clients and internal and external stakeholders on new products or services, or enhancements to existing products and services. Sales professionals demonstrate their value to clients by interpreting client needs and then sharing with them relevant, useful information that can enhance client productivity or that can lead to financial gains.

Continuous learning is important for sales professionals as part of the sales development process. The cornerstone of the sales development process is product knowledge. It is also essential for communicating product changes.

As you know, product literature should be kept current and should be displayed in a professional manner. Interactive Web sites are emerging as the standard for many industries. For example, the top automakers' Web sites provide opportunities to create a customized version of the new car consumers are researching and encourages them to look at different option packages, colors, and styles. Consider the following example to stimulate your thinking on how to keep clients updated.

Critical Situation: New Product Communications—Minimizing Costs

Situation: Each quarter we send out new product updates and any relevant service messages to all of our top clients. About four years ago we started including some type of promotional item with each new product roll-out. By developing a systematic and routine process for updating clients they grow to anticipate receiving the updates and when they don't arrive they can become irritated or upset which to us indicates the positive impact of including the promotional materials.

Development Issues: Setting up communication processes may require a great deal of planning and thought. However, thoughtful planning does pay dividends.

Action Tips:

• Establish a communications matrix regarding clients, communication methods, and frequency of communication. Ask each sales professional to complete and update an individual matrix plan annually.

• Brainstorm with your sales team about how to streamline and maximize client communication.

• Stress to sales professionals the need to write concise e-mails that they wouldn't be embarrassed for the world to see.

• Challenge your sales professionals to communicate with clients and others using e-mails no longer that one sentence.

DOES YOUR ORGANIZATION HAVE A PLANNED STRATEGY FOR PARTICIPATION IN TRADE SHOWS?

Trade shows can be effective for making first contact with clients. The value of a trade show is that, in a relatively short time, many potential prospects can be identified, researched, and rated as future sales opportunities. But when a strategic approach is not taken, trade shows can also be an expensive and ineffective method for selling products or services . Display costs, time, and travel expenses can quickly mount up. When too much time is spent at trade shows, sales professionals may see other sales opportunities lost because client calls or responses to information requests may be delayed.

First impressions are formed quickly at trade shows. Sales professionals must set themselves apart from other exhibitors in a professional way. One way to do that is to use a unique feature or article of clothing. Typical approaches might include using a distinctive company hat, shirt, or pin.

A second part of the trade show strategy is the premiums that can be distributed to potential clients and other visitors to the display booth. Developing memorable items that remain in the use of potential clients long after the show ends is a challenging task. Unique items that find their way back to potential clients' offices or homes remind them of your organization and helps them remember your organization's name when a follow-up call is made As part of the first impression, sales professionals working the show should have a scripted message that introduces them, explains their organization concisely, and provides a quick overview of the organization's signature products.

A press kit is another important part of a trade show strategy, and it can be extremely effective in securing free advertising and promotion. During a trade show, local newspapers or television stations will typically develop a story related to it. Since it is much easier to write a story about an organization that provides ready-made materials than one that does not, a press kit can help to capture press coverage. The press kit should contain company information, product information, and several news releases that lend themselves easily to a newspaper article or a television story.

If your organization is to make trade show appearances successful, then your sales professionals should focus on preparation. Goal setting is particularly important, and that permits the financial investment in the trade show to be measured. Trade shows offer an opportunity to meet many people in a short time. But if there is no follow-up afterward, then many potential sales leads are lost. Finding ways to make contacts with prospective clients and collect information about them is key. Each contact should be followed up on within two to three days of the show. Trade shows also offer sales professionals the opportunity to polish their skills in talking about their organization, showing the unique benefits of its products or services, and demonstrating how effective its working relationships with clients can be.

Trade shows are also a great opportunity to conduct market research on competitors. To that end, sales professionals should visit other booths, ask questions of prospective clients, and listen to what they hear about current or prospective competitors. Review the following situation and reflect on the development issues and action tips described in it.

Critical Situation: Planning Tradeshows— Developing an Image of Innovator

Situation: I'm in charge of sales and marketing for a mid-sized manufacturing company in a very competitive business. As a company we've had a long and rich history and solid customer base. However, while we have always thought of ourselves as innovators, we recently took a client survey through an independent group. Out of the top ten suppliers we ranked ninth in their perception of being an innovative company, which totally shocked us. As you can imagine, the pressure was on for us to establish ourselves and become more widely known as an innovator, for we know how quickly the market changes. The first thing we did was hire a well known advertising agency to help us in our strategy and initiate the campaign, "Ready With Innovations." To supplement this we created a family of brochures, all with a consistent modern look and feel. In our industry there are several major trade shows and for those trade shows, we decided to operate differently. Instead of putting all of our wares out for everyone to walk by and look at, as was our normal practice, we placed selected items in display cases under lock and key. Additionally, we prepared press kits outlining the features and benefits of our products and how they are innovative and distributed them ahead of time to all of the media. Guess what? We were inundated with reporters and photographers coming to look at and take pictures of our innovations. At the same time, we wrote orders for our traditional products at an accelerated rate.

Development Issues: Remember at trade shows to focus on two or three simple message points that you want to get across and support them with your materials. Second, prepare a press kit that includes new releases, photographs, and features new stories that you would like reported. Third, utilize this free source of advertising and promotion.

Action Tips:

- Develop an annual action plan for trade shows.
- Prepare a press kit checklist.
- Have sales professionals develop a list of common questions to ask clients: It will help them get the right answers.
- Reinforce to sales professionals the need to ask open-ended questions to uncover client needs, and to ask specific questions if they want a specific answer.
- Use associations, especially striking ones, to enhance your message.
- Consider preparing a set of customizable visuals to communicate desired sales messages.

DO YOUR SALES PROFESSIONALS ROUTINELY INTERACT WITH POTENTIAL CLIENTS AND OTHER SECONDARY STAKEHOLDERS?

Sales is not just about making sales calls and building selling relationships. It is a much broader effort intended to create a network of relationships leading to sales opportunities. However, sales professionals can quickly lose opportunities if they cannot tell the difference between occasions when business conversations are welcomed and when they are not.

Meetings of the chamber of commerce, Rotary Club, and trade organizations all present networking opportunities. Other social and professional events can also offer such opportunities. True sales professionals know how to present themselves in these settings in a natural way. But novices sometimes do not.

Informal selling at business, social, or professional gatherings can produce potential clients or leads to them that can be followed up later. Sales professionals may also discover intermediaries in such settings who could introduce the sales professional to potential clients or who could share their names and information with potential clients.

Effective networking at business, social, or professional gatherings—which can be as helpful in sales professional development as in making sales (Quinn, 1990)—requires planning and preparation. A good place to start that planning is by getting advance information on who will be attending the function. That can provide sales professionals the opportunity to pinpoint two or three new prospective client contacts to seek out at the meeting. It also permits some preparatory research among friends, colleagues, and other sources about the organizations of those prospective clients and about the individual backgrounds of prospective clients.

Reading the newspaper can also help sales professionals prepare for networking opportunites. Using information about current news events and sports can provide sales professionals with the basis for small talk to ease into conversations. Current news events also make it easy for others to carry on the conversation.

Of course, some topics can be risky to discuss. Generally, politics and religion should be avoided. Sports can provide a relatively safe conversation starter. For sales professionals who are not interested in sports, they may use such alternative topics as travel, gardening, or unusual hobbies as conversation starters. Consider the following situation. Note the development issues and action tips presented.

Critical Situation: Business Networking—A Part of the Job

Situation: The purchasing manager at the company was a young woman and I had been trying to meet her for the past three chamber social activities. I finally had my chance when we ended up in line next to each other for the buffet. I must admit it really wasn't an accident as I waited around until she got in line and then positioned myself right after her. After a minute or two I introduced myself and struck up a conversation. I love to play golf and inevitably I work it in to most social discussions. Well this is where it all started to fall apart. She just didn't look like a golfer and I had played a couple of times with the guy behind me so I started talking to him and sort of included her in the conversation. Well he started explaining to me about an eagle he had and I noticed she was paying attention. So I started explaining to her that an eagle in golf was different than the eagles that fly around outside and how you keep score in golf. Well I didn't know it but I was sinking myself fast. I just kept talking and she just kept listening and finally after about ten minutes of this I asked her if she had ever played. She smiled and told me she had a seven handicap and had played in college. We both laughed and I know my face was red as a beet. What a great example of talking too much!

Development Issues: Networking is a process. Just like being a detective, it takes planned investigation to be successful. Most seasoned sales professionals make it a habit to observe how a client or prospect's offices or surroundings are decorated. Such planned observations lead to the discovery of hobbies, work habits, and information on competitors. Effective communication, whether it be in a social setting or in a sales environment, is a two-way process. It is important to remember that open-ended questions can be a great way to get a conversation started. But the sales professional needs to remember when it is preferable to be quiet and let the other person talk. Gender stereotyping can get a sales professional into trouble very quickly. In this case the sales professional assumed the young woman did not play golf. Obviously it was a mistake and caused him to almost miss out on an opportunity.

Action Tips:

- Have your sales professionals identify their top ten clients or prospects and ask your sales professionals to observe and document what they see in their clients or prospects' offices or places of work.
- Based on identified client interests, ask your sales professionals to brainstorm a list of inexpensive mementos that might be given to clients with similar interests such as golf balls, pens, notepads, cigars, mouse pads, and so on.
- Good communicators make much better sales professionals.
- Use sales professionals that are most skilled at communicating as role models.

DO SALES PROFESSIONALS IN YOUR ORGANIZATION PLAN AND UTILIZE SPECIFIC SOCIAL ACTIVITIES AND EVENTS TO ENHANCE RELATIONSHIPS?

Some sales transactions may occur in a short time period. Others require longer-term investments in building client relationships based on trust and open communication. For some organizations, sales relationships can be enhanced when sales professionals participate in innocuous activities or events. Examples of such activities or events might include sporting events, theatrical productions, church events, or school events.

Decision makers in any organization must reach their own conclusions about how much of this informal networking to encourage. It may pay off. And then again it may not.

Critical Situation: Social Networking— Extra Effort Leads to More Sales

Situation: We were taking the train from Philadelphia to New York City to make a sales call. I was with this other salesperson who had worked in the city for several years and had always commuted on trains. That train trip was a real learning experience for me. He told me you can take two approaches when commuting. You can blow everyone off and pull out your laptop and write e-mails and work on a proposal for an hour and a half. Or you can do what he called "train sell." He explained all it took was enough nerve to just start talking to people even if they didn't look friendly, a supply of business cards, and a thick skin because it was inevitable that some people were going to ignore you or tell you to get lost. This seasoned sales professional also emphasized that this had to be a soft sell because you saw the same people on the train every day and you didn't want to wear out your welcome too fast. He said "Just give them enough info to tease them and then let them ask for more." So then he demonstrated for me how "train selling" worked. At the next stop he moved to a new seat by himself and sure enough a well-dressed young woman sat down next to him. I just watched and listened. At first she just stared into her newspaper and drank her latte. But after about fifteen minutes he dropped some papers and had to ask her to pick them up. Well, he had his opening and he broke the ice by asking her if she commuted every day. It turned she was traveling from Washington D.C. to New York for business. Well, as they talked he discovered she was heading to a meeting in a building he had worked in and he gave her directions and a shortcut. By the end of the trip they exchanged business cards and he promised to follow-up with her. I don't know if it ever led to any business for our company but it was a real learning experience for me on how to make contacts and use your time wisely to sell. The sales professional did assure me that they all don't go that smoothly and that people are just as likely to ignore you or give you the cold shoulder.

Development Issues: To sell things you have to communicate with people what you do and what the advantages are of working with you. A key for this type of situation is to not be a pest but rather give people the opportunity to start a relationship with you and ask you questions about your organization and the products or services you sell. Then the objective is to get their business card and set up a follow-up process, hopefully leading to a meeting where they understand the purpose of the meeting is to try and have them better understand your products or services—with your objective, of course, to make the sale.

Action Tips:

- During informal settings or social events, always have your business cards and a pencil with you for networking purposes.
- Establish a process to follow-up to cultivate potential business relationships. Send contacts inexpensive mementos with your name and number on them to remind them who you are, such as pens or post-it notes with your company name, logo, and pertinent information printed on them.

ARE YOUR SALES PROFESSIONALS USING YOUR WEB SITE AS A SOURCE OF INFORMATION FOR YOUR ORGANIZATION?

Web sites are a popular marketing tool for many organizations. And some organizations invest large sums in creating and maintaining such Web sites. The Web site may also be a major distribution channel as well as promotional venue. Of course, one key advantage of a Web site is that decision makers can easily track how many people visit such sites, how much they buy, and so forth.

Web sites have other uses. For instance, a Web site can serve as a repository of product knowledge that can be made available to present or potential clients, employees, and others. They also can facilitate international market development, since shipping information or people internationally can be expensive, but international clients can visit Web sites at relatively low cost.

Many decision makers still do not have much experience with Web sites. Some authorize creation of a static site that can end up presenting less of a positive and more of a negative image of their organizations. Others take an approach that is perhaps best summarized as "if we build it, they will come," and that is naive. Developing a Web site that reflects the needs of the organization's sales professionals and their clients is essential if it is to be regarded as a useful, continuing, up-to-date source of company, product, or service information.

While the content, graphics, search tools, tracking systems, and other elements of Web site development and administration are beyond the scope of this book, you should realize that the ultimate goal of every Web site is to create something that customers and employees alike want to bookmark and keep as a favorite. To that end, it may be necessary to conduct initial research to determine what information and features would be of greatest use to clients.

ARE YOUR SALES PROFESSIONALS E-COMMERCE LITERATE?

The rise and fall of the many dot.com organizations that flooded the landscape has been well documented. However, the reality is clear that organizations should adopt a strategic approach to e-commerce. Sales organizations must encourage sales professionals to acquire increasing knowledge of e-commerce and its potential impact on how they manage client relationships and conduct business. Sales professionals must possess at least some knowledge of e-commerce within the organization and have the ability to interact with clients at a level that clearly indicates they have the technological savvy needed to meet the client's needs. This includes developing an understanding of e-commerce language and technology. Can your sales professionals define the following e-commerce terms and definitions?

ASP:

LAN:

Portal:

KMS:

ISP:

Metatag:

HTML:

LMS:

If not, it may be time to focus on e-commerce as a topic for sales meetings and training.

DOES YOUR ORGANIZATION SPONSOR PROGRAMS TO ENHANCE MANAGING CLIENT COMMUNICATION?

Where should you start in your quest to enhance the process of managing client communication? This checklist identifies development activities that may help build competence among sales professionals in this area:

- ❏ Plan a schedule of regular informal meetings with clients (for example, lunch) to share ideas.
- ❏ Form a wide range of working relationships and associations and make them known.
- ❏ Keep a record of and analyze complaints, lost business, credit adjustments, missed deadlines, and overtime worked.
- ❏ Measure client satisfaction on a regular basis to track improvements and reactions to changes in performance and service delivery processes.
- ❏ Institute voice mail and toll-free telephone lines to make it easier for clients to reach sales professionals.
- ❏ Place simple client "report cards" in accessible areas to encourage feedback.
- ❏ Benchmark exemplary organizations to learn cutting-edge techniques to manage client communication.

☐ Listen to client needs by asking open-ended questions that require more than a yes or no answer.

☐ Before responding to clients, reframe the statement or message to confirm understanding and to provide time to formulate a response.

☐ Try to put yourself into the client's position and anticipate how your communication is likely to be received and accepted.

☐ Develop a clear vision in your mind of what you want to say to clients and then stick to it without rambling.

☐ Prepare sales presentation aids that will reduce your anxiety, keep your presentation to clients on track, and enhance the clarity of your presentation.

☐ Prepare concise e-mail messages to clients. Write them as if the world will read them.

☐ Develop a consistent proposal template that conveys messages in a clear and concise manner.

Ask your sales professionals to complete the checklist, checking those activities that they believe may be most useful to them and that could help to enhance client communication. Then consider how you might use the sample curriculum to build the competence of your organization's sales professionals on how to enhance managing client communications.

A Sample Program Outline to Guide Managing Client Communications

Title: Knowledge of Self

Competency Dimension: Managing client communications

Learning Objectives:
• Demonstrates active listening skills
• Can make clear and effective oral presentations to groups
• Able to manage telephone and e-mail communication
• Can develop appropriate proposals
• Demonstrates effective writing skills
• Can plan and execute appropriate follow-up

Potential Content Topics:
• Understanding, helping, and keeping clients
• Managing a dissatisfied client
• Building customer confidence
• Quality service improvement
• Measuring customer satisfaction
• Interview techniques

- Active listening skills
- Managing the telephone
- Handling questions, answers, and objections
- Business writing mechanics
- Applied business writing
- Proposals with impact

7

Enhancing Negotiating and Influencing Skills

While many people outside of sales may think that the work involves little more than taking orders, that is rarely true anymore. Today's dynamic business environment, characterized by increased restructuring and reorganization, can often mean that negotiation and influencing skills are essential to work effectively with internal and external clients. This chapter focuses on enhancing negotiation and influencing skills. To demonstrate this competency, sales professionals should be able to

- network with, and provide information to, clients, key groups, and individuals
- appropriately use negotiation and persuasion
- apply influencing skills to achieve objectives

Ultimately the effectiveness of sales professionals is measured by their ability to handle objections and close a sale. This chapter reviews proven strategies to create positive customer relationships to enhance closing rates and customer retention.

What are the development needs of your sales professionals in negotiation and influencing skills? Consult Figure 7.1 to see how the respondents to our survey

Figure 7.1
Behaviors Related to the Negotiating and Influencing Competency as Rated by Survey Respondents

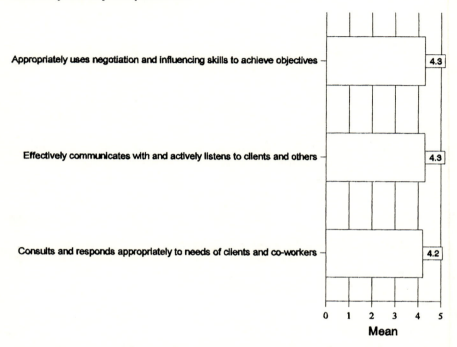

Source: From *A Survey about Sales Training Programs* by W. Rothwell, W. Donahue, and J. Park, 2001 (unpublished survey results), University Park, PA: Pennsylvania State University. Copyright 2001 by W. Rothwell, W. Donahue, and J. Park.

rated the relative importance of the behaviors associated with this competency. Then reflect on how you would rate sales professionals in your organization.

When you finish looking at Figure 7.1, complete the self-assessment as it applies to you and your organization. Each statement listed in this self-assessment is, of course, important. This chapter is organized around addressing the issues covered in these statements. Once you have completed the self-assessment, use the worksheet to organize your thinking about ways of building this competency among sales professionals in your organization.

Self-Assessment: Enhancing Negotiation and Influencing Skills

Directions: With your sales organization in mind, place a number on the line in the left column below that matches your level of agreement with each statement. Then add up the numbers and score your assessment.

Disagree   Agree

1   2   3   4   5   6   7   8   9   10

_____Your sales professionals understand and take advantage of business opportunities to negotiate.

_____Your sales professionals understand the concepts of effective negotiation.

_____Your sales professionals understand how to plan for negotiation.

_____Your sales professionals understand the difference between client needs versus wants and desires.

_____Your sales professionals understand how to structure a negotiation event.

_____Your sales professionals understand the different types of power and their use in influencing others.

_____Your sales professionals understand the impact of body language.

_____Your sales professionals understand the importance of controlling emotions and their impact on negotiation.

_____Your sales professionals take the opportunity to participate in internal project teams and positively influence others.

_____Your organization sponsors programs to enhance negotiation and influencing skills.

_____Total

How Did You Score?

Here is the key to enhancing negotiation and influencing skills. Add up your responses to get your score.

91–100   Great job! Congratulations! Your organization is effectively working to enhance negotiation and influencing skills.

81–90   Keep up the good work! You've probably had considerable success. But by using some of the tips in this chapter, you could improve your success.

71–80   Help is needed! There's room for improvement. You'll find this chapter helpful.

0–70   Warning! Your sales organization probably has some difficulty negotiating with and influencing clients. Read on!

A Worksheet to Organize Your Thinking about Enhancing Negotiating and Influencing Skills

Directions: In your opinion, what problems or challenges does your sales organization face in enhancing negotiation and influencing skills? Use this worksheet to organize your thinking about how to answer this question.

Notes:

DO YOUR SALES PROFESSIONALS UNDERSTAND AND TAKE ADVANTAGE OF OPPORTUNITIES TO NEGOTIATE?

Negotiation is an attempt by two or more people to settle differences and to reach agreement on important issues. As you know, negotiations can occur between a sales professional and a client over many issues. Negotiations can also occur within an organization when, for example, a sales professional is attempting to have a product produced or a service delivered on a much shorter time frame than normal.

Many opportunities to negotiate are overlooked or simply missed. As an awareness activity at a future sales meeting, ask your sales professionals to review this listing of business opportunities or reasons to negotiate:

❑ Discounts or premiums over list pricing for additional value-added services
❑ Special delivery dates and scheduling
❑ Storage or warehousing provisions
❑ Freight, shipping, handling, or transportation costs
❑ Terms of payment including discounts for early payment or no charge for extended payment
❑ Training and support
❑ Quantity or volume purchase
❑ Free advertising or testimonials
❑ Recognition programs
❑ Special assignments
❑ Other:

Ask each sales professional to share a story for each item appearing on the checklist based on his or her past experiences. Document relevant stories for inclusion in your resource guide for new sales professionals.

DO YOUR SALES PROFESSIONALS UNDERSTAND THE CONCEPTS OF EFFECTIVE NEGOTIATION?

Effective negotiation involves several stages and ultimately results in both parties feeling like they have negotiated a good deal. Negotiations typically transpire over time and often require the sales professional to be patient and focused on solving the problem if they are to be effective. Sales professionals can effectively negotiate with clients when they are in a position where the client has an interest in coming to some type of agreement and is interested in creating a situation where one party is not the overwhelming winner and the other party is the loser. Both parties must have something the other party wants if negotiation is to be effective. For a sales professional to attempt to negotiate with a client who is not negotiating in good faith or has very little interest in really buying, the time and effort are a waste. But how does a sales professional decide if the client is serious and worth the time and effort involved in negotiating a deal? This comes from the presales research and investigation completed when the sales professional is qualifying the client to determine if they are financially sound and a true prospect, not a suspect. Some clients may use the negotiation opportunity to determine how low they can drive the price and then use it for negotiation purposes with their current vendor. Again, these situations relate to how well the potential client has been qualified prior to the initiation of the selling process.

Success in negotiations begins with developing an understanding of our own negotiation style and how we react in specific situations. A sales professional's negotiation style can include ineffective factors that have developed over time and continue out of habit. These ineffective behaviors can continue to exist unless a systematic effort is made to change them.

Effective negotiators are able to move the discussion away from people issues and redirect them toward specific items or deliverables where common ground exists and options are available that allow each party to have room for give and take (see Alessandra & Barrera, 1993). Effective negotiation does not involve creating an either–or situation where agreement can only be reached if one side makes major concessions and is clearly the loser in the negotiation process. Identifying choices and multiple options is an effective negotiation strategy that allows the client to make choices that save them from being forced to choose the one right answer.

Consider the following situation. Note the developmental issues and action tips provided at the end of that situation as key points for helping sales professionals cultivate their talents.

Critical Situation: Opportunity to Negotiate—Mixed Opportunity

Situation: As the owner of a small company I wear many hats. Sometimes it's the sales manager, other times it's the purchasing manager as well as the technical expert for the company. Wearing these many hats gives me a unique perspective for sales professionals and things I've learned over the years. For one, sales professionals should realize that if a client asks for a concession on any particular point, the sales professional should be prepared to counter with some offsetting request. As an example, purchasing agents are taught to ask for a variety of free services that particularly inexperienced salespersons will almost always agree to. These could include free freight or shipping, handling, installation, support, as well as extended terms. There are many value-added services that sales organizations provide or that your organization may provide so it's important to have a clear understanding of what they are and the flexibility you have as a sales professional, and be prepared to "horse trade" if necessary to make sure you aren't taken advantage of. For example, let's say you know the client buys on price, and wants your best price. Before you give the best price or the range they desire, think about your situation. You may be able to deliver tomorrow but during your quote you may want to quote FOB (free on board) with a six-week delivery. Of course when they come back and say they want it tomorrow, you can quote a little higher price, knowing that you probably aren't going to get it, but then when you say that you can deliver it tomorrow they feel they have won a concession from you. As a novice purchaser of products and services, I was not accustomed to asking for free shipping, product training, and extended terms or payment as a regular course of business. However, now I ask for these as a normal course of doing business. Eighty percent of the time I get what I ask for without too much fuss or attempt to negotiate on the part of the sales professional. They are usually so hungry to make a sale that they don't ask for me to pay, even though, if challenged, I probably would have.

Development Issues: Sales professionals need to think and put themselves in the position of the purchasing agent. They need to know that their job is to get the best deal for their organization. What is it that they really want? Is it the price? Is it the delivery date? What is it that they really need? What role do you and your products and services play in their supply chain? Once you identify that, your negotiation options become very clear.

Action Tips:

- Take a supply chain management course and profile your various clients according to wants and needs.
- Outline the value-added products or services beyond your base product or service that you might offer that cost you very little to include.
- Encourage sales professionals to practice listening skills to read client needs and identify appropriate negotiation and influencing strategies.
- Teach sales professionals not to concede points without receiving something in return.

Effective sales professionals are able to identify what criteria or factors are important for the client and guide the client through an examination of the solutions in a way that does not solely focus on the bottom-line numbers but rather on what areas are of most interest to the client and how the sales professional's product or service match up with the criteria. Included in the following checklist are criteria to consider before sales professionals begin serious negotiation activities with clients:

☐ You understand that the other person's perception of the situation is his or her reality even if it is different from your reality.

☐ You make it clear in all negotiations that your goal is to reach a solution that both parties can live with.

☐ You are able to keep your emotions under control and not allow them to influence how you negotiate.

☐ You are able to take into account the other person's perspective and think through what he or she is trying to accomplish.

☐ You are able to recognize that differences will most likely exist on certain key issues.

☐ You are able to provide all necessary information needed to make a decision and if you do not have the authority to negotiate you clearly communicate this.

❏ Everyone involved in the negotiation process clearly understands their roles (good guy, bad guy, neutral observer) and responsibilities.

❏ You are able to identify when the person you are negotiating with is getting emotional and making decisions based on feelings and not facts.

To stress the importance of each factor, in a future sales meeting ask your sales professionals to share an experience they have had, positive or negative, relating to each factor. Document those experiences and summarize them in your resource guide for new sales professionals.

The negotiation environment is a critical factor in determining the possibilities for success. An environment where clients trust the sales professional and are open in their sharing of information creates an environment where both parties can openly share information on what it will take to complete the negotiation successfully. On the other hand, when the environment is distrustful both parties will play their cards close to the vest and share very little information about their desired outcomes. Sales professionals negotiating in a distrustful environment are much more likely to fail, and negotiations in this type of setting can quickly turn to bottom-line driven negotiations with the client expecting to be the "big winner." Negotiations of this type frequently result in short-term relationships with neither party willing to share information or make the effort to sustain the relationship over time.

DO YOUR SALES PROFESSIONALS UNDERSTAND HOW TO PLAN FOR NEGOTIATION?

Planning for successful negotiation begins with the sales professional clearly understanding what the issue is to be negotiated, whether it be with a potential client or with another member of their own organization. From there the sales professional must determine what their goal is for the negotiation and what achieving the goal will do to benefit the organization. Sales professionals must clearly identify how far they will go and what their bottom line is for the negotiation that they cannot go beyond. It is important at this point for sales professionals to step back and objectively think about their perspective on the negotiation and what the basis is for their final bargaining point. What issues are important and what is their order of priority? What points can the sales professional make concessions on without having an impact upon the ultimate goal? Once this has been identified and understood, sales professionals should begin to think about the party they are negotiating with.

It is important for the sales professional to recognize that the other party's interests may be different from those of the sales professional. Prior to the negotiation it is important to step back and try to understand where the other party is coming from and what will be most important to them. The sales professional should think about it from the client's position and ask "What would I do if I were in their shoes?" Some issues to consider in each negotiation are

- What impact will a successful or unsuccessful negotiation have on the other party's reputation?
- What precedent is being set if the other party accepts my solution?
- What is a fair solution? Who defines what is fair?
- How important is my personal relationship with the other person versus negotiating the solution?
- What people or departments will be impacted by the solution negotiated?
- Are there other interests (that is, political, cultural, business) that should be considered?

Tradeoffs are an important part of the negotiation process. As was mentioned earlier, establishing goals and identifying potential areas where concessions can be made in advance can help facilitate effective and successful negotiations. By identifying a best case and worst case scenario in advance sales professionals can establish a set of parameters within which they can negotiate. By looking at individual pieces of the issue and breaking it down into smaller subissues, opportunities for give and take can be identified. The sales professional is searching to identify solutions that satisfy all or most of the client's needs in a manner that they are satisfied with the negotiation; yet sales professionals do not have to go beyond the parameters they have set for the negotiation that also satisfy what they have identified as their minimum needs.

DO YOUR SALES PROFESSIONALS UNDERSTAND CLIENT NEEDS VERSUS WANTS AND DESIRES?

There is a distinct difference between wants and needs. I want a million dollars, but need one thousand. I want insurance to cover all risks, but need car insurance to keep my driver's license, and homeowners insurance to maintain a mortgage with my bank. Seeking clarification, identifying perceptions and hidden agendas requires asking the right questions. This checklist can help sales professionals clarify sales situations and gather valuable information and facts:

- ☐ What do we need (and want) out of this situation?
- ☐ What does the client need (and want) out of this situation?
- ☐ What are the critical issues, concerns, objections and consequences (1) for us, and (2) for the client?
- ☐ What are we willing, and not willing, to give up to satisfy the client's need?
- ☐ What would the ideal solution be and what actions are needed to come close?

DO YOUR SALES PROFESSIONALS UNDERSTAND HOW TO STRUCTURE A NEGOTIATION EVENT?

All too often, sales professionals don't invest the time to preplan important negotiation events and "wing it." Preplanning the proper location, setting the agenda, clarifying the issues, and inviting the appropriate individuals to the negotiation event are all factors to be considered before initiating the important negotiation event. To be successful, sales professionals should discuss points of agreement and disagreement with you and your sales leadership team. In addition, sales professionals should discuss anticipated responses to proposals and possible alternatives, as well as discuss techniques to overcome anticipated objections. Failure to preplan can be costly, especially when the client has been trained to ask for more and demand a lower price. At a future sales meeting, ask your sales professionals to consider the last time they conducted an important negotiation event and answer the questions that follow. Record and document best practices for inclusion in your resource guide for new sales professionals.

Have you

☐ prepared yourself and other members of your sales team for the negotiation event?
☐ determined roles and responsibilities of your team (good guy–bad guy)?
☐ created or established the right location and atmosphere?
☐ projected an appropriate image as knowledgeable and trustworthy?
☐ identified negotiation goals, strategies, and objectives?
☐ conducted the event in a professional manner?
☐ ended the event on a positive note, even if your team was unsuccessful?
☐ If unsuccessful, have you left the door open for future business discussions?

Critical Situation: Structuring Negotiations—Lessons from the Past

Situation: I've learned many negotiation lessons over the years, most of them the hard way. One of the most significant happened several years ago. I was negotiating in mainland China for the supply and delivery of a multimillion-dollar equipment package with support services. We were bidding against two other competitors on five major projects. Our approach was a very honest and sincere one, answering almost every question that was asked of us. We shared our manufacturing philosophy, drawings, and best practices in trying to win the award. After spending over half a million dollars on travel without a dime's worth of business, we started to realize that we were up against professional negotiators. Never in my life have I heard forty people in a room say in unison that our price was too high. And it dawned on me that we hadn't even given them a price yet. However, the straw that broke the camel's back was after a year of negotiation, they required us to come back during the Christmas holiday season for another round of negotiation where they said they wanted to talk price. They knew that while we would give a valiant effort we would all want to be back in the United States for the Christmas holiday and that before December 25 they would have our best price. And guess what? They did.

Development Issues: Consider the location, logistics, structure of your negotiation, and the environment conducive to your negotiation event. If possible, get the clients to a neutral location or on your home turf. This could involve inviting them to your location, playing golf, or taking them out to dinner or to a social event where you can get your main points across.

Action Tips:

- Determine your strategy according to the type of negotiation.
- Don't talk price until all of the other details are taken care of or the situation is understood.
- Learn as much as you can about the other party and their negotiation habits and strategies.
- Share only necessary information. Listen more than you talk.
- Have sales professionals set realistic sales objectives and abandon unrealistic ones.
- Encourage sales professionals to be flexible and patient. It is a sign of strength, not of weakness.
- Encourage sales professionals to study famed negotiators and share insights with you and other members of your team.

DO YOUR SALES PROFESSIONALS UNDERSTAND THE DIFFERENT TYPES OF POWER AND THEIR USE IN INFLUENCING OTHERS?

There are seven common types of power frequently identified in discussions related to the topic of negotiation and influencing people. Adapting and relating them to sales professionals, they are

1. *Coercive power.* This power is based on fear; one of the parties involved in the negotiation has the ability to deliver some type of punishment or retribution such as firing, withholding payment, threatening a law suit, or giving the business to another vendor, and so on.

2. *Connection power.* This power is based on who the person knows within the organization or the industry. Negotiations are based on the salesperson wanting to remain in the client's good favor to avoid negative feedback to other departments within the organization or to other potential external clients. As an example, "Hi client purchasing agent X, I was with your president Ms. Y yesterday in church and she speaks highly of you."

3. *Expert power.* In this case the sales professional may be the only supplier capable of delivering a particular product or service, or through years of personal experience is truly an expert in a particular product or service area.

4. *Information power.* This type of power focuses on the knowledge or information

one of the parties possess, and the value to the other party. The information could be critical for decision making or stand in the way of success. It could also involve a client sharing information on other potential clients.

5. *Legitimate power.* This power focuses on one's position in the organization and his or her ability to make decisions because of that position. Seasoned sales professionals know how to identify the true decision maker. As an example, many large engineering or technology firms have purchasing managers to manage the purchasing activities. However, the true decision maker for equipment related to specific projects is the assigned project manager.

6. *Referent power.* This power relates to the person's individual status in the organization or industry based on personal traits and the fact that he or she is well liked and held in esteem.

7. *Reward power.* This power is based on one party having the ability to provide rewards to the other involved in the negotiation. The client may believe that either the organization or themselves personally will receive something of value from the other person involved in the negotiation.

Understanding the importance of each of these types of power in the negotiation process is critical for effective negotiation. Whether it be real power or perceived power by the parties involved in the negotiation, power sources must clearly be understood and the impact of their use monitored. The negative use of power by sales professionals in negotiations with internal colleagues, whether they be in customer support or production, can be destructive to relationships and alienate people over the long term and create negative morale. In many of these cases the sales professional does not have any direct influence over the person (position or reward power), they are negotiating with and must rely on referent power or connective power as their basis for negotiation.

Creating positive relationships built on trust and developing a favorable reputation within the organization will allow the sales professional to accomplish things outside traditional methods in a timely manner. In negotiation with clients, in most cases the client holds both position power and reward power. In other words, they are either the gatekeeper to the decision maker or they have the ability to make the buying decision and can reward the sales professional with a purchase. Sales professionals must understand that unless their organization is the sole supplier of a product or service they must expect to have to negotiate on almost every sale they make.

Recognizing this during the selling process, sales professionals must create sources of power that they can use to negotiate. Expert power in particular can be a decisive factor in the negotiation process as the sales professional helps the client to solve problems based on product knowledge and ability to understand the client's business. Then their value to the client increases and plays a role in the negotiation process. Connective power also becomes part of the negotiation process. As sales professionals begin the relationship with the client they have another opportunity to show their value to the client through their ability to connect him or her to other resources within the sales organization that the client was not aware of, or to connect them with external opportunities for the client to sell their product or services.

As practice for your sales professionals, ask them to role play critical situations they encounter using the different types of power and influence they might use with a client.

DO YOUR SALES PROFESSIONALS UNDERSTAND THE IMPACT OF BODY LANGUAGE?

In communication books much has been written about the impact of body language on an individual's ability to communicate messages that either support or contradict the verbal message they are sending. For sales professionals, being aware of the nonverbal messages they are sending can either enhance their ability to develop relationships with clients, or a lack of understanding can create unforeseen problems that the sales professional is not aware of and could potentially stop a sale.

Nonverbal signs from a client can provide sales professionals messages. For example, they are beginning to oversell their product or they have overstayed the time the client has budgeted for the visit. Other nonverbal signs may indicate the client is positive about the negotiation and the sales professional should identify this as a sign to close the sale and ask the client to move forward with the purchase. However, sales professionals must recognize that many of their clients have studied the same books on nonverbal communication and fully understand how they can mislead or confuse the sales professional by sending mixed messages between their verbal and nonverbal message. During a future sales meeting ask your sales professionals to share their thoughts and experiences regarding the impact of body language on their sales success. Specifically, ask them to share examples of positive actions they should incorporate for each item included in this worksheet, and document their responses for inclusion in your resource guide for new sales professionals.

A Worksheet to Assess Positive Body Language for Sales Calls and Meetings

Directions: Use this worksheet to assess positive body language in sales calls and meetings. Count the frequency with which appropriate body language occurs in each area listed below.

Facial expressions

Eye contact

Gestures

Posture

Movement

Appearance and hygiene

Dress

Others

Consider having your sales professionals role play a typical sales call and videotape the performance. Ask them to demonstrate various nonverbal messages they have seen clients use. Incorporate exemplary role play video clips into your resource guide.

DO YOUR SALES PROFESSIONALS UNDERSTAND THE IMPORTANCE OF CONTROLLING EMOTIONS AND THEIR IMPACT ON NEGOTIATION?

Don't ever let them see you sweat! These are words of wisdom for any negotiation event. Seasoned negotiators know how to control their emotions. They also know how to observe and read the behaviors of others. No matter how difficult the situation may appear, your sales professionals should be prepared to remain calm and in control of their emotions. Sounds easy, but of course we all know it is not!

At a future sales meeting or training session consider asking your sales professionals to develop a list of unreasonable requests made by clients and brainstorm appropriate responses. Document your sales professionals' responses to unreasonable requests and incorporate them into your resource guide.

DO YOUR SALES PROFESSIONALS TAKE THE OPPORTUNITY TO PARTICIPATE IN INTERNAL PROJECT TEAMS AND POSITIVELY INFLUENCE OTHERS?

In many organizations a "we versus them" or "sales versus production" attitude and atmosphere exists. Do your sales professionals make reasonable requests of coworkers? Do they build trust and share information? You are all on the same team and should be working together to achieve the organization's highest priority goals and objectives.

Participating in internal project teams is one way of building positive working relationships with clients and coworkers. It is also a perfect forum to influence others by sharing your expertise and externally oriented sales perspective. After all, sales and customer service are everyone's job, and without sales, no one would have a job.

DOES YOUR ORGANIZATION SPONSOR PROGRAMS TO ENHANCE NEGOTIATION AND INFLUENCING SKILLS?

Where should you start in your quest to enhance negotiation and influencing skills? Consult the following list, which presents a checklist of developmental strategies to build competence in this area. Ask your sales professionals to check those development activities they believe should be integrated into a program to enhance negotiation and influencing skills for your organization.

- ☐ Know your sales objectives well and state them simply. Speak clearly and confidently.
- ☐ Practice sales interactions with peers who take a view of the long-term relationship and not just the immediate gains.
- ☐ Try to put yourself into the client's role and anticipate how your communication is likely to be received and accepted.
- ☐ If you are frequently misunderstood during sales interactions, ask your superior or peers for feedback on your negotiation style.
- ☐ Develop a clear vision in your mind of what you want to accomplish and say, then stick to it without rambling.
- ☐ Break complex sales interactions and negotiations down into smaller incremental negotiations.
- ☐ Observe effective sales professionals, politicians, or professional negotiators in action or on television. Analyze the sources of their effectiveness.
- ☐ Prepare sales negotiation data or aids that will reduce your anxiety.

Use this plan to help build the competence of your sales professionals in negotiation and influencing skills.

A Sample Program Outline to Guide Enhancing Negotiating and Influencing Skills

Title: Knowledge of Self

Competency Dimension: Enhancing negotiating and influencing skills

Learning Objectives:
- Can network with and provide information to clients, key groups, and individuals
- Understands different sources of power and influence
- Demonstrates appropriate uses of negotiation, persuasion, influencing skills to achieve objectives

Potential Content Topics:
- Negotiation skills
- Effective interviewing techniques
- Attaining skill in asking questions
- Listening and responding to others
- Developing skill in adapting negotiation style to differing sales situations
- Distinguishing between bargaining and principled negotiation

8

Resolving Sales and Interpersonal Conflicts and Coping with Change

When properly managed, conflict can be healthy and constructive for an organization. But when conflict is not managed, it can quickly lead to chaotic conditions and bad feelings. Both sales professionals and their managers should understand the strategies available to resolve conflict.

This chapter focuses on resolving sales and interpersonal conflicts and coping with change. To demonstrate this competency, sales professionals should be able to

- anticipate and seek to resolve possible confrontations, disagreements, and complaints in a constructive manner
- manage conflicts with other sales staff, operational people, and stakeholders in a constructive manner
- cope effectively with sales pressures and change

What are the development needs of your sales professionals for enhancing their conflict resolution skills? Consult Figure 8.1 to see how the respondents to our survey rated the relative importance of the behaviors associated with this competency. Then reflect on how you would rate the relative importance of those skills among sales professionals in your organization.

When you finish looking at Figure 8.1, complete the self-assessment as it applies to you and your organization. This chapter is organized around ad-

Figure 8.1
Behaviors Related to the Competency of Conflict Resolution as Rated by Survey Respondents

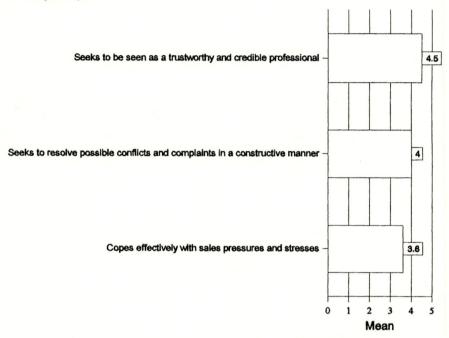

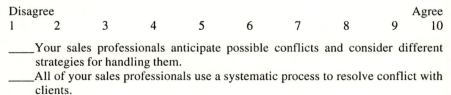

Source: From *A Survey about Sales Training Programs* by W. Rothwell, W. Donahue, and J. Park, 2001 (unpublished survey results), University Park, PA: Pennsylvania State University. Copyright 2001 by W. Rothwell, W. Donahue, and J. Park.

dressing the issues covered in the assessment. Once you have completed the self-assessment, use the worksheet to organize your thinking about ways of building this competency among sales professionals in your organization.

Self-Assessment: Resolving Sales and Interpersonal Conflicts

Directions: With your sales organization in mind, place a number on the line in the left column below that matches your level of agreement with each statement. Then add up the numbers and score your assessment.

Disagree									Agree
1	2	3	4	5	6	7	8	9	10

_____Your sales professionals anticipate possible conflicts and consider different strategies for handling them.

_____All of your sales professionals use a systematic process to resolve conflict with clients.

____Your sales professionals are able to identify the root cause(s) of conflicts.

____Your sales professionals are able to deal with openly hostile conflict situations.

____Your sales professionals understand how to use the right type of questions to resolve conflicts.

____All of your sales professionals effectively make their points with clients in conflict situations.

____Your sales professionals provide solid answers to the questions of clients and others involved in the conflict.

____Your sales professionals have the persuasive skills needed when conflict discussions need to be redirected.

____All of your sales professionals know how to listen and communicate to resolve conflicts with clients.

____Your organization sponsors programs to enhance resolving conflicts and coping with change.

____Total

How Did You Score?

Here is the key to resolving sales and interpersonal conflicts. Add up your responses to get your score.

91–100   Great job! Congratulations! Your organization is effectively working to resolve sales and interpersonal conflict.

81–90   Keep up the good work! You've probably had considerable success. But by using some of the tips in this chapter, you could improve your success.

71–80   Help is needed! There's room for improvement. You'll find this chapter helpful.

0–70   Warning! Your sales organization probably has some frustrations and conflict. Read on!

A Worksheet to Organize Your Thinking on Resolving Sales and Interpersonal Conflicts

Directions: In your opinion, what problems or challenges does your sales organization face in resolving sales and interpersonal conflicts? Use this worksheet to organize your thinking about how to answer this question.

Notes:

DO YOUR SALES PROFESSIONALS ANTICIPATE POSSIBLE CONFLICTS AND CONSIDER DIFFERENT STRATEGIES FOR HANDLING THEM?

When sales professionals are faced with resolving a conflict or disagreement with one of their clients the outcome can have a significant impact on current and future business with that client. It is critical that sales professionals be prepared for this type of situation because for all sales professionals it is inevitable that they will have to deal with conflicts during their careers. Using a systematic process for dealing with conflict in an effective manner is crucial for success. Conflicts can typically be resolved through one of five common strategies:

1. *Avoidance.* Recognize when the issue is trivial and not worth the aggravation or energy involved. The cost of continuing forward with the conflict may outweigh any potential benefits of resolution. In some situations a cooling off period may help both parties to put the issue in perspective.

2. *Accommodation.* At times a short-term accommodation to a client's demands can result in long-term gains. Preserving harmony in a relationship that has significant long-term value can frequently pay back significant dividends. The sales professional may or may not have made the mistake, but by owning the problem the sales professional can cement the relationship with the client and learn from the incident.

3. *Compromise.* The sales professional may decide that due to the nature of the conflict, the parties involved, or the time frame for the situation, it is better to compromise on a less-than-ideal solution versus forcing the issue and risking larger long-term negative consequences.

4. *Competition.* There may be times when the sales professional's best choice is to force the issue and push for a win–lose outcome to the conflict. It is important to recognize that when this strategy is chosen there will most likely be short-term and long-term implications. A competing strategy may be appropriate when the sales professional is sure he or she is right and the importance of potential negative consequences outweigh the value of the specific client relationship. Emergency situations may also warrant a competitive strategy when the time frame for the resolution of the conflict does not allow for anything other than a quick and decisive action.

5. *Collaboration.* A collaborative approach by the sales professional is one that facilitates a win–win solution to the conflict that both parties leave the discussion feeling positive about. Collaborative solutions are critical when the value of the relationship for both parties outweighs any give and take required to agree upon a solution to the conflict. Both parties must be committed to resolving the conflict in a way that is not totally to their benefit and, if needed, a less-than-optimal solution will be accepted.

Consider the following situation. Note the developmental issues and action tips provided at the end of that situation as key points for helping sales professionals cultivate their talents.

Critical Situation: Conflict Strategies—
Making a Mountain Out of a Molehill

Situation: I am head of a technical services organization for a mid-sized company. I've been selling equipment and technical services to a large manufacturing company. This multiyear multimillion-dollar contract has extended over the past several years. Basically we have had a great relationship. We have given the client absolutely everything they've asked for and the client has been very complimentary. On occasion, however, there have been minor delays or minor quality problems such as paint scratches or a missing manual over which my counterpart at the client, the vice president of operations, has gone through the roof. He has sometimes turned these minor problems into an international event to the point of embarrassment for us. Numerous times I have been tempted to tell the client to take his business and shove it, and have been baffled by the behaviors exhibited. Just about everybody in our organization has been aware of the demands placed on us and the uncomfortable position in which it has placed me and the rest of our sales staff. When we step back and analyze the situation, the vice president of operations is really just making a mountain out of a mole hill. Until recently, we thought it was just us that he was picking on, but as time has gone by we have heard that he does this to everybody. One thing it has taught us is that perhaps we were too quick to make the sale and should have spent more time documenting the actual details of the project ahead of time. Moreover, it has taught us the necessity of creating a formalized communication plan for major projects to maintain open and continual follow-up with our major clients.

Development Issues: First, while we are sometimes quick to make a proposal, sales professionals need to follow a systematic process of outlining what is included and not included in their proposal. Second, it underscores the importance of developing a formalized communication plan before the project begins to make sure that small problems don't become big problems. Third, sales professionals must recognize their job is to keep the client happy and that sometimes conflicts occur which can be very stressful. While it's easy to say "don't take it personally," it's difficult to do so. Sales professionals need to recognize that they are being paid to play a role and keep the client happy.

Action Tips:

- During stressful situations, it is a good idea to count to ten before responding to potential conflict situations and accommodate minor requests.
- Wait until the next day to respond to negative or critical e-mails.
- Write short concise e-mails. Saying too much can often times make a potential conflict situation worse.
- Ask your sales professionals to make a list of examples of typical conflicts they experience on a daily basis. Discuss how to avoid and plan for them.

DO YOUR SALES PROFESSIONALS USE A SYSTEMATIC PROCESS TO RESOLVE CONFLICT WITH CLIENTS?

Obviously which conflict strategy is appropriate for a given conflict situation depends on how important the situation might be and the ultimate consequences of your actions. If a client situation is important enough that your sales professionals cannot avoid or reasonably accommodate the situation, then we suggest a six-step process.

1. *Set ground rules*. Develop a formal or informal set of ground rules to guide the interaction with the client. This can start with the sales professional modeling effective conflict-resolution behaviors that include active listening, civility, no personal attacks, and a focus on the issues, not the parties involved in the discussion.
2. *Clarify goals*. Clarify what each party's goals are and what each person wants and needs to accomplish from the resolution of the conflict.
3. *Define problem*. Define the specific problem or situation that is the cause of the conflict. Identify the root cause of the problem, not the symptoms.
4. *Gather facts*. Gather all the facts related to the conflict that are relevant for developing a resolution. When possible, sales professionals need to do their homework and be prepared with all pertinent data and facts needed to objectively analyze the situation creating the conflict. Use open-ended questions to gain perspective on the client's point of view.
5. *Analyze*. It is easy to select the first solution that is identified. The sales professional should think through and identify all potential solutions and weigh the advantages and disadvantages of each. It is important to consider all of the potential direct and indirect consequences of each solution and the impact on all potential stakeholders.
6. *Take action*. As the sales professional works through the resolution of the conflict with the client it is important to clearly agree on what actions will be taken, by whom, and the time frame for the actions.

ARE YOUR SALES PROFESSIONALS ABLE TO IDENTIFY THE ROOT CAUSE(S) OF CONFLICTS?

The natural inclination in trying to resolve conflicts is to focus on the symptoms of the conflict and to overlook the root cause. It is much easier to focus on easily visible symptoms of a problem than to take the time and devote the resources needed to identify the root cause of the problem.

It is critical that the sales professional work with the client or other parties involved in the conflict to clearly agree upon what the conflict is about. Individual personalities or differences can quickly overshadow the real cause of the conflict. One person or group can quickly become the focus of a situation with blame for the problem placed at their doorstep. The sales professional must focus the discussion on the specific issues related to the conflict, not the people involved. As the facts and information related to the conflict are identified and recorded it is important for the sales professional to gauge the attitudes and emotions of the client and determine if the level of trust between the parties is sufficient to allow for a collaborative effort at resolving the conflict. As sales professionals work with the client to understand the source of the conflict they must express their confidence that things can be resolved in a positive and constructive manner. By focusing on the "why" behind the conflict the sales professional can peel back the layers of the situation and get to the root cause or causes. The sales professional should work toward developing a consensus with the client on the root cause of the conflict and then from there move the discussion to a focus on a set of outcomes that meet the client's expectations and allow both parties to part with positive feelings.

Client problems are usually the result of a series of events or actions, not one specific factor or activity. Delivery problems, manufacturing problems, or service problems usually occur because of a breakdown in a system or process, not as the result of any one specific event. A cause and effect diagram provides a framework through which problems can be reviewed and analyzed in a systematic manner. The diagram that follows focuses the analyses in six key areas that frequently are major areas where the root cause of a problem can be found. The process begins by defining what the problem is that needs to be solved. As the analyses continues and the diagram is completed, subcategories are brainstormed and recorded as participants' drill deeper to clarify what the root cause of the problem is. The following are categories of cause and effect analysis. They can, of course, be modified based on the unique issues affecting the organization or problem being analyzed.

1. *People.* Is there insufficient staff to complete the task? Do the staff need training?
2. *Methods.* Is the process used to complete the task wrong or outdated? Does the process not match the client's needs?
3. *Measurement.* Are you measuring the right data to define success for the client? Are the data we are using to make decisions proper and accurate?
4. *Money.* Are we neglecting maintenance because of a lack of money? Was the shipping done in two days and not overnight to save money?
5. *Materials.* Did we receive substandard raw materials? Were the parts from the supplier installed in the piece of equipment faulty?
6. *Machines.* Was it a technical problem? Is the equipment not capable of meeting the client's specifications?

Cause and effect diagrams are a good tool to slow down the process of resolving a client conflict and redirecting the client's energy from blaming a specific person or group. The cause and effect process can help to diffuse a tense situation as all parties involved focus on solving the problem and maintaining the relationship versus venting anger and focusing on individual people. The cause and effect diagram is only one part of the problem-solving process and it is important for the sales professional to recognize the value of a cause and effect diagram and also that to solve the problem may require more time and the collection of further information and data before a solution can be offered. As an example and activity for a future sales meeting, brainstorm the possible causes of a late postal delivery (see Figure 8.2). Then, focus on a critical client problem your sales organization is experiencing and work to determine the root cause.

ARE YOUR SALES PROFESSIONALS ABLE TO DEAL WITH OPENLY HOSTILE CONFLICT SITUATIONS?

Emotional attacks and openly hostile statements by clients to sales professionals can quickly destroy relationships and leave both parties unhappy and feeling ineffective. Some severe types of hostility are beyond the influence of sales professionals. However, there are some specific actions sales professionals can take to diffuse potentially explosive situations. Personal attacks and threats usually occur as the result of incomplete information, past negative interactions, fear of unknown consequences, or a perceived high-risk situation. Frequently the hostility is not directed at the specific sales professional but rather toward the organization or the specific situation in question.

Figure 8.2
Cause and Effect Diagram

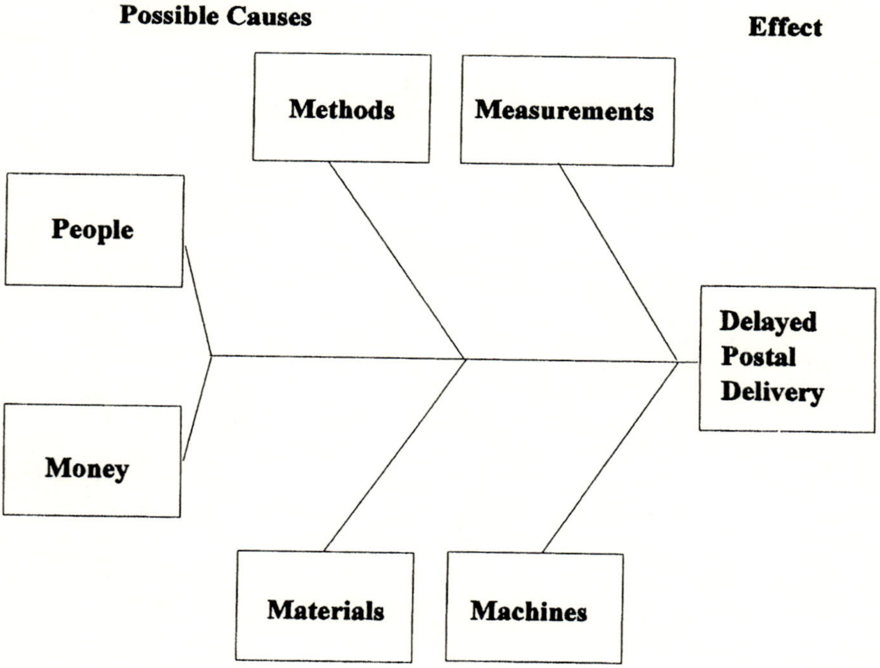

First and foremost, sales professionals must maintain control of their own emotions. Trading insults and derogatory comments does nothing but add more momentum to the conflict. Sales professionals cannot afford to lose their own tempers or show any breakdown in their ability to control their emotions. Responding to personal attacks in a positive and controlled manner sets the tone for the interaction and will eventually deliver the message to the client that the sales professional's goal is to resolve the conflict and salvage the relationship. If the attacks are personal in nature then it is critical for the sales professional to deflect the negativity and focus the discussion on relevant issues and to use open-ended questions to surface positive factors and areas of common interest that can be used to move the discussion forward toward resolution.

If the sales professional sees little progress in turning the discussion in a positive direction it may be time to bring in a third party to facilitate the discussions in an unbiased environment. Or the sales professional may work at diffusing the situation by postponing any actions until additional information and facts can be collected and reviewed by all parties involved. Ultimately the sales professional may have to concede that the relationship has been damaged so severely that a mutually acceptable solution cannot be identified. In this type of situation it is best for the sales professional to limit losses and end the relationship in a professional and civil manner, recognizing that the client may be lost and the organization's reputation damaged.

Critical Situation: Managing Hostile Clients— Paid to Keep Them, Not Love Them

Situation: I couldn't believe the way the lady was talking to me! We have been one of her key vendors for about three years and we always seemed to get along just fine. She was one of the more professional purchasing managers I had to deal with. Once or twice over the past three years we had a little problem with late deliveries but she just sort of shrugged it off and didn't make a big deal about it. Wow, did things change! When I got in to the office one Monday morning about 7:30 there were already two voice mails from her waiting for me and she was definitely not happy. She was threatening to cancel everything we had going with her company and tell everyone in the world she knew what a lousy company we were. Apparently the last order I had sold her hadn't arrived yet and it was two days late. I had checked on things the week before with the folks in logistics and everything looked like it was on target for on-time delivery so I had forgotten about it and was focused on doing some new client development. Before I gave her a call I headed to logistics to see what was going on and from there I grabbed a cup of coffee and sat down in the cafeteria to think this through. This was one of my top three clients and with the way the economy is I couldn't afford to lose them. I gave the purchasing manager a call at about 8:05 A.M. and I didn't even get my name out of my mouth before she started lighting into me. It was not pleasant and she was obviously not pleased with our company. The more we talked the more she seemed to calm down and be more of her old self. I had checked on the shipment and it had left our plant right on time for delivery on Friday—actually a little ahead of schedule—but somewhere things had broken down. I found out two of the four packages had been delivered and it turned out the shipping company had delivered two of the packages to their other plant. She also shared with me that the new plant manager had been giving her a hard time lately.

Development Issues: In many conflict situations taking a little extra time to collect all of the facts and information can be a big plus for the sales professional trying to deal with an upset client. Sometimes sales professionals end up catching the flak for things that are beyond their control. They can either smile and work through the situation with the client or get defensive and risk losing the business.

Action Tips:

- Remind sales professionals that in hostile conflict situations they have to sometimes think of themselves as actors, not get defensive, and play the role of client advocate. They are being paid to keep clients, not lose them.
- Ask your sales professionals to describe the biggest conflict they have experienced in their sales career, how they handled it, and what they would do differently. Take time to debrief and document.
- Ask your sales professionals to share how they spot conflict warning signals and take appropriate actions to avoid conflict when necessary.

DO YOUR SALES PROFESSIONALS UNDERSTAND HOW TO USE THE RIGHT TYPE OF QUESTIONS TO RESOLVE CONFLICTS?

Even with the most effective training on conflict resolution and systematic strategies to approach the situation a client can move a sales professional off track and focus a discussion on areas not productive to resolving the conflict. Using meaningful and pertinent questions is an excellent strategy for clarifying the issues behind a conflict and redirecting a discussion in a positive direction that will result in positive outcomes. Simply asking the client to describe, from their perspective, what the cause of the conflict was and how it got started can provide valuable information to the sales professional and also provide the client with an opportunity to reflect on what actually started the entire event. From there, clarifying all of the individuals involved in the conflict can shed light on some of the underlying issues involved in the conflict. The sales professional can further draw clients into the conflict resolution process by asking them to identify potential solutions and what they see as the advantages and disadvantages of each potential solution. The sales professional must explain why they are asking each question. For example, clarifying specific points, gathering more background information, understanding the time frame, and determining the special factors involved are all potential explanations for asking questions.

Questions should be presented in a neutral and nonthreatening manner that does not belittle or attack the client. Having sincere and valid reasons for the questions and presenting them in a respectful and courteous manner is essential. Ultimately the sales professional must reinforce that the goal is to resolve the conflcit in a positive and professional manner.

CAN YOUR SALES PROFESSIONALS
EFFECTIVELY MAKE THEIR POINTS WITH
CLIENTS IN CONFLICT SITUATIONS?

Making the point and effectively communicating in client conflict situations can be difficult. Dealing with clients who do not agree with the sales professional's perspective can be stressful. Sales professionals must thoughtfully plan for this type of communication and identify what two or three major points are most important for the client to understand and grasp. The sales professional must communicate the major points in clear and easily understandable terms. Each point must be supported with facts and data and reinforced as a positive factor. The data used to support each point must be valid and the client able to understand how the data were developed and collected. State the key points, support them with data and then restate them. When possible restate quotes or positive points the client made that support the direction the sales professional is taking the discussion. Visual aids such as graphs and charts that visually support the sales professional's key points should be used to clarify and support key concepts.

As the sales professional works to resolve the conflict, inclusive terms such as "we," "all of us," and "you and I" should be used to encourage the sense that the sales professional and the client can work together to resolve the conflict and maintain the relationship. Technical jargon should also be avoided as organization-specific terms can create barriers between the sales professional and the client. The client can interpret jargon as an attempt by the sales professional to talk down to them or a strategy for confusing the situation and the details of the problem.

CAN YOUR SALES PROFESSIONALS PROVIDE
SOLID ANSWERS TO THE QUESTIONS OF
CLIENTS AND OTHERS INVOLVED IN THE CONFLICT?

Sales professionals should expect to have to address some tough questions as they work with a client or internal colleague to resolve a conflict. As you know, the wrong response to a client question can quickly stop any momentum that is being gained toward resolving the conflict. Questions can quickly take a discussion off track. All questions should be addressed and if they are not relevant to the discussion then they should be acknowledged by the sales professional and redirected or tabled until a later time. Talking down to the client or person asking the question or belittling them in any way is certain to take the discussion from positive to negative. As the sales professional works with the other individual to resolve the conflict it is critical to remain positive, patient, and in control of the discussion. Hostility should be expected and it is up to the sales professional to maintain control of the discussion and continue to move it toward a positive resolution.

Questions can be viewed as a threat to the sales professional or as an opportunity to reinforce the key points and guide the discussion in a favorable direction. Clients typically ask questions for some specific reasons; they want to confirm what they heard, they are trying to belittle or attack the sales professional, they didn't believe what they heard and are trying to challenge the speaker, they are trying to stretch out or delay the discussion, they are trying to turn the focus from the speaker to themselves, or they have poor listening skills and were not paying attention. Sales professionals must expect difficult behaviors and questions of this nature any time they are in a conflict situation. Anticipating what questions might be asked and preparing responses in advance can have a significant impact on the sales professional's ability to keep control of the situation and move the discussion in a productive direction. However, not every question can be anticipated or planned for and inevitably questions will come up that the sales professional does not have an immediate response for. Before responding in this type of situation the sales professional should take the time to restate the question and give the other person the opportunity to confirm that in fact the sales professional heard the question correctly. This also gives the sales professional an opportunity to think through the response and consider the implications of what he or she is about to say.

Overanswering a question can be as problematic as providing an incomplete or inaccurate answer. Sales professionals should accurately answer the question they have been asked in a clear and concise manner. They should also recognize that, if they do not know the answer or do not have all the data at that point in time, it is better to say so then to give confusing or incomplete responses.

Sales professionals must evaluate their audience and, when using facts or data, make sure that they are correct and accurate. Inaccurate use of data can quickly erode all credibility and trust. Also, using statistics or tables when the sales professional does not fully understand the implications of the data can be dangerous. Individuals involved in the discussion with more background can quickly dispute data or turn what was intended to be positive to negative.

Finally, if the sales professional moves the discussion toward resolution of the conflict and the questions they were anticipating do not surface, it is acceptable for the sales professional to pose questions of their own even if they are qualified as being hypothetical. The sales professional's questions can serve as an icebreaker and encourage clients to voice any reservations or concerns they had been holding back about the situation.

DO YOUR SALES PROFESSIONALS HAVE THE PERSUASIVE SKILLS NEEDED WHEN CONFLICT DISCUSSIONS NEED TO BE REDIRECTED?

Not all attempts at conflict resolution with clients or internal colleagues go as expected. The sales professional may be faced with the challenge of convincing clients or others in the organization that the solution needed to resolve the conflict is not the one that everyone involved expected. This type of persuasive salesmanship is similar to taking a cross-country trip in that the journey must be completed in smaller segments; and even though a specific amount of travel was planned for each day, factors may develop that were not planned for. Redirecting a conflict resolution discussion may have to be accomplished through a series of small incremental moves that require resiliency and patience on the part of the sales professional as they work to salvage the relationship and keep the groups involved recognizing that the final solution may not be ideal in the eyes of all parties. As the sales professional works through the conflict any concessions they can make to move closer to their client's perspective are helpful and can give the client the feeling that the sales professional does want to treat them fairly and honestly, not because it is good for business but rather because it is the right thing to do. The sales professional should strive to paint a picture of the solution they are striving for and help the client to see how that picture satisfies their needs and leaves them feeling like the conflict was resolved to their satisfaction.

When carefully collected and explained, facts and data can have considerable influence in redirecting those involved in a conflict situation toward an alternative solution. Carefully displaying the data and including clear and succinct explanations with each piece of the data can help both sides to better understand the cause of the conflict and the impact of different solutions. Background information on similar situations that occurred in the past and how they were resolved can also help to build the case for a particular solution to the conflict. As the sales professional shares information with the parties involved in the conflict resolution process it is important that the most important and significant pieces of information be shared first and presented in a clear and logical sequence. The sales professional should also finish strong and reinforce the key points made at the beginning of the discussion to assure that everyone understood why the conflict should be resolved in a positive manner. The sales professional's credibility and the perception that he or she is attempting to do what is best for all parties involved is critical if any give and take is to occur on either side of the conflict.

DO YOUR SALES PROFESSIONALS KNOW HOW TO LISTEN AND COMMUNICATE TO RESOLVE CONFLICTS WITH CLIENTS?

In normal circumstances most people comprehend a fraction of the information that is presented to them. Whether it is because of external distractions like other conversations or from internal distractions like daydreaming, many important ideas and major points are missed under normal circumstances. Add the stress of a heated conflict over the late delivery of a shipment, for example, and it is easy to see why sales professionals must be very focused and attentive when working to resolve a conflict situation with an important client. Effective listening skills are not only important for the sales professional when attempting to resolve a client conflict, they are truly critical any time a sales professional is involved in the sales process. By being recognized as an excellent listener sales professionals can enhance their image with the client and earn their respect and trust as they build their own self-confidence in their ability to handle any situation they encounter. The more opportunities the client is given to communicate the more information the sales professional can gather about the situation and the better they can understand the client's perspective.

Whether using a hand-held personal assistant or a notebook and pencil, maintaining an accurate set of notes of the discussion helps to keep the sales professional focused on the discussion at hand and, after the fact, accurate notes can prevent misunderstandings or errors. Note taking also helps the sales professional to maintain a mental map of the points the client has been making and enhances their ability to retain the key points made in the discussion. Some clients and colleagues may be intimidated by note taking, feeling the sales professional is taking notes for documentation purposes or as evidence for a future event. In a conflict situation it is always best to explain the purpose of the note taking as a technique for helping the sales professional to stay focused on the situation and to make the offer to clean-up the notes after the meeting and share them with the other parties involved as a summary of what occurred.

Asking clarifying questions and providing positive nonverbal feedback are also techniques for keeping the sales professional focused on the client and actively involved in the discussion. Statements that acknowledge the other person's perspective, "I can see your point and understand why you would be upset," can send a message that you are interested in resolving the situation and will do what you can. These techniques clearly send a sign to the client that the sales professional values what the client is saying. Providing feedback and restating key points also provide an opportunity for the other person to confirm if the sales professional truly understood the points that were being made and the client's rationale for being dissatisfied. By restating the key points in a nonthreatening manner the sales professional gives the client an opportunity to cool down and also confirms to them that this discussion is important and that the sales professional is really listening to what is being said. This is an opportunity to make the client feel important and valued by the sales professional and their organization.

Effective listening skills come naturally to some people while others have to work to develop and maintain the skills necessary to be successful. To be an effective listener in a conflict situation the sales professional should be doing more listening than talking. If that is not the case then it is most likely that the sales professional is more concerned about getting their perspective across than listening to the client and understanding his or her perspective. Being quiet and silent at times during the discussion can also enhance the effectiveness of the discussion. The natural inclination for many people is to quickly fill up any empty space with conversations. Remaining silent while someone takes the time to think through an important point or contemplate a response to a question can be difficult. Silence on the sales professional's part can be perceived by the client as an invitation to continue talking and an opportunity for the sales professional to learn more about the client's perspective on the resolution of the conflict.

Consider the following situation. Note the developmental issues and action tips provided at the end of that situation as key points for helping sales professionals cultivate their talents.

Critical Situation: Controlling Emotions—Cool Under Fire

Situation: I consider myself a seasoned sales professional but sometimes lose my cool when I am hit with what I think are unreasonable client demands. Recently I observed another sales professional in our organization come under fire over some unexpected changes. Instead of immediately responding she waited till the next day and simply asked the client "If you were in my position, what would you do?" He suggested a few minor changes and the problem was over. It really made me stop and think about how I would have handled the situation. I am afraid I would have not handled the situation as smoothly as she did.

Development Issues: Patience is a virtue. Try to control emotions and stay focused on potential solutions. There has never been a time in the history of the world that change has been so rapid. We must learn to deal and cope with the stress of change.

Action Tips:

- If your sales professionals experience conflict or resistance from clients or other stakeholders, encourage them to ask themselves why. Never assume you know what people think. Ask them.
- Identify those in your sales organization who manage and cope with conflict and stress in a constructive manner and use them as role models.
- Keep in mind that technology is changing more today than it has in the history of mankind. Reinforce that resolving interpersonal conflicts and coping with change is part of every sales professional's job.

DOES YOUR ORGANIZATION SPONSOR PROGRAMS TO ENHANCE RESOLVING CONFLICTS AND COPING WITH CHANGE?

Where should you start in your quest to enhance the competence of sales professionals in resolving conflicts and coping with change? Consult the following checklist of developmental strategies to build competence in this area.

- ☐ Use oral communication when exploring complex sales issues in order to achieve and check your understanding of important issues.
- ☐ Try to put yourself into the client's role and anticipate how your communication is likely to be received and accepted.

❑ Take a conflict resolution course to develop your interpersonal skills for communicating one-on-one in hostile situations.

❑ In hostile sales situations be concise. Use short, simple words and short, clear sentences.

❑ If you are frequently misunderstood in sales situations, ask your superior or peers for feedback on your conflict-resolution style.

❑ Break complex sales topics down into smaller ideas and present your ideas incrementally.

Ask your sales professionals to check those development activities they believe should be integrated into a program to enhance their ability to resolve conflicts and cope with change. Then use this plan to help build the competence of your sales professionals in resolving conflict and coping with change.

A Sample Program Outline to Guide Resolving Sales and Interpersonal Conflicts and Coping with Change

Title: Knowledge of Self

Competency Dimension: Resolving sales and interpersonal conflicts and coping with change

Learning Objectives:
- Can anticipate and seek to resolve possible client confrontations, disagreements, and complaints in a constructive manner
- Able to manage conflicts with other sales staff, operational people, and stakeholders in a constructive manner
- Can cope effectively with sales pressures, stress, and change

Potential Content Topics:
- Conflict resolution
- Interpersonal communication styles
- Coping with communication challenges
- Enhancing your understanding of yourself and others in the sales process
- Understanding the process of organizational change and its influence on sales
- Developing individual and group resilience
- Negotiation skills
- How to use power and influence
- "Win–win" negotiating
- How to be more assertive
- Using nonverbal techniques for persuasion
- Power without authority
- Dealing with rejection and other sales-related stress

PART **III**

KNOWLEDGE OF PRODUCTS AND SERVICES

The chapters in Part III focus on four core competency dimensions related to knowledge of products and services. Each competency is treated in a chapter. Each chapter introduces the competency, offers an opening assessment activity, and then encourages the reader to think about how each question posed in the opening assessment activity relates to the key characteristics needed by sales professionals.

9

Establishing Ongoing Client and Stakeholder Informational Processes

Exemplary sales professionals exude confidence. They know how to develop programs to communicate about organizational methods and procedures, and they take responsibility to rectify problems. Their confidence stems from their ability to establish and communicate proper boundaries and guidelines of operation. Once established and communicated, salespeople can use their discretionary power to assess the significance of potential situations, identify alternative solutions, and exercise their judgment for the good of the organization and the client.

Establishing ongoing client and stakeholder informational processes is thus important in the success of sales professionals. This competency means that sales professionals possess the ability to

- create an ongoing process to keep clients and stakeholders informed
- communicate organizational methods and procedures
- introduce a range of products and services and resources available to support the selling process

What are the development needs of your sales professionals for establishing ongoing client and stakeholder informational processes? Consult Figure 9.1 to see how the respondents to our survey rated the relative importance of the behaviors associated with this competency. Then reflect on how you would rate sales professionals in your organization.

Now complete the self-assessment as it applies to you and your organization.

Figure 9.1
Behaviors Related to the Competency of Client and Stakeholder
Informational Process as Rated by Survey Respondents

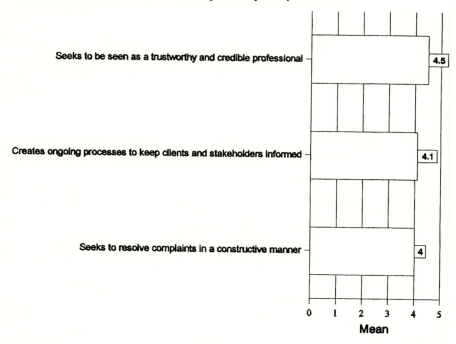

Source: From *A Survey about Sales Training Programs* by W. Rothwell, W. Donahue, and J. Park, 2001 (unpublished survey results), University Park, PA: Pennsylvania State University. Copyright 2001 by W. Rothwell, W. Donahue, and J. Park.

Self-Assessment: Establishing Ongoing Client and Stakeholder Informational Processes

Directions: With your sales organization in mind, place a number on the line in the left column below that matches your level of agreement with each statement. Then add up the numbers and score your assessment.

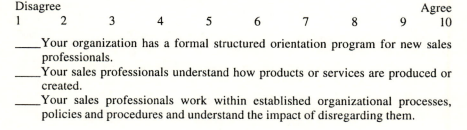

____Your organization has a formal structured orientation program for new sales professionals.

____Your sales professionals understand how products or services are produced or created.

____Your sales professionals work within established organizational processes, policies and procedures and understand the impact of disregarding them.

____Your sales professionals understand their role in maintaining a positive work environment including labor–management relations and the impact they have.

____Your sales professionals understand your internal accounting, budgeting, and pricing processes and their responsibilities in each area.

____Your organization has a formal process for collecting client feedback on all products and services.

____Your organization has a process or system in place for analyzing client feedback and using it to make organizational changes.

____Your organization communicates to clients and stakeholders how product and service decisions are made.

____Your organization sponsors programs to enhance ongoing client and stakeholder informational processes.

____Total

How Did You Score?

Here is the key to establishing ongoing client and stakeholder informational processes. Add up your responses to get your score.

91–100 Great job! Congratulations! Your organization is effectively working to enhance informational processes and self-development.

81–90 Keep up the good work! You've probably had considerable success. But by using some of the tips in this chapter, you could improve your success.

71–80 Help is needed! There's room for improvement. You'll find this chapter helpful.

0–70 Warning! Your sales organization may have difficulty keeping your clients and stakeholders properly informed. Read on!

Once you have completed the self-assessment, use this worksheet to organize your thinking about ways of building this competency among sales professionals in your organization.

A Worksheet to Organize Your Thinking on Establishing Ongoing Client and Stakeholder Informational Processes

Directions: In your opinion, what problems or challenges does your sales organization face in enhancing your organization's informational processes? Use this worksheet to organize your thinking about how to answer this question.

Notes:

DOES YOUR ORGANIZATION HAVE A FORMAL STRUCTURED ORIENTATION PROGRAM FOR NEW SALES PROFESSIONALS?

A thoughtful and systematic orientation program is a key informational process and one of the cornerstones of a successful sales development program. An effective orientation program helps employees make the transition into the organization, understand the value of the organization's products and services, gain an appreciation for the keys to success, and is the first step in helping the employee identify with the organization and become a long-term high performer.

First impressions are critical in the sales process and equally as important in setting the stage for the training of new sales professionals. An orientation program is a time to inform new employees of important organizational issues, specific job roles and responsibilities, key policies and procedures, and how the organization's culture functions. Including an overview of the organization's strategic plan, if available, can play an important role in helping a new sales professional understand the context and importance of their position in sales to the success of the organization. Orientation programs are most effective when they are presented over a period of time in a systematic and phased manner versus an intensive one or two-day forced session. By extending the orientation program new employees have the opportunity to ask follow-up questions and the orientation program serves as a support system during the first month or two of work, providing them with access to resources and other new employees who could be experiencing similar issues or questions. Mentoring or buddy programs are also an important part of the orientation program.

Supporting documentation either in traditional paper form or on a Web site that provides ongoing support for the new sales professional is an important factor in the orientation process. All materials regarding benefits and policies and procedures should be carefully reviewed with the new sales professional. Many organizations are requiring employees to sign off that they have read and understood all policy information. This can be a precautionary measure for documentation in case of future legal action if an employee leaves or is asked to leave the organization.

A mix of one-on-one and small group training sessions are usually most effective in the teaching and presentation of the orientation materials. Sound adult teaching principles should be applied with role plays, case studies, small group discussions, self-assessments, and videos all being integrated in to the program. As orientation programs become much more of an integral part of the new sales professional development program, postprogram testing of knowledge and skills is also being used to evaluate participants.

Learning about and understanding the depth and breadth of the new organization they have just joined is an important part of a new sales professional orientation program. Having a framework to guide this learning can be helpful in ensuring that the sales professional has taken the time to review the organization in a systematic manner. This list of categories could serve as a table of contents for a resource guide:

1. Business of the organization and history
2. Industry analysis
3. Sales and marketing activities
4. Organizational culture and design
5. Human resources policies and procedures
6. Finance and budgeting
7. Leadership
8. Products and services
9. Miscellaneous (for example social activities, dress policy, ethics, and so forth)

By focusing on these areas in the orientation process the sales organization can facilitate a learning experience for the new sales professional that is comprehensive and ensures that they understand the importance of their role in comparison to the broader organization. An effective orientation program for sales professionals can set the tone for future performance and is an important factor in the long-term success and retention of employees.

DO YOUR SALES PROFESSIONALS UNDERSTAND HOW PRODUCTS OR SERVICES ARE PRODUCED OR CREATED?

Product and process knowledge and understanding can quickly set top-level professional salespeople apart from the rest of the field and enhance the client's perception of product value. For sales professionals involved with some type of a production or manufacturing operation, taking the time to understand the complexities of the operation and its capabilities can make it much easier to answer questions about customization capabilities or to be able to make realistic commitments for rush orders. Understanding product and process capacity can help the sales professional to better link potential clients' needs with the products or services they sell in a positive problem-solving manner.

Clients can test or play games with sales professionals to gauge their product knowledge and understanding of the business or industry they are working in. Knowledgeable clients can quickly determine if sales professionals actually know the business or are faking their way through a discussion. Sales professionals who have been cross-trained to understand the strengths and weaknesses of the organization's production processes can confidently respond to technical questions.

Critical Situation: Product Understanding—Become an Expert

Situation: When I asked the guy about the motherboards in the laptops he looked at me as if I was speaking a foreign language. Here he was representing his organization at one of the major trade shows in the world and he was about as prepared to answer questions as my dog. Honestly, I really didn't know much more than him about what I was asking him but I was more interested in asking the right question and letting someone else impress me with how much they knew, pretended to know, or, in this guy's case, how little they knew and were willing to admit. When I asked him to explain a couple of fairly basic things about the processes his company was using he floundered around for a bit and then finally he was honest enough to admit that he was clueless and that his technical person was out to lunch. By that point he had totally turned me off on buying anything off of him and it made me wonder about the company in general if he was the best they could produce for an event like this.

Development Issues: Sales professionals don't need to be technical wizards, but they do need to have a base line of knowledge about the processes used to develop the products they are selling. Having a standard set of FAQs is a great way to prepare sales professionals for dealing with a technical audience. And, if you are filling in or substituting for someone, say so.

Action Tips:
• Establish FAQs for your products and services.
• Establish guidelines to ensure everyone is treated equally, fairly, and with respect.

DO YOUR SALES PROFESSIONALS WORK WITHIN ES-TABLISHED ORGANIZATIONAL PROCESSES, POLICIES, AND PROCEDURES AND UNDERSTAND THE IMPACT OF DISREGARDING THEM?

Sales professionals pushing the limits and skirting on the edge with what they perceive as trivial organizational policies and procedures is fairly common. What organization wouldn't love to have a department full of hungry, aggressive, overachieving sales professionals who once in a while bend the rules a bit to get the job done? However, there is a fine line between bending the rules a bit to get things done and totally disregarding organizational policies and procedures due to a lack of knowledge or, worse yet, a lack of caring. In particular, ignoring or not adhering to policies regarding expense accounts, billing practices, and credit checks can be costly in real hard dollars and morale to an organization.

Knowledge and understanding of expense account policies and procedures should be part of the new sales professional's orientation. Beyond compliance with tax guidelines for expense accounts, organizational policies on per diems, or mileage rates can be unique for each organization. However, with changes in tax laws many organizations are becoming more structured in their policies and restricting the types of activities they will support on an expense account.

Allowing select members of an organization to violate or disregard specific organizational practices can quickly destroy a manager's credibility with the workforce. Isolated incidents of overcommitting on finance terms or juggling billing dates for clients can be problematic for an organization but something organizations can live with if sales are strong and the company is profitable. However, this type of activity occurs more often when sales have been tracking downward and salespeople are willing to do whatever they can to get the sale and make their quota. As all businesses have learned from time to time, making the sale can come much easier than waiting for that late payment or turning an account over for collection. Sales professionals must understand the impact of their actions on the overall success of the organization, not just specifically focus on the sales organization.

DO YOUR SALES PROFESSIONALS UNDERSTAND THEIR ROLE IN MAINTAINING A POSITIVE WORK ENVIRONMENT INCLUDING LABOR–MANAGEMENT RELATIONS AND THE IMPACT THEY HAVE?

The sales profession is a stressful and challenging occupation. Sales professionals are under pressure to produce results and it is easy to become internally focused and to lose touch with what is important in life and in a business organization. Treating sales colleagues and other employees across the organization in a respectful and civil manner is one of the key components of creating a positive work environment. Positive organizations are able to retain employees and create a work setting that is friendly and open. Relationships between sales professionals and others around the organization in customer service, manufacturing, or logistics are critical to their success. Sales professionals must be especially sensitive to how they interact with employees in union organizations. A lack of awareness and knowledge of how sales professionals should, for example, discuss a delivery problem or a problem with product specifications with a union member is not a viable excuse. Union policy may prohibit sales staff from directly approaching a shop employee with a particular problem without first going through proper channels. A lack of knowledge is not a valid excuse; grievances can be filed as the result of failure to follow proper procedures. Sales professionals should be informed as part of the sales development program as to proper procedures for dealing with union employees.

Creating and maintaining a positive work environment takes time and energy on the part of managers and employees no matter what level they are in the organization. Positive organizations have the following characteristics:

☐ Sales professionals feel like they are part of the organization and what they do is contributing to the overall success of the organization.

☐ Performance issues are handled in private. Poor sales performance and feedback on errors or mistakes are handled in private—not in front of the entire sales group in a way that is attacking or demeaning.

❏ Sales professionals have established goals and are rewarded for achieving those goals. Also, when the overall organization reaches its goals everyone in the sales organization shares in that achievement and understands how how incentives or rewards are tied to those goals.

❏ The sales organization has a clear purpose and vision. Leaders have communicated their vision to everyone in the sales organization and everyone is in alignment with that vision.

❏ Sales professionals in the organization focus on treating others the way they like to be treated. Abusive or mean behaviors are not accepted or tolerated.

❏ Mistakes are viewed as an opportunity to correct something and the focus on mistakes is fixing them and correcting the process, not blaming an individual sales professional.

How does your organization compare? Check the preceeding statements you believe to be true about your sales organization.

A positive work environment does not guarantee the financial success of an organization. However, it is certainly a contributing factor when you examine organizations that have had long-term success in reaching their financial goals, retaining employees, and being a safe and friendly work environment. In unionized environments establishing positive labor–management relationships can have a positive impact on employee grievance situations and productivity.

DO YOUR SALES PROFESSIONALS UNDERSTAND YOUR INTERNAL ACCOUNTING, BUDGETING, AND PRICING PROCESSES AND THEIR RESPONSIBILITIES IN EACH AREA?

Ultimately the primary goal for most organizations is to generate a satisfactory return on investment for the owners or stockholders of the organization. Unlike some departments within an organization the effectiveness of the sales department has a direct impact on the achievement of this goal. Although sales professionals' day-to-day sales productivity may not be impacted by their ability to understand company budgeting and pricing and accounting principles, their long-term value to the organization and their ability to move into other roles within the organization will be influenced by their ability to understand the broader organization and the impact of their success on the overall organization. Sales professionals who have a broader business knowledge are also better able to add value to their client organizations, as they can be looked at as a broader resource than solely a vendor or provider of a product or service.

The groundwork for understanding the budgeting and accounting practices guiding the organization can be found in the annual report generated by the organization if it is publicly held. Most organizations are placing all or most of their key financial information on their Web sites. This is an excellent place for sales professionals to begin in their understanding of an organization's key financial indicators. Sales growth, net income, and earnings per share are all common indicators of the health and financial viability of most organizations. Most clients today expect sales professionals to have an awareness of their organization's current financial performance and it is important for all sales professionals to be able to address questions about the financial stability and viability of their organization in today's turbulent economic environment. Sales professionals may also be asked how their organization's financial condition compares to the competition, so it will be important for sales professionals to monitor the financial performance of their top competitors when that knowledge is available through the organization's Web site or other sources. Beyond their key financial indicators it can be informative to examine how competitors' cost structure, investments, and net operating results compare.

A sales professional's income and expense projections can be a critical component of a sales organization's budgeting process and have a direct impact on accounting practices. Inflated or underrepresented projections can have a tremendous impact on budgeting and distribution of resources.

DOES YOUR ORGANIZATION HAVE A FORMAL PROCESS FOR COLLECTING CLIENT FEEDBACK ON ALL PRODUCTS AND SERVICES?

Measuring customer satisfaction begins with determining what critical factors should be measured and what the right questions are to ask clients to determine how effective the organization is in meeting their needs in the critical areas. To provide great customer service to your client organizations, your business must identify and understand how they define great customer service. This information must in turn set the vision and tone for customer service in the organization. Without a clear understanding of how excellent customer service is defined it is difficult to determine if the organization is providing it to clients.

Surveys and market research are two of the many tools needed to truly understand an organization's clients. Market data is as good as the data collection process and the people providing the input. Truly, if all organizations that needed to roll out successful new product lines used market research, then every company would be extremely profitable, and the Fortune 500 companies would be the same as they were in 1980s. We all know that is not the case. Market research and client satisfaction surveys provide a portion of the information needed to understand client satisfaction, however, they still do not replace face-to-face conversations with clients.

As clients' needs change their perceptions of what they value in a product or service and their expectations also change. In the auto industry, for example, items such as an automatic transmission or air conditioning that were once considered options are standard equipment in most cars. Understanding what is important to clients and what value they place on specific products or services is an ongoing process that requires continuous feedback. Monitoring clients' purchases can provide valuable information on their level of satisfaction with a particular product or service. The following checklist provides examples of data that can be immensely useful in assessing client satisfaction:

☐ Has the average purchase size for all clients changed?

☐ What is happening with the purchases of the organization's top ten clients? Are their purchases increasing or decreasing?

☐ How many clients purchase our products one time and do not buy again?

☐ Are our clients providing referrals?

Sales managers can be one of the most valuable sources of client information. Periodic visits with sales professionals to clients can provide an opportunity to share information and provide input on the client's level of satisfaction with the organization's products or services. Many clients interpret the manager accompanying the sales professional as an indication that they are considered a valuable client that warrants a call from the manager. This perception can in fact serve to free up the client to talk in detail about the organization and their level of satisfaction with the products and services being provided.

DOES YOUR ORGANIZATION HAVE A PROCESS OR SYSTEM IN PLACE FOR ANALYZING CLIENT FEEDBACK AND USING IT TO MAKE ORGANIZATIONAL CHANGES?

In many cases collecting data for problem solving is the easy step. Turning that raw data into pieces of information that can be used for decision-making purposes can be much more difficult. The same can hold true of client feedback. Collecting client data is only one step in the process of being a customer-focused organization. The data must be analyzed and reviewed for themes and trends that indicate a need for change. Sales professionals can play a valuable role in helping to understand the context of client feedback and the client's frame of mind when it was provided. Understanding what needs to be changed to address client concerns can be difficult. Client satisfaction teams composed of sales professionals, customer support staff, logistics staff, and manufacturing or service delivery personnel can provide valuable feedback and solutions for addressing client concerns and feedback. Using problem-solving techniques, client data can be analyzed for trends and themes and then utilized to drive process reviews and potential changes.

Change can create stress and anxiety in people. Sales professionals must recognize that change is a constant reality for them and in the current environment an organization's ability to change to meet customer needs is a prerequisite for any type of profitable long-term survival. Changes to address client feedback may need to be abrupt and immediate or the change may need to be more planned and gradual. Whatever the change, it is critical that the change be reviewed and analyzed to help the organization identify and understand the broader implications to the organization and to the client. If abrupt changes are warranted then the organization must recognize that potential conflicts can arise and plan accordingly. With more gradual long-term change, pilot programs can be conducted to evaluate client and organizational impact with client and stakeholder feedback driving adaptations to the change initiative.

DOES YOUR ORGANIZATION COMMUNICATE TO CLIENTS AND STAKEHOLDERS HOW PRODUCT AND SERVICE DECISIONS ARE MADE?

Beyond newsletters, whether they be paper or electronic, product literature mailings, news postings to the company Web site, sales, or more formal personalized correspondence, salespeople are the primary conduit of information to clients and stakeholders. How they deliver information and communicate organizational changes, such as price increases, can have a tremendous impact on sales growth and company profitability. In particular the context of how price increases are communicated to clients can often determine the client's acceptance or inclination to seek out pricing from the competition. Price increases that drop from the sky unexplained are hard for clients to accept and even more difficult for sales professionals to justify. When sales professionals understand the context of how decisions on price increases are made and they are able to communicate this to clients, then even if the increases are still unwelcome at least the clients can better relate what is happening to their own situation.

Organizations that make decisions in a vacuum from formal research can expect limited ownership in these decisions from clients and stakeholders. Clients that understand the organizational structure and decision-making processes can better provide their input on issues such as new product development or service enhancements to the company at the appropriate time and at the right level.

The more clients understand where sales professionals fit into the organization the better they can relate to them and understand their role in the decision-making process. How an organization communicates the rationale for decisions can have a strong influence on the level of client and stakeholder acceptance or dissatisfaction with the decision and the overall organization.

Involvement brings ownership with it. Clients who are asked to provide feedback prior to decision making are much more likely to feel ownership in the decision and be supportive, while decisions made in a dictatorial manner with no feedback are much more likely to face resistance and distrust from clients. Some decisions, no matter what level of feedback or input is solicited, will remain unpopular and poorly received. Sales professionals must be prepared to deal with negative feedback on specific decisions that are beyond their control, just as the rejection of sales proposals should not be personalized. Negative feedback on decisions beyond the sales professional's control should be accepted in a gracious manner and not personalized.

Critical Situation: Client Communication—
How Products Are Made, The Product College

Situation: Are you the quality supplier of commodity products and services? How do you differentiate your products from those of your competitors when seemingly they all look like? As an example, how would you differentiate a roll of toilet paper, plastic containers for beverages or food products, or aspirin without adversely talking about your competitors? One innovative company decided to start an annual three-day Product College primarily for client purchasing agents where they showcased their extensive research and development department and superior manufacturing practices. The program was conducted by various department heads within the company and was not promoted as a public relations event but rather an educational course for its clients. However, while the company didn't specifically promote its products and services, rest assured, all participants from its client organizations left with jackets and other memorabilia from their three-day experience and a clear understanding that not all suppliers could provide the same level of support. The purchasing agents also developed a variety of lasting personal relationships with their supplier's department heads and sales professionals.

Development Issues: Creating an ongoing informational process highlighting your products and services in a positive way should be an ongoing initiative. Developing a symposium, short course, or even an informal educational event can help to educate not only your clients but new employees within your organization. It also provides the opportunity for seasoned veterans to showcase their expertise and knowledge.

Action Tips:
- Ask your department heads to prepare and conduct an educational segment of a larger event highlighting the products or services of their departments or work units.
- Consider conducting, at least annually, a short course or symposium focused on your products and services and invite selected clients and new employees to attend.
- Communicate to each person based on his or her experience or educational background.
- Prohibit sales professionals from talking negatively about other units in your organization (sales versus production).
- Invite and establish an interaction forum of stakeholders.

DOES YOUR ORGANIZATION CREATE AND
MAINTAIN PRODUCT AND SERVICE SPECIFICATIONS
OR CAPABILITIES DOCUMENTATION
FOR SALES PROFESSIONALS AND CLIENTS?

Easily accessible, accurate, and current product specification and capabilities documentation are important support materials that can set a sales organization apart from the competition. As you know, outdated or inaccurate information can have an immediate negative impact on an organization's professional image and can cause a sales professional to lose a sale. Client expectations in this area continue to elevate. Having current information available via a Web site is no longer a luxury for organizations—it is a required necessity. Product catalogs and support documentation must be available in multiple formats; that is, traditional paper, compact disk, Web site, and downloadable from PDF files. Some clients will continue to avoid the Web and expect paper copies of information.

Creating and maintaining product information is a challenging and potentially costly endeavor. Database-driven repositories of this critical organizational information should be created in a manner that allows them to be updated in a timely and efficient manner. Using a database as a framework for the repository allows the administrator of the database to make changes in one place, which then appear throughout the document.

DOES YOUR ORGANIZATION SPONSOR PROGRAMS TO ENHANCE ONGOING CLIENT AND STAKEHOLDER INFORMATIONAL PROCESSES?

Where should you start in your quest to enhance ongoing client and stakeholder information processes? Consult this checklist of developmental strategies to build competence in this area:

☐ Practice asking open-ended sales questions that require more than a yes or no answer.

☐ Before responding to clients, reframe the statement or message to confirm understanding and to provide time to formulate a response.

☐ Keep a log of the technical questions and problems that clients ask you for assistance with.

☐ Analyze what client situations you were able to help with to determine what your strengths and weaknesses are. Share them with other sales professionals.

☐ Try to become the expert in your organization in one or more technical areas. Keep a list of relevant technical resources.

☐ Maintain a climate of continuous learning within your sales organization by drawing on the expertise of your coworkers and having them share their knowledge through demonstrations, presentations, and written papers.

☐ Encourage other sales professionals to use you as a sounding board for their ideas.

☐ Share relevant technical articles and sales-related information among members of your sales organization.

Ask your sales professionals to check those development activities they believe should be integrated into a program to enhance ongoing client and stakeholder information processes for your organization. Then use the following plan to help build the competence of your sales professionals in enhancing ongoing client and stakeholder informational processes.

A Sample Program Outline to Guide Establishing Ongoing Client and Stakeholder Informational Processes

Title: Knowledge of Products and Services

Competency Dimension: Establishing ongoing client and stakeholder informational processes

Learning Objectives:
- Can create ongoing process to keep clients and stakeholders informed
- Able to communicate organizational methods and procedures
- Can communicate range of products and services to clients and stakeholders

Potential Content Topics:
- Developing an organizational intelligence system
- Applying tools for improving operations and managing resources
- Understanding the technical transfer process
- Managing upward
- Leading cross-functional teams
- Project management
- Creating a climate for teamwork, cooperation, and involvement
- Approaches to building high-performance teams
- How to make meetings work

10

Identifying and Communicating Product Features and Benefits

An effective sales professional understands what kind of—and how much—product(s) or services add value for a client. Developing a systematic process for the matching of client needs with products or services is a critical component of successful sales. Systematically responding to clients' needs is also essential to cultivating long-term, sustainable relationships. This chapter reviews tools that may be used to communicate features, benefits, and value-added services to clients. By using these tools, your sales staff become product experts, and that can make them indispensable to clients.

This chapter focuses on identifying and communicating product features and benefits. To demonstrate this competency, sales professionals should be able to

- demonstrate technical understanding of product features and benefits as well as limitations
- understand client needs
- communicate the value of products and services
- respond appropriately to clients

What are the development needs of your sales professionals for identifying and communicating product features and benefits? Consult Figure 10.1 to see how the respondents to our survey rated the relative importance of the behaviors associated with this competency. Then reflect on how you would rate sales professionals in your organization.

Complete the self-assessment as it applies to you and your organization, using the worksheet to organize your thinking about ways of building this competency among sales professionals in your organization.

Self-Assessment:
Identifying and Communicating Product Features and Benefits

Directions: With your sales organization in mind, place a number on the line in the left column below that matches your level of agreement with each statement. Then add up the numbers and score your assessment.

Disagree									Agree
1	2	3	4	5	6	7	8	9	10

_____All of your sales professionals are able to identify and analyze the product or service needs of clients.

_____All of your sales professionals demonstrate technical understanding of your products and services.

_____Your sales professionals understand the relationship between needs, benefits, and features.

_____Your sales professionals communicate and sell benefits over features.

_____Your sales professionals have the tools they need to communicate features and benefits and respond appropriately to clients.

_____All of your sales professionals understand and utilize value-added selling techniques.

_____Your sales professionals are skilled at overcoming objections.

_____Your sales professionals understand the capabilities and limitations of your products and services.

_____Your organization works to position your sales team as the product or service experts.

_____Your organization sponsors programs to educate and prepare sales professionals to properly communicate product features and benefits.

_____Total

How Did You Score?

Here is the key to identifying and communicating product features and benefits. Add up your responses to get your score.

91–100 Great job! Congratulations! Your organization is effectively working to communicate product features and benefits.

81–90 Keep up the good work! You've probably had considerable success. But by using some of the tips in this chapter, you could improve your success.

71–80 Help is needed! There's room for improvement. You'll find this chapter helpful.

0–70 Warning! Your sales organization probably has some challenges communicating features and benefits. Read on!

Figure 10.1
Behaviors Related to the Competency of Identifying and Communicating Product Features and Benefits as Rated by Survey Respondents

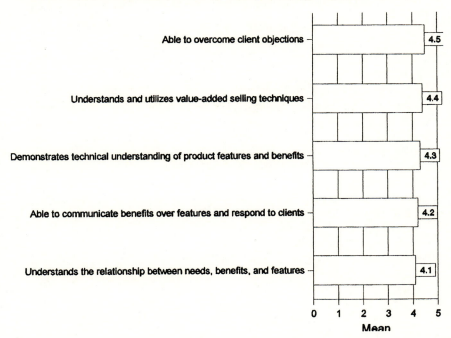

Source: From *A Survey about Sales Training Programs* by W. Rothwell, W. Donahue, and J. Park, 2001 (unpublished survey results), University Park, PA: Pennsylvania State University. Copyright 2001 by W. Rothwell, W. Donahue, and J. Park.

A Worksheet to Organize Your Thinking about Identifying and Communicating Product Features and Benefits

Directions: What challenges does your sales organization face in identifying and communicating product features and benefits? Use this worksheet to organize your thinking about how to answer this question. Use the space appearing below to record your thoughts.

Notes:

ARE ALL OF YOUR SALES PROFESSIONALS ABLE TO IDENTIFY AND ANALYZE THE PRODUCT OR SERVICE NEEDS OF CLIENTS?

It all starts with the communication process. If sales professionals are not trained in how to assess needs then it is a hit or miss as to how they work with clients to understand the client's organization and help the client to solve problems related to utilizing the sales organization's products or services. Active listening as described earlier in this book is a key competency dimension in the assessment of needs. During the needs-assessment phase of the sales process sales professionals must maintain their focus and concentration on the clients' needs and not slip in to a selling mode. Clients often do not share all of the information necessary to understand their needs with sales professionals in the first meeting and in subsequent follow-up meetings unless they are encouraged and prompted to do so. The information collected by the sales professional will only be at a superficial level unless clients are allowed to and encouraged to share their underlying needs. As you know, sales professionals must learn as much as they can about the client's organization and their decision-making criteria, whether it be formal or informal, for selecting vendors prior to the sales call and this will allow them to prompt the client to go into more depth in their description of the organization's needs.

True needs rarely surface unless the sales professional is able to establish a level of trust with clients where they will share information; for example, a particularly bad experience they had with a competitor's product, how they would change an existing product or service to better meet their needs, what price range they feel is fair, or what services they truly value. Sales professionals can generate this key information by not rushing the sales process, but rather by continually nudging it forward and being able to bring closure to the fact that their organization can satisfy each of the needs identified.

To keep moving the process forward sales professionals must be able to validate for the client their understanding of each of the needs identified. This validation of understanding happens as the sales professional summarizes and restates the need, giving the client the opportunity to confirm that the sales professional understood the need. As the client becomes confident that the sales professional understands each need he or she will continue and share additional needs that, when understood, give the sales professional the information necessary to formulate a proposal. This proposal is packaged in a manner that makes it obvious to clients that the sales professional has been listening and has taken the time to understand their specific needs.

The solution that the sales professional suggests should be explained, but it should be evident that all of the clients' needs are clear to the sales professional and they feel that the solution presented is the best way to meet those needs. The sales professional then needs to give the client the opportunity to provide feedback on the solution or proposal.

DO ALL OF YOUR SALES PROFESSIONALS
DEMONSTRATE TECHNICAL UNDERSTANDING OF
YOUR PRODUCTS AND SERVICES?

Technical competency begins for sales professionals by understanding the language of the industry they are working in. *Technical knowledge* means that sales professionals have the ability to talk with confidence about specific product processes and specifications across the product or service line they sell. Technical knowledge and understanding are important competencies in the development of a comprehensive value proposition for clients. When sales professionals are creating a value proposition for a client that differentiates them from the competition technical competency becomes critical. If the organization's sales strategy is built on lowest price then technical competency is of lesser importance. However, as we have discussed at other points in this book, many clients are looking for the organizations that provide the best value relative to price. Technical understanding and competency are an important factor that can have an influence on the client's perception of the sales professional's ability to add value to the sales transaction.

Technical competency allows the sales professional to position himself or herself as a professional resource that the client or potential client can call on for sound advice and trust that the information provided is accurate and on target. Sales professionals can leverage small successes over time and build their reputation with the client as a trustworthy source of information and support.

Consider the following situation. Note the developmental issues and action tips provided at the end of that situation as key points for helping sales professionals cultivate their talents.

Critical Situation: Product Features and Benefits—Don't Wing It

Situation: I own a small real estate development firm and need vehicles to transport clients to various sites. I decided to target three different dealerships, trying to find that right blend of a professional yet practical vehicle. One of my agents accompanied me and we also decided, in advance, to observe the selling skills of the salespeople, always looking for a new tip or two. Our feet had barely touched the ground as we got out of our car when the salesman started asking us how he could help us. It was an understatement to say he was being attentive to us. I must admit I do know a little more than the average automobile consumer, having grown up working on cars and around a dealership. So, I gave him the opportunity to sell me on the features and benefits of the car to see what he could do. Of course selling to salespeople is tough because we already had all of that training on asking for the order and closing the deal. It was a situation where the more he talked the bigger the hole he dug himself and the more obvious it became that he knew very little about the car he was trying to sell us. After about ten minutes of this he finally admitted that he really didn't know much about the cars since it was his first week on the job.

Development Issues: Sales professionals need to do their homework. There is no replacement for investing the time and effort into learning about the products you sell. Customers will quickly figure out that the sales professional really knows little about the product or services. It is better to admit you are new and learning things about the products versus trying to wing it and losing the confidence and trust of the potential client.

Action Tips:

- Develop a list of questions for new sales professionals to consider asking clients that are anchored to your product or service's features and benefits.
- Develop a family of specification sheets outlining features and benefits.
- Create a client-needs questionnaire based on or anchored to the features and benefits of your products and services.

DO ALL OF YOUR SALES PROFESSIONALS UNDERSTAND THE RELATIONSHIP BETWEEN NEEDS, BENEFITS, AND FEATURES?

Many sales professionals discuss the importance of listening to their clients and identifying needs. The reality for new sales professionals is that once they have made it past the gatekeeper and finally have that ten-minute appointment with the company decision maker they have a tendency to listen for a few minutes and once that first or second need has surfaced the tendency is for the sales professional to be off to the races and overwhelming the potential client with a shotgun approach that throws everything they have in their product or service portfolio out there for the client to take a look at. Many times the real needs are missed in the hurry to get the features and benefits in front of the client. The sales professional does not take the time to ask the right questions and transform the session from one of information transmitting to that of listening, analyzing, and problem solving. To establish long-term relationships the sales professional needs to focus on identifying needs and convince the client that the product benefits of his or her organization cannot begin to be understood in only ten minutes. The purpose of developing needs is to gather information about the potential client's organization and who is currently supplying the product or service the sales professional is trying to sell to the client.

As sales professionals work to involve the prospect in the discussions it is critical that they have a clear understanding of the *features* (the specific components, tasks, or actions the product or service they sell has or does) and the *benefits* (specific tangible actions or activities that would accrue to the client derived from the use of your product). A sunroof would be a feature in a new car versus the benefit of the sunroof could be the ability to enjoy the sunshine and fresh air while you are stuck in busy afternoon rush-hour traffic.

Once sales professionals have an in-depth understanding of their own product or service benefits and features it is also important that the sales professionals have an extensive understanding of their competition's products and services and the benefits and features that they sell. What are they focusing on? Is it price? Quality? Or are they taking a broad value-added perspective? By understanding the benefits and features of the competition sales professionals can better craft their proposals in such as way as to to address potential objections.

As sales professionals examine each of the products or services they provide to clients and identify features and benefits, it is also important to think through the questions clients will ask about each product and benefit. Planning for and cataloging these questions can help to ensure sales professionals are not caught off guard by a potential client.

Use the following worksheet to identify features and benefits systematically for your organziation.

A Worksheet to Organize Product Features, Benefits, and FAQs

Directions: Use this worksheet to organize your thinking about product features, benefits, and frequently asked questions.

	Product	Features	Benefits	FAQs
1				
2				
3				
4				
5				
6				

DO YOUR SALES PROFESSIONALS COMMUNICATE AND SELL BENEFITS OVER FEATURES?

An interesting question to ask your organization's sales force is "If you could only say one thing about this product what would it be?" Comparing the results of this activity among the members of the sales force can provide opportunities for them to think about benefits differently and also to begin to develop a list of additional benefits that had not been previously identified. If the sales team struggles with this exercise then it is indicative of a need for information and training on the products and services being sold.

Understanding features helps a client to measure the value of the sales professional's product or service. However, in the client's overall perception of product value the product's benefits are more important in the decision-making process. As the client compares products, his or her ultimate question is, "What's really in this for me?" By understanding product benefits, clients can better make the connection between purchasing the product or service being offered and meeting their needs. When clients purchases a product or service, they expect their organization to benefit in some way—either economically, personally, or by providing a competitive advantage.

DO YOUR SALES PROFESSIONALS HAVE THE TOOLS THEY NEED TO COMMUNICATE FEATURES AND BENEFITS AND RESPOND APPROPRIATELY TO CLIENTS?

Brochures and product literature must be created with the audience in mind and be similar to an effective business plan in that the key points must jump out at the reader. If product materials are too rich in text and technical jargon clients will not take the time needed to read them. Integrated in a strategic marketing initiative, sales support materials can be an effective part of a sales professional's client call or, if improperly used, can distract potential clients from providing information about their needs. New sales professionals have a tendency to use support materials as a crutch and can quickly slip into a routine of reading a brochure to a client versus being focused on listening to the client and identifying needs. A shotgun approach of spreading several brochures or catalogs on a client's desk will turn the client call into a presentation, not a discussion and opportunity for the sales professional to identify needs.

Product support materials built at a level not appropriate for the primary audiences can become negative for sales professionals. If materials or electronic information are too complicated or simple for the client they can quickly lose interest. Confusing, outdated, or poor quality program materials can be more of a distraction or a hindrance than help for sales professionals.

Critical Situation: Product Features and Benefits— Using Support Literature

Situation: I never really received any sales training until I had been in my job for a couple of years. It was basically "Here, go sell this stuff." The manager I worked for had been promoted up through the ranks and his perception of selling was that you just go knock on doors and good things happen. Of course he rarely made any calls and was more focused on creating and reading reports. When he took me on my first sales call he took along about fifty brochures and flyers. He had a folder stuffed so full with every brochure the company had that he put rubber bands around it to keep them inside. When we got there and had introduced ourselves the first thing he did was hand the brochure folder to the potential client like it was a hot potato. After that the client said "I'll look over this stuff and give you a call," then he proceeded to skim through the materials while we sat there and tried to talk to him while he was reading. Well, guess what, that client never did call us back. I am sure he threw the folder on his credenza and never got to it, and I couldn't blame him. No two brochures looked alike, and three-fourths of the stuff wasn't even relevant for him—so why should he waste his time trying to sift through the stuff looking for what was important to his needs. Well, that taught me a lesson that has been reinforced in different training sessions I have attended in the twenty-plus years since then I have spent in sales. I rarely hand out any brochures or product material until I am ready to leave and then when I do I hand the person each piece individually and give them a brief explanation of what is in the brochure and how it relates to their organizational needs.

Development Issues: Brochures and other types of product information when direct mailed to a potential client are meant to sell products or services. However, when used by a sales professional on a face-to-face sales call brochures should be secondary to the face-to-face communication with the client. In that case sales professionals are focused on listening to the client, identifying needs, and finding matches with the products or services they sell.

Action Tips:
- Reinforce to sales professionals that product literature is secondary to face-to-face communication and integrated as show-and-tell to support a sales call.
- Sales professionals should hand out each piece of literature individually to clients and give them a brief explanation.
- Brochures and product information rarely make the sale, rather sales professionals make the sale.

More is not always better when it comes to brochures. Overwhelming clients with volumes of materials almost guarantees they will not look at all of the pieces and inevitably the ones that are most relevant get overlooked. Brochures and other product information should be focused, easy to read, and targeted to specific audiences.

Providing new sales professionals with a standard set of features and benefit statements that they in turn can customize to their particular style and the client's needs can ensure a more consistent message across the company. Also, when sales professionals do leave the organization the new hires can more easily understand the features and benefits of each product as part of the overall value proposition. These statements should be consistent between brochure materials and the message points delivered face to face. Creating a database for the management of features and benefit statements can ensure that this type of corporate knowledge is managed and effectively leveraged across the entire organization. In the case of national and multinational organizations this can be especially challenging.

DO YOUR SALES PROFESSIONALS UNDERSTAND AND UTILIZE VALUE-ADDED SELLING TECHNIQUES?

Clients are essentially analyzing each buying decision they make based on three key factors. There may be other considerations that have an impact on buying but ultimately it comes down to the total cost of the product, whether your product meets the base line for quality and what type of service your organization provides before, during, and after the purchase. Since the quality movement of the 1980s and 1990s, quality cannot be counted on as a way to differentiate an organization from the competition. Few organizations that could not produce a quality product survived the business shakeouts of the past two decades.

Good quality will not necessarily keep clients from leaving for a competitor but quality problems combined with average pricing and poor service is a guarantee that clients will jump to the competition. Organizations that have built their business reputation on being the consistent low-cost provider must expect on an ongoing basis that every time one of their competitors lowers their price a few cents that a portion of their client base will flee to the competition. While price is a key factor in the decision-making process, it is more a means for organizations to get a ticket to the game and once they are there figure out how the other portions of their value proposition help them to maintain clients.

Customer service through sales and support staff is an area where organizations can create a perception of product value that sets them apart from the competition. Product value is based on the perceptions of clients and their feeling that the total package they are receiving (price, quality, service) is meeting or exceeding their needs and what they are getting in return for their investment is a fair value. Sales professionals must be able to understand these factors and communicate them face to face and through their proposals to clients.

ARE YOUR SALES PROFESSIONALS SKILLED AT OVERCOMING OBJECTIONS?

Price, historical problems, and product and delivery issues are frequently used as the basis for client objections to buying and to slow down or discourage the sales professional. "The price is too high" is perhaps the most frequent objection voiced by potential clients. Overcoming objections and repositioning the client to buy is an interesting challenge. Sales professionals must be prepared to address each objection the client addresses as they come up in the discussion. Ignoring or leaving a discussion on objections to later definitely has a negative impact on the possibility of success.

When sales professionals experience no objections their first inclination is to smile and breathe a sigh of relief. However, this is not always such a positive sign as the client may in fact have already decided it is not a good match with your organization. In this type of case the challenge for the sales professional is how to pull the real objections out from the client. This can be accomplished by using a series of open-ended probing questions that force the clients to think about what they want to accomplish. Use the following checklist to help you identify useful questions to surface possible client objections:

☐ What criteria are you using to make your decision?

☐ How will decisions regarding this purchase be made?

☐ Will other people in the organization be involved in the decision-making process?

☐ Does your organization work to position your sales professionals as product or service experts?

☐ What is your time frame for making a decision?

☐ What type of budget process are you using for this decision?

☐ Who ultimately will make the decision?

As you know, once the sales professional has identified an objection, it must be addressed or it will become the client's focus and prevent the sales professional from moving forward in the selling process. Understanding the objection can start with the sales professional repeating his or her understanding of the objection to the potential client and allowing that client to agree with the summary or to correct the sales professional's perspective. A sales professional should work to define objections and break them down. It should be made clear whether other objections still exist. In many cases price will also surface at this point as clients tend to hold pricing information close until they feel comfortable with the sales professional. If no other objections surfaces then the sales professional should work to clarify how to handle the objection.

One technique is to test the client by asking "If we could take care of X, would you be willing to move forward with the purchase?" Asking for the order enables the sales professional to send the message that he or she wants to work with the prospect; and if that one objection is all that is preventing the close of the deal, then it can be made to happen.

Variations of the "feel, felt, found" technique are commonly talked about in many sales programs that provide a systematic and canned approach for dealing with objections. The technique presses the sales professional to respond to each objection by first empathizing with the prospect and relating to them on a feeling level. Some variation of "I understand how you could feel that way" is used and then the sales professional goes on to explain that the prospect is not alone in that concern and that other people have also felt that way. From there the technique transitions into how other people who became clients had the same concerns, and once they learned more about the product or service they discovered or found out that the concern disappeared and it was worth the effort. Using this technique to handle objectives can be effective based on the type of listeners and their training and background in sales. Attempting to use this technique with experienced purchasing managers or other sales professionals can be embarrassing and indicative of a lack of sophistication on the part of the sales professional. It can quickly backfire and sales professionals can see their appointments ended or see the experienced sales professionals toying with the newer people to learn more about their products or services.

As the sales professional works to address objections by the prospect it can allow both parties to get directly down to business and allow the sales professional to make a decision regarding whether to continue to pursue the prospect or to concede and move on to the next opportunity.

DO YOUR SALES PROFESSIONALS UNDERSTAND THE CAPABILITIES AND LIMITATIONS OF YOUR PRODUCTS AND SERVICES?

Overselling the capabilities of a product or service is an easy trap to fall into for new or relatively inexperienced sales professionals. In many cases sales professionals eager to make the sale may have enough understanding of product capabilities to be dangerous. Without an understanding of product or service capabilities it is difficult to develop any valid type of features or benefit statements and truly understand their significance and alignment with the client's needs. As part of the training process it is critical that sales professionals see firsthand how products are created in a manufacturing environment or, in the case of services, how specific factors relate to the overall process and learn firsthand what is critical for the success of the client's operation.

Just as damaging for new sales professionals can be a lack of understanding of the total capabilities of a product. Underselling capabilities or confusion over capabilities is a telltale sign for clients of an inexperienced or ill-prepared sales professional. For example, in the rapidly changing technology field product capabilities can change on almost a weekly basis. Failure of sales professionals to stay current on product changes can be a warning sign to potential clients that the company has a poor support network and could make the client question whether that apparent lack of support could carry over to postpurchase customer support.

DOES YOUR ORGANIZATION WORK TO POSITION YOUR SALES TEAM AS THE PRODUCT OR SERVICE EXPERTS?

Perception is reality. Think of the effect of a Sears lifetime guarantee on the Craftsman tool line, or your image of the Maytag repairman. These organizations have positioned themselves as experts in their respective market areas.

Check out the cosmetics counter of your local department store. There you will find beauty consultants all encouraging you to sit down and try their products and receive a free beauty consultation. These consultants usually receive extensive training and become an indispensable product or service expert. All will be selling the benefits of their products.

How about your local insurance agent or real estate firms? Many carry a full range of products and services and are promoting themselves as being able to handle your comprehensive needs, including financial services. In order to establish themselves as product and service experts they are giving public presentations, seminars, or making conference presentations related to their products and services.

What about your local building or home supply center? Most offer a seminar series on the products and services they carry. This establishes them and their network of vendors as product or service experts in the minds of the consumer. What can your sales organization do to establish your sales professionals as product experts?

DOES YOUR ORGANIZATION SPONSOR PROGRAMS TO EDUCATE AND PREPARE SALES PROFESSIONALS TO PROPERLY COMMUNICATE PRODUCT FEATURES AND BENEFITS?

Where should you start in your quest to enhance how well sales professionals properly communicate product features and benefits? Consult the following checklist of developmental strategies to build competence in this area. Ask your sales professionals to check those development activities they believe should be integrated into a program to help them properly communicate product features and benefits.

- ☐ Evaluate the technical competence of each member of your team. Provide training programs for your sales professionals in areas of new technologies.
- ☐ Subscribe to appropriate magazines, electronic bulletin boards, and technical journals. Appoint specific sales professionals to scan specific publications and note articles that apply to your organization and circulate those articles to members of your team.
- ☐ Help sales professionals develop technically oriented networks with employees in other areas of the organization and with suppliers.
- ☐ Compile a list of resources and job aids for technical areas related to your products and services.
- ☐ Maintain a competitor library containing relevant product literature.
- ☐ Encourage your sales professionals to network with others in your field to discuss and exchange ideas relevant to advances in your field.
- ☐ Nurture relationships with individuals in organizations spawning new products and services to maintain awareness of the technological or marketing opportunities that could help your sales organization.
- ☐ Encourage vendors of new products, services, or technologies to make presentations to your sales organization.
- ☐ Participate actively in professional organizations and trade associations.

Now use this plan to help build the competence of your sales professionals in enhancing ongoing client and stakeholder informational processes.

A Sample Program Outline to Guide Identifying and Communicating Product Features and Benefits

Title: Knowledge of Products and Services

Competency Dimension: Identifying and communicating product features and benefits

Learning Objectives:
- Demonstrates technical understanding of product features and benefits as well as limitations
- Able to understand client needs
- Can communicate value of products and services
- Demonstrates ability to respond appropriately to clients

Potential Content Topics:
- Planning skills
- Process of innovation
- Innovative problem solving
- New product planning
- Technical writing
- Advertising and promotion

11

Establishing and Maintaining
a Competitive Analysis Process

This chapter focuses on the core sales competency of establishing and maintaining a competitive analysis process. That process requires sales professionals to

- stay informed of industry trends
- capture and maintain competitor information
- understand the impact and uses of different sources and types of information
- use that information in decision making

This chapter also explains how to make use of a process approach to rank competitors and strategies for identifying key decision points and how to establish a team effort to identify and create a database of competitor information.

What are the development needs of your sales professionals for establishing a competitive analysis process? Consult Figure 11.1 to see how the respondents to our survey rated the relative importance of the behaviors associated with this competency. Then reflect on how you would rate sales professionals in your organization.

Complete the following self-assessment as it applies to you and your organization.

Figure 11.1
Behaviors Related to the Competency of Maintaining a Competitive Analysis Process as Rated by Survey Respondents

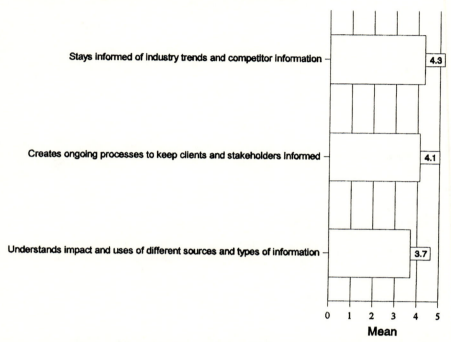

Source: From *A Survey about Sales Training Programs* by W. Rothwell, W. Donahue, and J. Park, 2001 (unpublished survey results), University Park, PA: Pennsylvania State University. Copyright 2001 by W. Rothwell, W. Donahue, and J. Park.

Self-Assessment: Establishing and Maintaining a Competitive Analysis Process

Directions: With your sales organization in mind, place a number on the line in the left column below that matches your level of agreement with each statement. Then add up the numbers and score your assessment.

Disagree									Agree
1	2	3	4	5	6	7	8	9	10

____Do your sales professionals stay informed of industry trends?
____Does your organization actively benchmark against the best?
____Does your organization solicit competitive information?
____Does your organization capture and maintain competitor information?
____Does your organization clearly communicate with employees the importance of maintaining key information confidential and out of the hands of the competition?

____Do your sales professionals understand how to conduct basic market research?

____Does your organization track their ease to do business with?

____Does your organization use competitive information once you have collected it?

____Does your organization have a policy on ethical behavior regarding the collection of competitor information?

____Does your organization sponsor programs to help establish and maintain a competitive analysis process?

____Total

How Did You Score?

Here is the key to establishing and maintaining a competitive analysis process. Add up your responses to get your score.

91–100	Great job! Congratulations! Your organization is effectively working to establish and maintain a competitive analysis process.
81–90	Keep up the good work! You've probably had considerable success. But by using some of the tips in this chapter, you could improve your success.
71–80	Help is needed! There's room for improvement. You'll find this chapter helpful.
0–70	Warning! Your sales organization probably has some difficulty maintaining information on competitors. Read on!

Use the worksheet to organize your thinking about ways of building this competency among sales professionals in your organization.

A Worksheet to Organize Your Thinking for Establishing and Maintaining a Competitive Analysis Process

Directions: In your opinion, what problems or challenges does your sales organization face in establishing and maintaining a competitive analysis process? Use this worksheet to organize your thinking about how to answer this question.

Notes:

DO YOUR SALES PROFESSIONALS STAY
INFORMED OF INDUSTRY TRENDS?

A systematic approach for keeping sales professionals informed of broad industry developments and changes is a critical competency for building an organization's value proposition for clients. Sales professionals lacking broader industry knowledge can be less effective in their ability to place the organization's products in relation to the competition and highlight strengths. Clients can also interpret a lack of industry knowledge as a lack of interest and professionalism on the part of the sales professional.

Creating and maintaining industry knowledge must be a shared responsibility between the sales organization and the sales professional. The sales organization must create a strategy that identifies targeted opportunities for sales professionals to learn and grow, including financially supporting membership in specific associations and organizations. Sales professionals must proactively reach out and work to establish relationships.

Membership in relevant trade associations and organizations can be a key source of industry information. The related publications created by trade associations are a valuable source of information on pending developments and changes in the industry. Trade associations exist on a local, regional, and national level. Membership and involvement at each level has potential benefits. Local participation in any type of association or club always has the potential for producing opportunities to meet new clients plus opportunities to meet and talk with other professionals dealing with similar challenges and opportunities. Regional and national participation provides broader opportunities for learning and knowledge gathering. Association trade shows provide a tremendous opportunity to take a broad firsthand look at new developments, innovations, and changes.

Participation in other local or regional organizations can also provide valuable information on broader economic changes or political activity for sales professionals. Chambers of commerce, economic development groups, and even charity boards can all help sales professionals to keep in touch with what's happening in the area. As you know, plant closings or layoffs can be signs of pending problems or opportunities depending on the financial well-being of the sales professional's own organization. What professional associations do your sales professionals participate in? Does your organization encourage and support involvement in professional organizations?

DOES YOUR ORGANIZATION ACTIVELY
BENCHMARK AGAINST THE BEST?

As discussed earlier in this book, benchmarking is an important characteristic of successful learning for organizations seeking opportunities to grow and improve. Effective benchmarking begins with an internal focus and then turns to external sources of information for comparison purposes. Benchmarking requires organizations to first examine internal processes and procedures to establish a base line of understanding of the current realities of the organization. Once this internal assessment is conducted your sales organization can focus externally and begin identifying potential benchmarking partners who are recognized as a leader in their field and have similar or related processes that could be evaluated, analyzed, and compared to the organization.

The selection of benchmarking partners can be time consuming and complex. Opening your doors to another organization to review processes and procedures can be risky and potentially disruptive. In light of discussion in this book on competitive knowledge many organizations are extremely cautious of whom they allow inside plants or facilities, recognizing that confidential information can easily fall into the wrong hands. Benchmarking relationships should be established with a clear set of expectations on the part of all organizations involved. Defining a criteria for benchmarking partners can be one of the most important first steps in developing a sustainable benchmarking study. Most benchmarking arrangements are undertaken with the understanding that all parties involved in the relationship will benefit in some way. Understanding the importance of the relationship providing value to both parties is critical in the planning phase of the benchmarking process. Otherwise, benchmarking relationships that are one-sided in nature tend to be one-time activities that are short-lived and not sustainable.

Determining the qualifications of quality benchmarking partners should be a thoughtful process. Evaluating secondary data collected from formal sources such as annual reports, published industry rankings, personal relationships with clients or other knowledgeable industry professionals is all part of the process. Criteria often used to identify and rank potential benchmarking partners can be

- Financial performance
- Financial stability
- Sales volume
- Type of sales
- Industrial Standards Organization (ISO) Certification or other type of certification
- Quality award nomination and selection (state or local awards, Baldrige Award)
- Leadership turnover
- Form of ownership
- Client satisfaction system and rating
- Employee turnover
- Process stability
- Positive press and stories in trade journals

Many professional organizations, universities, and consulting firms are sponsoring targeted benchmarking studies. This type of benchmarking activity can be costly, but the data provided can be significant and the opportunity to participate in the meeting of partners facilitated by an unbiased third party can be valuable. Data collected through paid relationships can be much more in-depth and although the analysis is typically provided in a more generic format the unbiased perspectives of the sponsoring organization can reduce or eliminate any chances of a single person influencing the decision-making process.

DOES YOUR ORGANIZATION SOLICIT COMPETITIVE INFORMATION?

Accurate and timely competitor information can be an extremely valuable asset to organizations. As you know, sales professionals can take on a key role in the collection and analysis of competitive information. Competitive knowledge can help sales professionals build their own value proposition for their clients as well as help them to better counteract the efforts of the competition. Sales professionals can readily collect valuable information simply by asking the right questions and understanding the importance of reciprocating with information when appropriate. Sales professionals must always be aware of the power they have when moving among similar organizations who are serving the same or similar markets. In this type of situation sales professionals can quickly lose the trust of clients if it is discovered that they are sharing any type of inappropriate information among clients who are potential competitors.

Establishing a process for the collection, analysis, and distribution of competitive information on a timely basis is an important sales support process. Most sales professionals will gladly share customer information they acquire in discussions with clients, vendors, or through newspaper or other media coverage. However, the process for collecting this information must be efficient and not burdensome to the sales professionals or they will not participate. One strategy is to routinely distribute an electronic form via e-mail that can be quickly completed and returned. Another is to simply designate a single point of contact for competitive information and ask sales professionals and others to call or direct information to that person.

An important factor in soliciting competitive information from sales professionals is that they must see their efforts are being appreciated and the data are being used. Otherwise, they will quickly lose interest in participating in providing information and focus their time and energy elsewhere.

DOES YOUR ORGANIZATION CAPTURE AND MAINTAIN COMPETITOR INFORMATION?

Competitive research and information gathering should be a standard business practice for all organizations regardless of the type or size of organization they are. Many times businesses have misconceptions about who their real competition is, how they compare, and the features and benefits of the competition's products or services. Competitive research can help sales professionals to understand what the competition truly does well and where their weaknesses are.

However, gathering competitive intelligence can quickly spin out of control if the organization's ethics and values do not remain in the forefront of decisions regarding this type of activity. There is a fine line between tracking and collecting data from a variety of sources and corporate spying and espionage. Delving into activities like "dumpster diving" where company garbage is scoured for any potentially valuable source of information is one example of how organizations have gone overboard in their pursuit of information and a competitive edge. Others have gone as far as misrepresenting themselves as reporters or media consultants collecting information for stories as their cover to access confidential company information. The field of competitive-intelligence gathering has become very complex with professional associations springing up across the country and attendees at their conferences numbering in the thousands. There has also been a designation established, Competitive Intelligence Professional (CIP), to certify interested individuals in the field, and continuing education courses are offered each year. The point of this background on competitive intelligence is to highlight the growing emphasis on its role in organizational planning, market strategy, and new-product development.

Relying on external sources for competitive information can be costly. However, the value of having an independent source collect, analyze, and prioritize information can save a considerable amount of internal time and effort. There are organizations that scan trade journals, magazines, newspapers, and the Web for competitor information. To be most efficient, it must be organized into a concise format like the following example.

A Worksheet to Organize Competitive Information

Directions: Use this worksheet as a format to organize information about competitors.

	Date	Source	Key Points	Relevance
1				
2				
3				

Critical Situation: Organizing Competitive Information— Simple Is Good

Situation: For years we got our name on every mailing list and database we could so that we would receive competitors' flyers, catalogs, and brochures. But the reality was all we did with them was scan every third or fourth one for anything that jumped out and then piled them in the corner. I'll bet at one time we had over a thousand brochures and catalogs piled in a corner of the stockroom. Some of them were four or five years old. Finally, after we moved the stuff around a couple of times, we decided there had to be a better way.

What we did was empty a bookcase and start a minilibrary, organizing the brochures and catalogs in alphabetical order by company and then cross-referenced them by product. After doing this for a couple of years and actually taking the time to look at the stuff once in a while we finally got serious about tracking trends and changes in our competitors' products. We went to the local university and were lucky enough to qualify for an internship program for MBA students. Well, we now have everything stored in a database and you can sort by date, time, title, subject, and a couple of other things. But the important point is that we regularly pull out data and talk about changes and trends in our monthly sales meetings. All of our sales staff access the materials as well as contribute to the cause.

Development Issues: Having excessive amounts of competitive data in a raw, unusable form is of little value; and the effort and energy expended on collecting it if it is never used can be a waste. There are effective and economical resources available to help organizations develop competitor databases that can present valuable information that can contribute to organizational planning and strategy development. Databases can be housed on the Web and made available to a geographically dispersed sales force.

Action Tips:
- Determine what competitive information you need and want and develop a database template or format for your sales professionals to use.
- Establish a minilibrary of competitor information.
- Ask sales professionals to select specific market areas, and be responsible for monitoring trends and keeping their team informed.

Critical Situation: Confidential Information—The Heartland Study

Situation: We are a Fortune 500 company, and several years ago we embarked on an extensive competitive-intelligence campaign. Part of the campaign included commissioning consultants to legally collect information about our competitors. To do this they structured a phone interview script that stated who they were and what they were commissioned to do for an independent organization that wished to remain anonymous. Their process was to call the operations managers of selected competitor plants across the country and ask a series of targeted questions, such as what they made, type of equipment, number of employees, and so forth. We were skeptical that they could obtain the type of information that would be useful so as a cross-check we included a sampling of our own plants across the country. Wow, were we wrong. The information they were able to collect on the competitors and us was both amazing and disturbing. Essentially they were able to describe every job that was running at each plant, the part weights, how fast, on what equipment, as well as the manning. As you might imagine this sent shock waves throughout our organization as most of the information they collected we considered confidential. The next day we sent out a directive to all of our plants and employees outlining procedures for handling callers as well as a description of information we considered confidential.

Development Issues: All new employees should be educated about the competitive nature of business, confidential information, and trade secrets. In addition, maintaining security and a safe and civil work environment is the responsibility of every employee.

Action Tips:

- Inform all sales professionals and staff about the necessity of keeping confidential information confidential.
- Make a checklist of what specifically your organization considers trade secrets and review with your staff. Conversely, ask them to be on the lookout for similar information about competitors.
- Establish a database repository for competitor information and designate a single point of contact.

DOES YOUR ORGANIZATION CLEARLY COMMUNICATE WITH EMPLOYEES THE IMPORTANCE OF MAINTAINING KEY INFORMATION "CONFIDENTIAL" AND OUT OF THE HANDS OF THE COMPETITION?

In many industries and services there are very few competitive advantages, while in other industries proprietary equipment or processes present a strong barrier to entry. For example, in certain specialty chemical manufacturing or powdered metal product lines, proprietary processes can truly differentiate an organization from the competition.

Businesses have historically recruited and hired employees away from the competition solely to learn about a specific process or piece of equipment. This may be viewed as less than ideal by some ethicists, unless the employee signed some type of noncompete agreement or statement of confidentiality, because there is little that can be done by the former employer.

Product and service confidentiality is an area that should be addressed during the hiring process and reinforced during the sales professional's orientation. Also, during early company sales calls with their manager or trainer, assumptions cannot be made about a new sales professional's understanding of the impact of sharing information. Unless issues and processes that warrant confidentiality are clearly defined and addressed the intentional or unintentional sharing of information can easily occur.

Formal written noncompete agreements can be a more formal strategy for controlling company information and employee knowledge. Legally prepared and binding noncompete agreements have historically been used to deter employees from taking client or process information with them to a competitor or a new start-up when they leave an organization. The potential for legal action can deter or cause sales professionals to rethink leaving the organization for a competitor. Questions regarding the legality and enforceability of noncompetes should be directed to the leagal counsel of each business to ensure all state and federal factors are taken into account.

DO YOUR SALES PROFESSIONALS UNDERSTAND HOW TO CONDUCT BASIC MARKET RESEARCH?

Market research can allow sales professionals to analyze who their current and potential clients are, where they are located, special characteristics (company age, political background, values), revenue, and income. Marketing research is about identifying and solving a marketing-related problem or opportunity. Marketing and sales are about identifying and satisfying a company's needs. Marketing research provides organizations with up-to-date information on current trends and looks toward the future. The following checklist can serve as a useful framework to guide the market research process.

❑ Clearly define the problem or opportunity you are doing research on.
❑ Analyze the environment and issues surrounding the problem.
❑ Define what data and information are needed and available.
❑ Create a data collection plan (primary and secondary data).
❑ Gather the data and analyze for themes or trends.
❑ Make changes or seize new opportunities.

Market research and preplanning are important for preventing problems. Understanding the environment surrounding a problem or opportunity frames up the market research and provides the context in which the data should be examined. Looking at data out of context with its environment and where they were collected can be dangerous and can allow organizations to make incorrect assumptions or correlations.

Most organizations have a wealth of information on clients and their transactions. However, this information is frequently disjointed and not available in any type of useful form that allows for systematic analysis and decision making. By first determining what data are most appropriate and important for the research, countless hours can be saved and duplication of efforts avoided.

Market surveys are the most common method for collecting primary marketing data from clients or stakeholders. Surveys can provide specific factual data about businesses such as number of employees, revenue, and satisfaction with current vendor. Surveys can also include open-ended questions designed to allow those responding to discuss in more detail the problems they face.

Critical Situation: Conducting Market Research—Price or Delivery

Situation: As a sales professional and sales manager I'm accustomed to hearing our price is too high. My clients say that, while price is important, it is not the most important thing to many of them. Simple market research identified that for many clients delivery according to specified schedule was the most important for them. We learned over the years to listen very carefully to clients to find out what their specific need is. By conducting simple survey research and asking several focused questions we determined that many of our clients judged our performance mainly on timeliness. We know that if our products weren't there on time their production operation would come to a halt. Therefore our top priority is delivery, not price. Over the past several years we have gained clients based on our delivery reputation and many clients don't even ask the price anymore. We've made it a standard practice among our sales professionals to say to clients, "I know both price and on-time delivery are important to you, but which is more important?" and then allow the client to think about this for a few minutes.

Development Issues: It is important to peel back the onion, so to speak, to separate wants from needs. It is helpful to conduct basic market research and develop a series of simple but specific questions aimed at zeroing in on the most important variables to the client.

Action Tips:

- Conduct simple market research with clients by developing a series of specific open questions that encourage clients to separate their true needs from wants.
- Questions to separate how important delivery and how important price are to the client might include "What happens in your organization if delivery is delayed for some reason?" or, "If you could take a whole truckload, we could give you a better price, is this attractive to you?" Doing this will separate how important delivery and price are to the client.

Critical Situation: Market Research—The Unspeakable Bottle

Situation: A number of years ago I worked for one of the world's largest packaging companies. One of their divisions manufactured glass bottles. The company was very successful and known as a technology leader in its industry. One of their strategic research and development thrusts was to develop a lightweight unbreakable container. After spending several years and millions of dollars they developed several process concepts that they estimated would add about 20 percent to the cost of the container. Unfortunately, instead of conducting extensive market research they excitedly moved to commercialism. While the product was considered a technological success, it was also a market failure as the market would not accept the 20 percent cost premium.

Development Issues: Sales professionals can become excited and quite emotional about new-product development activities. However, it is important for your organization to have a process of checks and balances. Simple market research can save millions.

Action Tips:

- Develop a checklist of action steps to guide new-product development that includes market research.
- Have your sales professionals conduct simple market research on selected products or services to demonstrate understanding and stress importance.

Not all data can and needs to be primary data collected directly from current or potential clients. Secondary data pulled from industry sources or academic resources can be obtained less expensively and, depending on the context of the research, may be sufficient to allow for informed decision making. In this case caution must be exercised that the sources are valid and current.

Just collecting or having data does not insure proper decisions will be made. The data must be analyzed and meaning made out of the data in a way that prompts changes or adaptations. New opportunities for sales professionals to go after a new or different market segment that had previously not been considered may surface in the data analysis. There are cases where the data produce results that are crystal clear and support a dramatic change or action. But just as frequently the data are not clear-cut in their message and incremental changes may be warranted that require careful observation and testing.

DOES YOUR ORGANIZATION TRACK THEIR EASE TO DO BUSINESS WITH (ETDBW)?

Successful sales professionals recognize that a key factor in the client decision-making process is how easy it is to do business with their organization. Communication barriers, inflexible contracts, logistical difficulties, and payment constraints are only a few of the factors that can come into play when clients evaluate their buying experience and how easy the organization is to do business with. Typically these issues may not be under the influence or control of the sales organization. However, dissatisfaction in any of these areas should prompt the sales professional to begin collecting market research that supports the need for change. Many of these factors may not initially prompt a client to purchase from the sales professional but they will certainly surface when decisions are made regarding the renewal of a contract or allowing competitors the opportunity to present their products or provide a proposal.

In particular, small companies can benefit from innovations in their ETDBW and create service benefits that differentiate them from their larger competition. Speed and flexibility of new product or service development can be a differentiating factor that sales professionals can capitalize on.

DOES YOUR ORGANIZATION USE COMPETITIVE INFORMATION ONCE YOU HAVE COLLECTED IT?

Just as collecting client data and not turning them into client information that can be used as a basis for decision making is a waste, the same holds true for competitive data and information. Making marketing decisions without relevant data can be disastrous. Competitive information can be valuable in the development of marketing strategies and for new-product development.

DOES YOUR ORGANIZATION HAVE A POLICY ON ETHICAL BEHAVIOR REGARDING THE COLLECTION OF COMPETITOR INFORMATION?

Overzealousness can quickly get newer sales professionals into uncomfortable or even illegal situations when it comes to collecting competitor information. While dumpster diving on private property is most likely illegal, conducting the same activity on public property could be viewed differently and, depending on the community, be interpreted as legal or illegal. In either case having an employee caught in this type of activity and appearing on the evening news would be disastrous.

Investing in consultants and other external sources of competitive information can be a viable alternative for smaller organizations that are financially sound but lack the staff needed to collect and analyze competitive information.

Pricing information is one area that most organizations consider confidential. While it would be unethical for a sales professional to call up a competitor under an assumed name and ask pricing information, sometimes clients will volunteer such information. Obviously, a good salesperson is "all ears." Managers must work with sales professionals beginning at orientation to clearly communicate acceptable behaviors.

DOES YOUR ORGANIZATION SPONSOR PROGRAMS TO HELP ESTABLISH AND MAINTAIN A COMPETITIVE ANALYSIS PROCESS?

Where should you start in your quest to help sales professionals establish and maintain a competitive analysis process? Consult the following checklist of developmental strategies to build competence in this area.

❒ Be aware of emerging technological advances that could impact your products, services, and market.

❒ Keep a list of relevant resources.

❒ Invite experts from academia, trade associations, suppliers, and others from the public or the private sectors to make presentations in your organization. Ask them how you stand relative to the competition.

❒ Maintain proficiency in your sales area of expertise by remaining involved in your profession and by keeping up on the technical literature and developments.

❒ Attend professional meetings and network with other sales professionals in your field.

Ask your sales professionals to check those development activities they believe should be integrated into a program to establish and maintain a competitive analysis process. Now use the following plan to help build the competence of your sales professionals in enhancing ongoing client and stakeholder informational processes.

A Sample Program Outline to Guide Establishing and Maintaining a Competitive Analysis Process

Title: Knowledge of Products and Services

Competency Dimension: Establishing and maintaining a competitive analysis process

Learning Objectives:
- Demonstrate knowledge of trends
- Able to capture and maintain competitor information
- Understand impact and uses of different sources and types of information
- Demonstrate use of information in decision making

Potential Content Topics:
- Managing with information technology
- Developing an organizational intelligence system
- Networking
- How to benchmark
- Competitive analysis
- Supply-chain management
- Technical transfer process
- Process of innovation

12

Linking Sales and Marketing Strategies

Sales professionals are frequently charged with turning sketchy sales plans into market realities. Their ability to react to an opportunity or a problem in a timely manner can frequently spell the difference between staying in business or going out of business. In an age of mergers and acquisitions and changing client bases, sales professionals become an organization's eyes on the future. What they learn and how they present their learning to others in the organization provides a foundation for an organization's overarching marketing plan and strategy.

This chapter focuses on linking sales and marketing strategies. To demonstrate that competency, sales professionals should

- stay informed of market trends
- link market strategies and activities to sales and promotion
- understand the relationship among sales, marketing, and business results

What are the development needs of your sales professionals for linking sales and marketing strategies? Consult Figure 12.1 to see how the respondents to our survey rated the relative importance of the behaviors associated with this competency. Then reflect on how you would rate sales professionals in your organization.

Figure 12.1
Behaviors Related to the Competency of Linking Sales and Market Strategies as Rated by Survey Respondents

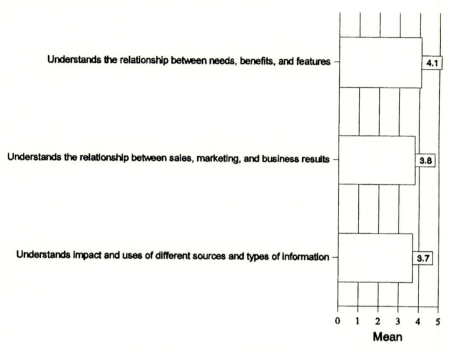

Source: From *A Survey about Sales Training Programs* by W. Rothwell, W. Donahue, and J. Park, 2001 (unpublished survey results), University Park, PA: Pennsylvania State University. Copyright 2001 by W. Rothwell, W. Donahue, and J. Park.

When you finish looking at Figure 12.1, complete the self-assessment as it applies to you and your organization.

Self-Assessment: Linking Sales and Market Strategies

Directions: With your sales organization in mind, place a number on the line in the left column below that matches your level of agreement with each statement. Then add up the numbers and score your assessment.

Disagree									Agree
1	2	3	4	5	6	7	8	9	10

____Your organization has a sales plan linked to an overall marketing plan.
____Your sales professionals have a historical understanding of marketing.
____Your sales professionals stay informed of individual market trends.
____Your sales professionals understand the four Ps of marketing.

_____Your sales professionals understand the impact of different distribution channels.

_____Your sales organization offers programs for orienting and developing market channel partners.

_____Your organization leverages advertisement and promotion activities to support face-to-face sales efforts.

_____Your organization leverages free publicity to support sales initiatives.

_____Your sales professionals understand the concept of market segmentation and value pricing.

_____Your organization sponsors programs to help link sales and marketing strategies.

_____Total

How Did You Score?

Here is the key to linking sales and market strategies. Add up your responses to get your score.

91–100   Great job! Congratulations! Your organization is effectively working to link sales and marketing.

81–90   Keep up the good work! You've probably had considerable success. But by using some of the tips in this chapter, you could improve your success.

71–80   Help is needed! There's room for improvement. You'll find this chapter helpful.

0–70   Warning! Your sales organization probably has some frustrations linking sales to market strategies. Read on!

Once you have completed the self-assessment, use this worksheet to organize your thinking about ways of building this competency among sales professionals in your organization.

A Worksheet to Organize Your Thinking about Linking Sales and Market Strategies

Directions: In your opinion, what problems or challenges does your sales organization face in linking sales and marketing? Use this worksheet to organize your thinking about how to answer this question.

Notes:

DOES YOUR ORGANIZATION HAVE A SALES PLAN LINKED TO AN OVERALL MARKETING PLAN?

The effective integration of a sales plan with a broader marketing plan allows the sales organization to stay focused on the development of new clients and the maintenance and satisfaction of existing clients (Grant & Schlesinger, 1995). Competition continues to intensify as markets reshape themselves in a global economy. E-business is also a factor that must be considered as marketing and sales plans are created. The sales plan should flow from the market research and analysis conducted for the marketing plan. A sales plan should contain information like in the following checklist. Use the checklist to double-check any sales plans submitted.

☐ Total sales goal with an ongoing comparison of actual to planned

☐ Total sales costs and an ongoing comparison to actual

☐ Number of projected and actual sales calls to new and existing clients

☐ Ratio of sales calls to actual sales

☐ Goals on percentage of market share as compared to total market volume

☐ Sales per product line, territory, client, salesperson

☐ New sales dollars versus repeat business dollars

☐ Client satisfaction data and ratings

☐ Other:

Critical Situation: Sales and Marketing—Creating a Family Image

Situation: I am in charge of sales and marketing for a division of a very large and complex organization with an international reputation for quality. As managers we are aware that our jobs depend on maintaining our image, and tarnishing the image is cause for dismissal. Our "logo gods" are very powerful. Every piece of literature, news articles, business cards, and even our formal proposal template had to be approved in order to maintain a consistent sales, marketing, and brand image. While at times some of the requirements appear extreme, the strategy has led to us having one of the most recognizable brands in the world.

Development Issues: Linking market strategies to sales and promotion activities requires discipline and an understanding of its importance.

Action Tips:

• Document and communicate marketing strategies.

• Ask sales professionals to align their sales goals and promotional plans with market strategies. Make sure they understand why image is so important.

• Develop a family image and guidelines for all sales and promotional materials that fit with your overarching market strategies.

• Establish specific marketing metrics and reporting scorecard.

Marketing activities should support personal selling and increase the probability that sales professionals will be successful in their efforts to meet individual and departmental sales goals. Marketing efforts should influence buying decisions and enhance organizational image and brand recognition.

It is important for everyone in the organization to understand that each of its members are involved in the sales and marketing process. Sales and marketing are everyone's job and that philosophy should drive the entire organization from the maintenance staff through the president's office. The sales plan should support the overall marketing initiative of the organization and should also enhance teamwork (Cespedes, Doyle, & Freedman, 1989). Meeting sales goals should be one measure of the success of a marketing strategy defined in the marketing plan. Brand recognition, product awareness, and brand loyalty are all key factors that are beyond the realm of sales but important components of the marketing plan that have a tremendous impact on sales. Each of these areas should be aligned with the benefits being sold in face-to-face selling efforts.

DO YOUR SALES PROFESSIONALS HAVE A HISTORICAL UNDERSTANDING OF MARKETING?

Marketing is the broad concept of creating and maintaining the mutually beneficial exchanges of ideas, products, or services between a business and its clients. Marketing is broader than just selling. It also includes the promotion and advertising of a product or service. Sales professionals must leverage marketing support in their sales efforts and understand the advantages of timing calls to be aligned with ad campaigns. Marketing efforts should build on message points delivered in print, via the Web, or other delivery methods and take advantage of brand recognition created by their colleagues in the marketing department.

Over the past 100 years the focus and orientation of marketing efforts have changed and shifted. During the early 1900s the focus was on the availability of products and the efficiency with which they were developed and manufactured. Customer needs were secondary and the approach to marketing was focused on creating products that were easily available and accessible.

Beginning in the 1930s and the time of the Great Depression in the United States companies focused on selling existing stocks of products or those that they had been producing. New product development was limited due to capital constraints and client needs were secondary as availability of products drove the selling process.

During the postwar era of the 1950s and up through the 1970s customers became much more selective in their purchases and the expectations for client service increased. Consumers were becoming more selective in their purchases as their options increased and demand flattened out.

Beginning in the 1970s and continuing through the 1980s organizations began to concentrate on their competition and to turn their focus from an internal one to an external analysis of what the competition was producing and how their products compared. Organizations have recognized the need to stay close to their customers while also closely monitoring and tracking their competition. Any and all competitive advantages are sought out and all organizations, whether they are large or small, are closely evaluating every process in the organization to drive out waste and ensure the highest quality possible. The focus on short-term profitability has gradually been refocused to consider the long-term sustainability of organizations.

As sales professionals focus on their own individual performance and results it is natural to overlook the broad organizational marketing efforts and the relationship between specific sales efforts and organizational performance. It is critical that the sales development efforts continue to emphasize the importance of organizational understanding and a historical perspective to prepare sales professionals for ongoing learning and growth.

DO YOUR SALES PROFESSIONALS STAY INFORMED OF INDIVIDUAL MARKET TRENDS?

Market shifts and changes have been occurring rapidly and sharply. In the global marketplace abrupt changes in political or economic factors can quickly shift a product focus or emphasis. Leadership changes in governments or pending elections can have an impact on multiple levels of a market segment. For example, deregulation and privatization are occurring in health care and energy providers across North and South America; services or industries that were historically government-regulated or controlled are being reshaped and opportunites created.

New markets are emerging and sales opportunities are developing that did not previously exist. Mergers, acquisitions, and plant closings can all quickly change the landscape of a specific product market or even an entire industry. Sales professionals must be constantly scanning the environment for events or trends that could have an impact on their relationships with clients. National and international newspapers, magazines, news programs, and Web sites are all sources of information that require constant scanning for signs of upcoming developments and changes. Developing support systems and processes that allow sales professionals easy access to information encourages involvement and commitment to the scanning process.

Sharing market trend information should be an ongoing component of the sales development program. Web-based tools for collecting the information and bulletin boards or e-mail-based listservs are the most effective tools for distributing information on trends and related activities to sales professionals not located in a single geographic location.

To support the collection of information on market trends, sales development programs must make newspapers, magazines, and other resources available to sales professionals. Second, once the information has been collected sales professionals must see that it is being distributed to others and used to make decisions about sales strategies for the organization. If these elements do not occur sales professionals will quickly shift their energy and efforts elsewhere, away from monitoring market trends.

DO YOUR SALES PROFESSIONALS UNDERSTAND THE FOUR Ps OF MARKETING?

The four Ps of marketing are product, price, promotion, and place. These four key elements provide the framework for the development and marketing of any product or service. Understanding how the four Ps are linked and the impact they have on each other can broaden a sales professional's focus beyond looking at the sales volume for an individual product line or market segment.

1. *Product* is any type of item or service that a business provides to a consumer that fulfills a need. Products are some tangible item that has size and substance while a service is an intangible event or happening that lacks any physical form but meets a consumer need. Products typically flow through a cycle of events over their lifespan from the development stage through growth and in most cases eventual decline. By tracking a product's life cycle organizations can make decisions regarding reinvestment in product updates and also make decisions on investments in new product development. Marketing investments should also be aligned with the product life cycle. Bringing new products or services to market requires a significant investment in marketing to properly promote and place the product in the market. In later stages of the product life-cycle sales volumes may remain constant but profit margins begin to deteriorate. As products enter the final stage of the life cycle where sales and margins are both on the decline, strategic decisions must be made to determine the return on investment of reinventing the product versus abandoning the product and replacing it with something new. Research and investments in new product development should be ongoing and integrated into the marketing plan.

2. *Place* is how the product will be distributed to clients and consumers. Distribution channels are driven by the needs of the client and the realities of the product or service being provided. Trends toward direct distribution from the manufacturer to the consumer continue to move forward, but the most popular distribution channel continues to be manufacturer to wholesaler to retailer to consumer. Understanding the impact of distribution channels on the sales process can help sales professionals to understand the competition's business and opportunities for capturing additional market share.

3. *Price* has been and will continue to be a key element in the success of sales organizations. Sales dollars and the corresponding profits are driven by the prices developed for products or services. Organizations totally focused on pricing to drive their marketing strategy can be more susceptible to the impact of price wars where competitors build market share based on lowest price. Building a pricing structure around product value can reduce the impact of price wars, as sales professionals focus on the overall value of the relationship and the additional benefits provided beyond the actual product or service such as free delivery, product support, or other special factors.

4. *Promotion* is much broader than only advertising—it also includes personal selling. The advertising component of the promotion element is the communication of product or service benefits to current and potential customers through the use of the mass media. Promotion efforts should be aligned with personal selling efforts and focus on creating brand image and awareness, brand allegiance and loyalty, and to encourage potential clients to make purchases.

Each of the four elements of marketing should be an important consideration in the creation of the marketing plan. When combined the four Ps provide a framework for decision making and the allocation of resources.

DO YOUR SALES PROFESSIONALS UNDERSTAND THE IMPACT OF DIFFERENT DISTRIBUTION CHANNELS?

Distribution channels are the methods businesses use to move their products or services from their production or storage facility to the end user or client. Distribution channels can either be controlled by the producer or supplied by a third party intermediary. The intermediaries provide the product or service to the client for purchase at a place or time that is most convenient and suitable for them. Meeting client channel requirements can enhance sales volume and client satisfaction as well as reduce costs for both the sales organization and the client.

As technology has grown its role in the distribution element of marketing has changed significantly. Home shopping channels on television, the Web, direct mail, and even the mobilization of services such as animal clinics are a few examples of how traditional retail operations have had to rethink their business models. Traditional bricks-and-mortar-based organizations have gone to a bricks-and-clicks business model where they are using traditional retail outlets as well as Web sites and e-commerce as distribution channels.

As sales professionals work with a variety of clients it is important that they collect feedback on the alignment of current distribution channels with their client's needs. Many organizations have made significant investments in the development of Web sites to support e-business only to see little or no impact on the bottom line in response to these investments, while other organizations have reinvented themselves and successfully transformed their distribution channels to capitalize on e-business. Sales professionals provide one of the most valuable sources of information on the alignment of distribution channels with client needs.

DOES YOUR SALES ORGANIZATION OFFER PROGRAMS FOR ORIENTING AND DEVELOPING MARKET CHANNEL PARTNERS?

Partnerships are not something sales organization should just talk about. In the global environment the creation of a planned effort to establish channel partners can provide significant opportunities for sales growth, especially in the international marketplace. Successful partnerships begin with the creation of a strategy for dealing with partners and the identification of which products or services the organization is interested in distributing through nontraditional channels. Sales professionals can broaden their sales scope through the creation of partnership arrangements that benefit the organization and help them to meet their individual sales targets. Strategically selecting partners can open up new markets or reduce the costs of serving existing markets.

Critical Situation: Channel Partners—Cultivating International Partners

Situation: We had conducted in-depth market analysis and were confident there was a market for our product in South America. Over the past three years we had sent our sales manager and several sales professionals on business development trips to Peru, Chile, Brazil, and Argentina with little success. Every one of them came back even more convinced that there were opportunities for us if we could just figure out how to break into the market. We decided that we could not successfully distribute our products in South America without local help. We needed to develop a distribution channel or series of sales agent relationships that had local contacts in the areas. After that we developed a set of criteria we were looking for in partners and before we invested too much time in a relationship we did a background check to see how financially sound the organization was. Well, after a couple of failed attempts where we spent considerable time and effort creating relationships we have finally developed relationships with two well-known organizations that are selling our products across South America. It has not been a great success but we have had two or three contracts come through and we have several others in the works. At this point we are cautiously optimistic and have set some achievable sales goals for next year.

Development Issues: Developing relationships takes time and effort. Developing distribution partners or agents in foreign countries can be difficult, time consuming, and expensive. By developing a clear set of expectations and criteria ahead of time many potential partners can be eliminated early in the process. It is also important to remember that there are many resources available through state and federal government to support international growth.

Action Tips:

- Visit state and federal trade offices. They are valuable sources of business development help.
- Develop realistic expectations and forecasts of desired new business.
- Conduct focused market research and develop distribution channels that provide access to local contacts.

DOES YOUR ORGANIZATION LEVERAGE ADVERTISEMENT AND PROMOTION ACTIVITIES TO SUPPORT FACE-TO-FACE SALES EFFORTS?

Promotion and advertising activities can open the doors for sales professionals to make company contacts and sales calls. However, advertising can also be an expensive drain on organizations with poor or mixed results. Advertising can allow smaller organizations, at a reasonable cost, to reach out beyond the scope of their sales force to influence the purchases of potential clients. By matching target audiences with the correct medium the return on investment can be enhanced.

Sales professionals should coordinate their contacts with advertising campaigns to leverage brand recognition and image. Use the following checklist to help you align sales and advertising efforts. Ask your sales professionals to select one of your products and services and answer the key questions.

☐ Is the overall goal or purpose of the ad to generate direct sales or enhance the sales professionals' ability to sell?

☐ What are the specific objectives to be achieved?

☐ What is the geographical overlap between the sales professional's area and the different media's distribution or circulation area?

☐ Is the alignment between the media audience and the target customers?

☐ How often must the ad appear before it has an impact on the target clients?

☐ How will the impact of the advertisements be tracked against sales?

☐ Does the advertisement focus on specific product lines?

☐ How much new business can realistically be achieved?

One-time or the short-term use of advertising media such as newspapers or television typically has very little impact on the ability of sales professionals to sell a product or service. However, longer-term sustained advertising and publicity can have a positive impact on brand recognition and the effectiveness of sales professionals. Sales development programs must emphasize the importance of coordination between sales efforts and advertising campaigns to have any type of significant impact.

DOES YOUR ORGANIZATION LEVERAGE PUBLICITY TO SUPPORT SALES INITIATIVES?

Publicity is the media coverage organizations receive as part of television, newspaper, radio, or Web reporting of what are perceived as newsworthy organization-related events or activities. Publicity is free media coverage. Many times the positive effect of publicity exceeds that of paid advertisements as the news media are looked at as objective sources of information. However, positive publicity does not happen by accident. Organizations must have proactive and focused attention on the telling of their stories and messages if they expect to receive positive publicity on a regular basis. Sales professionals must be made aware of any relevant publicity items and, just like paid advertising, must leverage the brand name exposure to get first appointments with potential clients.

Public service activities, continuing education course completion, promotions, new-product development, or the hiring of new employees are all examples of organizational activities that when properly communicated to the media can create publicity opportunities. However, reporters and media staff must be able to quickly see why the story would be of interest to others beyond the company. Brand identity and name recognition can pave the way for sales professionals to create new relationships.

Organizations that are able to cultivate a positive public image through their publicity efforts can create client perceptions of the organization that are positive and conducive to personal selling calls from sales staff.

DO YOUR SALES PROFESSIONALS UNDERSTAND THE CONCEPT OF MARKET SEGMENTATION AND VALUE PRICING?

Market segmentation allows organizations to analyze their potential markets and break them down into separate groups based on factors such as geography, product usage, buying volume, or purchasing processes. There are several reasons why organizations should consider segmenting markets and sales professionals should understand the value of the concept:

- New products can be more closely aligned with client needs.
- Advertising and promotion campaigns can be designed to tightly focus on specific needs and benefits.
- Marketing and sales resources can be more closely allocated to markets according to growth opportunities or other trends.
- The industry knowledge and awareness required of sales professionals can be more focused and narrowed.

Each reason for segmenting can improve a sales professional's ability to understand and reach potential clients. By strengthening the sales professionals' ability to identify, understand, and meet client needs their level of productivity and effectiveness increases. Working in defined market segments allows the sales professional to have greater industry knowledge and understanding of client needs.

As you know, businesses must also offer their products or services for sale at a price clients are willing to pay and at a profit level that will meet owners or stockholders expectations regarding their return on investment. The challenge becomes identifying the maximum price clients will pay based on their perception of the product's worth and value. These perceptions frequently begin with a comparison with the competition. Understanding customer perceptions of the value of products or services sold by a business in relationship to prices charged can help sales professionals be more effective in their ability to close sales. From a price-negotiation standpoint, the more knowledge and understanding sales professionals have of what the product or services they sell customers that value, the better they can work to match needs to products at what is perceived by the client to be an appropriate price. The message is clear. If clients will not pay for an organization's products or services at a price that reflects costs plus a fair profit then the business needs to step back and evaluate its costs of doing business, its definition of a fair profit, and determine if it should rethink the products or services it provides. Value-based pricing focuses on matching the price being charged for a product or service with the client's perception of its value. From a sales perspective the challenge is to not price the product beyond its perceived value and thereby cause clients to look elsewhere to meet the need.

The following checklist offers key questions related to value-based pricing.

☐ Are there similar products or services that meet the same client needs?
☐ What are the features and benefits that differentiate your products and services from competitor offerings and how valuable are they to your clients?
☐ Is it more cost or time effective for the client to outsource the product or service to your organization than to keep the function in-house?
☐ Does the use of your product or service help to differentiate your clients from their competition?
☐ Do your clients perceive that your organization has a positive value-to-price ratio?

Ask your sales professionals to select a specific product or service and answer the questions contained in the checklist. Each of these questions can help organizations to step back and objectively analyze their pricing practices and structure. For sales professionals, understanding how prices are set can facilitate their ability to handle objections and close sales.

DOES YOUR ORGANIZATION SPONSOR PROGRAMS TO HELP LINK SALES AND MARKETING STRATEGIES?

Where should you start in your quest to link sales and marketing strategies? Consult the following checklist of developmental strategies to build competence in this area.

☐ Offer a "fundamentals of marketing" training course.
☐ Review advertisements and make it a point to try and determine the target audience and message points.
☐ Conduct a benchmarking analysis.
☐ Ask sales professionals to visit local retail establishments and bring back creative ideas for your organization to consider and discuss at future sales meetings.
☐ Ask local advertising organizations to conduct a seminar on their services to your sales organization.

Ask your sales professionals to check those development activities they believe should be integrated into a program to link sales and marketing strategies. Then use the program outline to help build the competence of your sales professionals in this area.

A Sample Program Outline to Guide Linking Sales and Market Strategies

Title: Knowledge of Products and Services

Competency Dimension: Linking sales and market strategies

Learning Objectives:
- Relate knowledge of trends to market strategies
- Able to link market strategies to sales activities
- Able to link market strategies to promotion
- Describe relationship between sales, marketing, and business results

Potential Content Topics:
- Strategic sales management
- Assessing your competitive sales advantage and market position
- Learning the difference between planning, strategy, and tactics
- Fundamentals of marketing
- Essentials of sales
- Selecting methods of advertising and promotion

PART IV

KNOWLEDGE OF CLIENTS AND BUSINESS

The chapters in Part IV focus on four core competency dimensions related to knowledge of products and services. Each competency is treated in a chapter. Each chapter introduces a competency, offers an opening assessment activity, and then encourages the reader to think about how each question posed in the opening assessment activity relates to the key characteristics needed by sales professionals.

13

Forecasting, Planning, and Prospecting for Clients

All good sales professionals feel the pressure to produce. Their ability to forecast, plan, and deliver sales does not come by accident. Successful prospecting for new clients results from applying disciplined techniques and focused research. In that process, it is particularly important to know how to reach decision makers. To forecast, plan, and prospect for clients successfully, sales professionals can

- network with, and seek information on, key groups and individuals
- understand the impact of different sources of information
- appropriately use information to forecast, plan, and achieve goals
- screen and prioritize clients

What are the development needs of your sales professionals for forecasting, planning, and prospecting for clients? Consult Figure 13.1 to see how the respondents to our survey rated the relative importance of the behaviors associated with this competency. Then reflect on how you would rate sales professionals in your organization.

Use the following self-assessment and worksheet to organize your thinking about ways of building this competency among sales professionals in your organization.

Figure 13.1
Behaviors Related to the Competency of Forecasting, Planning, and Prospecting for Clients as Rated by Survey Respondents

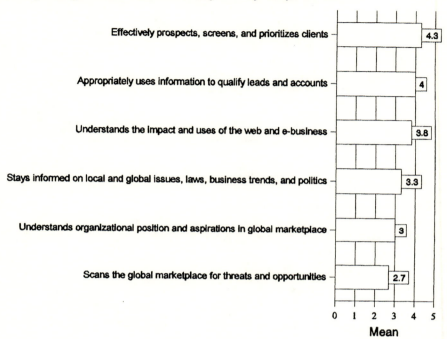

Source: From *A Survey about Sales Training Programs* by W. Rothwell, W. Donahue, and J. Park, 2001 (unpublished survey results), University Park, PA: Pennsylvania State University. Copyright 2001 by W. Rothwell, W. Donahue, and J. Park.

Self-Assessment: Forecasting, Planning, and Prospecting for Clients

Directions: With your sales organization in mind, place a number on the line in the left column below that matches your level of agreement with each statement. Then add up the numbers and score your assessment.

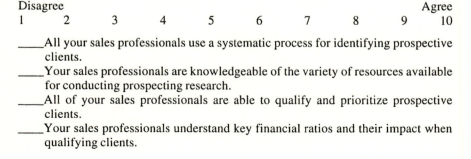

Disagree   Agree
1   2   3   4   5   6   7   8   9   10

____All your sales professionals use a systematic process for identifying prospective clients.

____Your sales professionals are knowledgeable of the variety of resources available for conducting prospecting research.

____All of your sales professionals are able to qualify and prioritize prospective clients.

____Your sales professionals understand key financial ratios and their impact when qualifying clients.

_____All of your sales professionals maintain and update their key prospect files.

_____Your sales professionals create accurate sales forecasts.

_____All of your sales professionals are aware of sources for international client information and market development assistance.

_____Your sales professionals are aware of international industry trends and innovations related to your industry.

_____All of your sales professionals understand your organization's global strategy and plans.

_____Your organization sponsors programs to help forecast, plan, and prospect for clients.

_____Total

How Did You Score?

Here is the key to forecasting, planning, and prospecting for clients. Add up your responses to get your score.

91–100 Great job! Congratulations! Your organization is effectively working to enhance interpersonal selling skills and self-development.

81–90 Keep up the good work! You've probably had considerable success. But by using some of the tips in this chapter, you could improve your success.

71–80 Help is needed! There's room for improvement. You'll find this chapter helpful.

0–70 Warning! Your sales organization may have some confusion. Read on!

A Worksheet to Organize Your Thinking about Forecasting, Planning, and Prospecting for Clients

Directions: What challenges does your organization face in forecasting, planning, and prospecting for clients? Use this worksheet to organize your thinking about how to answer this question.

Notes:

DO YOUR SALES PROFESSIONALS HAVE A SYSTEMATIC PROCESS FOR IDENTIFYING PROSPECTIVE CLIENTS?

Success in sales today is not a guarantee for next year or even next month. Markets change, businesses close or are acquired, and purchasing managers move on to new opportunities. Successful sales professionals recognize that they must be continually prospecting for new clients. Prospecting must be conducted on a regular, systematic, and disciplined basis. There are many different approaches to prospecting. The following factors should be considered in the development of a prospecting system and its integration into a sales development program.

The identification of potential prospects is the first step in the process. Prospect lists can be either primary or secondary in nature. The sales professional or a member of their sales team develops primary lists. Primary lists can include former clients who are currently inactive; personal contacts developed through networking at social events, professional associations, and business clubs; cross selling from the purchase of other products within the company; research from newspapers, Web searches, or other media sources. Secondary sources come from outside the sales professional's organization. Secondary lists can include mailing lists purchased from a direct-mail marketing company, lists obtained from economic development associations or industrial directories, lists obtained through membership in chambers of commerce or other business organizations, trade show participants lists, or even by systematically reviewing the business pages in telephone directories.

Prospecting is one of those unglamorous, time-consuming tasks that is critical to a sales organization's success that can be overlooked or underemphasized. In good times prospecting may be placed to the side, as current clients demand all of the sales professional's energy and time, while in bad times sales professionals are focused on making calls and can be more concerned with the number of calls they make versus the quality of those potential leads. Sales professionals are evaluated on results and prospecting takes time and effort. Prospecting for clients typically does not result in an immediate sale; rather it is one piece of the client development and selling process.

Former clients can be an opportunity or a headache and time waster for sales professionals. The history behind why a client leaves an organization and seeks another vendor can become distorted and confusing with time. Personnel, product and service offerings, and business conditions are constantly changing and factors that may have prompted the former client to look elsewhere for a vendor may no longer exist or be important. Salvaging or renewing relationships can be accomplished by applying the same skills necessary in any successful sales relationship: listening and helping the client to identify needs, becoming a trusted provider of value to the potential client, and providing a product or service that meets a need. However, the challenge becomes proving to clients it is going to be worth their time to meet with the sales professional. This can be an example of where a sales manager or regional director could accompany the sales professional on the call to confirm to potential clients that the sales professional's organization values them and would like to work with them to develop a new relationship.

Referrals can be one of the most effective and easiest methods for sales professionals to develop potential clients. Referrals can come from a multitude of sources. Some sources of referrals to consider are listed:

☐ Current, new, and long-term clients

☐ Other prospects who say no (it never hurts to ask if there is someone else who could benefit from your product)

☐ Other sales professionals who sell complementary or noncompeting products

☐ Vendors

☐ Service providers (accountants, attorneys, and consultants)

☐ Employees in other departments in the organization

☐ Friends or social acquaintances

☐ Others:

Ask your sales professionals to mark the sources on the checklist that they use most frequently.

One of the keys to receiving referrals from other professionals is the concept of "give-to-get." Sales professionals must be willing to provide quality referrals or leads to other sales professionals if they expect to receive the same courtesy in return. All leads, whether or not they turn into a sale, should be acknowledged with a personally written thank you. Cultivating a network of colleagues and professional associates that regularly provide leads can have a positive return for most sales professionals. Golf outings and event tickets, whether they be for a show or a sporting event, lunches, or a copy of a current best-selling business book can all be small ways to show appreciation to another professional for opening the door with a potential client. However, it is critical that these types of relationships are not one-sided and that both parties understand that the relationship is built on trust and friendship first and that no pressure should be applied by either party for leads; rather leads are provided out of respect and friendship. Win–win relationships between sales professionals should be developed and valued.

Referrals also frequently come from satisfied clients who share the sales professional's company or name with a business associate. In particular this type of lead can be valuable, as potential clients have already identified some of their needs and the sales professional's credibility has already been partially established through the referral by the satisfied client.

As discussed earlier in this book, trade shows can be a potential source of leads. Participants who stop at a booth can be given a premium in return for throwing a business card in a box or completing an information card. The more information that can be gathered in that face-to-face setting the easier it is for the sales professional to qualify potential clients and determine if they are prospects or suspects who are gathering competitive information for their own business or a consulting client.

As the sales development program is created, internal and external training seminars and meetings provide an opportunity for sales professionals to network. Internal networking can result in cross-selling opportunities. When sales professionals manage specific territories, they can share leads in training. When selling is conducted by product line, training can also provide a venue to share contacts.

Critical Situation: Qualifying Prospects— Promotional Giveaways That Work

Situation: Part of my role as an applicant recruiter for a very large financial services company is prospecting for qualified applicants. As part of our prospecting campaign we strategically plan promotional initiatives at various sporting events and selected high-traffic areas and events such as at malls at holiday seasons, and so forth. Some people might think of promotional items as being gimmicks, however we very carefully plan out our strategy. We look at the particular time of day, time of year and match the promotional item with the needs of the particular target customers or clients. Our real purpose is to attract potential clients, qualified prospects, and quality referrals. As an example, during the early fall season we target football games, where we first give out hats, t-shirts, and visors which have all been very popular. As the season goes on we move to heavier clothing, long-sleeved t-shirts and stocking caps. During back-to-school days which are high-traffic areas at malls we found that three-color highlight markers have been a popular item. What we promote is, "Come obtain the free promotional giveaway for supplying us with names of serious quality prospects for our financial services products." In order to ensure the integrity of information we require the people that supply information and referrals also show their ID. We also require they be at least eighteen years of age. At a particular sporting event it's not unusual for us to collect over a thousand quality leads for which we subsequently follow-up with efforts to market our financial services.

Development Issues: Prospecting is a planned event with a clear objective, which is to obtain quality leads and essential contact information.

Action Tips:
- Think about your promotional items and use them as an incentive to collect information, not just as a giveaway.
- Ask clients for referrals.
- Ask each sales professional to develop and maintain a listing of prospects and to prioritize.
- Review each listing on at least a monthly basis.

ARE YOUR SALES PROFESSIONALS KNOWLEDGEABLE ABOUT THE VARIETY OF RESOURCES AVAILABLE FOR CONDUCTING PROSPECTING RESEARCH?

There is an overwhelming amount of research information available to those savvy sales professionals and organizations that know where to look. Public and university libraries can be a tremendous source of prospecting information at little or no cost to the researcher. Professional association publications, newspapers, and annual reports are all rich sources of information that can help sales professionals to identify and qualify prospective clients. On-line databases, information reports like *Value Line*, and directories such as the one published by *Harris* contain contact names, financial performance, key personnel, product information, and other valuable marketing information. For larger corporations and a growing number of smaller organizations product information, annual reports and bios on key personnel can be downloaded from company Web sites. The following partial list of the resources available to sales professionals illustrates the large number of organizations that regularly collect and distribute marketing-related company and client information. Ask the sales professionals in your organization to mark on the checklist the sources they use most frequently.

☐ Chamber of commerce directories (national and international)

☐ Dun & Bradstreet Business Solutions and Marketing Services

☐ *D & B Million Dollar Directory: America's Leading Public and Private Companies*

☐ *Thomas Register*

☐ Standard and Poor's Corporate Records

☐ Moody's Manuals (Industrial, Government, Utilities, Transportation)

☐ *Ward's Business Directory*

☐ *Everybody's Business: A Field Guide to the 400 Leading Companies in America*

☐ *Business Ranking Annual*

☐ *Value Line*

☐ Others:

There is a tremendous amount of information available through Internet searches and reviewing industry and professional association Web sites. Most of the resources listed can be accessed through their Web sites. When efficiently used the Web can produce vast amounts of information from very diverse sources that sales professionals would traditionally not have had access to. However, caution must also be used as the validity and reliability of data provided by the Web is not guaranteed. In many cases there is no one monitoring the accuracy or truthfulness of information posted on the Web.

As we described earlier, prospecting and conducting client research is a tedious and time-consuming job that many sales professionals do not look at as a productive use of their time. Thus, the sales manager has several choices available to enhance the client-prospecting process: Retain an external research organization, include formal prospecting as a component of the sales professional's job and consider it in the performance evaluation process, create an internal research and prospecting department, or outsource prospecting and client qualification to one of the professional firms providing this service.

ARE YOUR SALES PROFESSIONALS ABLE TO QUALIFY AND PRIORITIZE PROSPECTIVE CLIENTS?

Once the list of potential clients has been collected and identified the process is only partially completed. Enormous amounts of time, money, and energy can be wasted on poor prospects that have no need for your products or a contact who is not the organizational decision maker. The client-qualifying process must be conducted in a thorough and efficient manner based on a set of criteria that is aligned with the characteristics of the target markets the sales professional is pursuing. Ask your sales professionals to mark the questions on this checklist that they use most often when qualifying prospects:

- ❏ What is the prospect's potential?
- ❏ Is their organization financially sound?
- ❏ Do they pay their bills?
- ❏ How much of a need do they have?
- ❏ What is their short- and long-term potential for buying?
- ❏ Do we have a product or service that could fit their needs?
- ❏ When might they need our product?
- ❏ Are they currently using a similar product or service provided by a competitor?
- ❏ Would their purchase require any special manufacturing or service support?
- ❏ Other:

These sample questions focus on key areas that should be addressed in the qualifying process. Some of the information may be readily available from the business's Web site, or, if they are a publicly traded company, from their annual report. Other qualifying information may be collected from sources such as local or regional newspapers, purchased services like *Value Line* or Dun & Bradstreet, or from chambers of commerce member guides. In the case of qualifying clients the more information that can be collected and analyzed the better decisions can be made on the likelihood of success. Recognize that ultimately the decision must be made whether calling on this potential client is a good investment of time and energy on the part of the sales professional.

Prioritizing clients is a critical component of the sales function, whether it is for the identification of prospective new clients or for developing a schedule for follow-up calls on existing clients. Once the first level of clients has been contacted, the sales professional must look to that second tier of potential clients who may have similar needs to the early innovators but are not able to realize they have needs. The challenge for the sales professional is to establish a trusting relationship with those clients and help them to recognize they have needs and that some or all of those needs could be met by the products or services being sold by the sales professional. The following worksheet provides a simple template to follow to track monthly prospecting activities.

A Worksheet for Organizing a Prospecting Activity Report

Sales Professional_____ Month Ending_____

	Product or Service	Potential Annual Income Volume	Possible Closing	Action Needed
Best Prospects				
Good Prospects				
Current Clients: Additional Activity				
Long-Range Target Account				

Critical Situation: Prospecting at Trade Shows— The Big Fish Are Always There

Situation: We don't really sell a product, we actually sell a management system that is supported by a product or series of products. The tough thing for me when prospecting is not looking at where the business is at this point but rather at their long-term potential. Rarely do I walk in and make a sale, it is long-term stuff and it can take up to two years from the first contact until I actually close the sale. I struggle with deciding on making more frequent calls on larger clients that all of the competition calls on, or going after the smaller clients that could have real long-term potential. The strategy I use is to make the calls on the large companies and try and also focus on them at any trade shows or association meetings I go to because they are always represented. And then I budget more time for those smaller, high-potential companies with the idea that they will give me a big return on my investment some time down the road.

Development Issues: Sales are about meeting short-term goals but not at the sacrifice of the long term. Sales professionals need a mix of clients and those clients need to be in various stages of the development process. Big is not always better when it comes to clients. Frequently the large companies draw the attention of all the sales people in the market area and can be tough to sell.

Action Tips:

- Use trade shows as prospecting opportunities to target large organizations.
- Purchase or obtain tradeshow directories in advance and prioritize planned prospecting efforts.
- Recognize the value of having multiple clients at different stages in their organizational life cycle.

ARE YOUR SALES PROFESSIONALS ABLE TO UNDERSTAND KEY FINANCIAL RATIOS AND THEIR IMPACT WHEN QUALIFYING CLIENTS?

Sales professionals who are capable of quickly reviewing key financial ratios and understanding their impact on a client's financial health can avoid wasting time with prospects who are shopping for longer payment terms, changing vendors to avoid payment of bills, or who may be interested but not capable of buying at this time. Financial information for publicly traded companies can be found in annual reports or through purchased service providers such as Dun & Bradstreet.

An in-depth discussion of financial ratios is beyond the scope of this book. However, the following information provides a brief introduction and description of some key ratios that can be important for sales professionals when dealing with smaller business clients. The financial analysis of larger clients can be beyond the scope of sales professionals' understanding and may require additional resources.

The acceptable range and implications of specific ratios differ based on the client's type of business and the economic environment. Industry-specific information and examples should be collected and integrated into the sales development program. There are several ratios to consider.

The current ratio provides a snapshot of a business's ability to pay current bills and meet any unexpected demands or opportunities out of current assets. The current ratio is calculated accordingly: current assets ÷ current liabilities = current ratio. This ratio provides insight into a business's ability to liquidate its assets and pay all debts and cover outstanding liabilities.

The debt ratio provides insight into the potential client's current and long-term debts as it indicates the percentage of total assets financed. The debt ratio is calculated thus: total debt or liabilities ÷ total assets = debt ratio. Total debt consists of current short-term liabilities plus any outstanding longer-term notes. How businesses leverage and manage their debt and what is acceptable can differ significantly across businesses.

The average payable period ratio indicates how rapidly a business resolves debts and settles their accounts payable. Successful businesses are able to manage the payment of bills to extend the use of their cash. However, consistent late payments that do not take advantage of payment terms can be indicative of limited cash or poor cash management by the business. Before determining the average payable period ratio the payables turnover ratio must be calculated: cost of purchases ÷ accounts payable = payables turnover ratio, then the average payable period ratio can be calculated: number of days in accounting period ÷ payables turnover ratio = average payable period ratio. Comparing these data to industry averages of the typical payment terms the potential client would have access to can be helpful in determining how aggressively to pursue the sales opportunity.

The value of particular ratios in qualifying a potential client can differ depending on the type of business or service they are involved in. Identifying which ratios are most valuable in the analysis of potential clients should be considered as the sales training curriculum is created. The ratios presented are only a small sampling of the ratios that can be used to qualify clients. Industry-specific ratios may be more appropriate indicators of a client's potential value. There are many sources of financial data available in both broad and industry-specific contexts that should be analyzed. However, sales professionals must be trained in the significance of the data if it is to be used as part of the client qualification process.

DO YOUR SALES PROFESSIONALS MAINTAIN AND UPDATE A KEY PROSPECT FILE?

Some sales can occur almost overnight while others may take months or even years. For the successful sales professional it is critical that his or her portfolio of potential clients have a cross section of prospects from those who are close to buying to those potential clients who are out in the future and need cultivation and relationship building before they can even be considered real prospects. Each region or market segment has key clients whom every competitor in the sales professional's business or service sector would love to have. These A+ clients are on every competitor's list because of the amount or type of purchases they make. The challenge for sales professionals is developing a relationship-building strategy for key clients. How do you create opportunities to meet the right people? How do you determine who the key clients are? Size or current buying potential cannot always determine key prospects. Key prospects can also be those industry influencers in the area that may be smaller, but once they adopt a product or a process, the "keep up with the competition" factor kicks in and other organizations become interested in the sales professional's product line or services because the word has spread.

A key-prospect database should be developed as a source of knowledge available for all sales staff. Specific information regarding opportunities to meet decision makers should be collected. Any buying information, key contact names, personal data on the key contacts, or important company information should be included. Many organizations are including this information as part of their customer relationship management system.

DO YOUR SALES PROFESSIONALS CREATE ACCURATE SALES FORECASTS?

Some sales managers suggest that forecasting is more art than science. The development of realistic and relevant sales forecasts requires time, an understanding of the sales environment, and extensive client, business, and industry knowledge. Accurate and relevant sales forecasts can make valuable contributions to the budgeting, inventory planning, and cash-flow management processes of an organization. Forecasting can also be an exercise in futility and wasted effort. Tracking productivity over time and evaluating the circumstances and context of sales success can help organizations to do realistic historical forecasting. Forecasts of existing products or services that have a proven track record can be created using a variety of quantitative analysis formulas and techniques. Forecasting the revenue for sales professionals involved in the rollout of new products or services is more difficult. Comparisons can be made within the organization to similar new-product events in the past or estimates can be made based on comparisons to the efforts of other organizations. Trade associations and chambers of commerce are two sources of data.

Even the most careful analysis and research do not guarantee accuracy of sales forecasts. Many organizations develop three sales scenarios—"best case," "worst case," and the "most likely to occur." This provides ranges for the budgeting of operational expenses and planning for cash flow. In small businesses this type of sales information is critical for managing the flow of cash for bill payment and for making decisions regarding inventory and purchases during the course of the year.

Calling on sales professionals to forecast sales figures based on their perceptions of the current marketplace and their predictions on what will occur in the future can be difficult and at times very inaccurate. However, by involving them in the process sales professionals better understand the impact of their efforts on the financial success of the organization. Integrating forecasting awareness training into the sales training program can further enhance the sales professional's ownership of organizational sales goals.

Consider the importance of forecasting and budgeting for your organization. Check the forecasting factors in Figure 13.2 that you believe your sales organization adequately considers in your operating environment.

Figure 13.2
The Importance of Sales Forecasting and Budgeting in Your Operating Environment

Forecasting Factors	Sales Forecasts and Budgets	Variable Costs Budget
Sociocultural Political and Legal Economic Technological Industry Marketplace Your organization Individual clients	Overhead Costs Budget	Overall Budget

Critical Situation: Forecasting Sales— Eating the Elephant One Bite at a Time

Situation: As sales managers of a mid-sized manufacturing firm we found that sometimes forecasting can be overwhelming. We serve many different markets with our numerous products and in order to be successful we've learned that we must segment each market and product category to its simplest form. Several of our sales professionals joke that it's like eating an elephant. You need to take one bite at a time. We typically try to identify as many prospects and potential users of each of our products as we can. We then plot them on a map indicating their size by using different color-coding systems. We then create a series of overlays to indicate the type of products they require. We also produce another series of overlays of where our clients and prospects ship their end product, as a method of evaluating vertical integration and possibly another source or pool of prospects. Then we examine and focus on selected geographical areas where concentrations occur and profile each potential prospect in that geographical area. A Web search and a few phone calls usually provide sufficient detail to then plan a series of face-to-face calls on the prospects. Our sales professionals then categorize the prospects into four categories: best prospects, good prospects, long-term prospects, and a fourth category which is current clients who don't currently use the particular product but potentially could. We then use this information to create three sales forecast scenarios: optimistic, pessimistic and most likely. We update our forecasts monthly.

Development Issues: What gets planned gets done. Operating procedures and accountability must be built in to an organized prospecting process in order to be successful.

Action Tips:
- Require sales professionals to plan and report their activities on a routine basis.
- Establish a formalized reporting structure that can be easily consolidated and reviewed by the sales manager on a weekly and monthly basis.

ARE YOUR SALES PROFESSIONALS AWARE OF SOURCES FOR INTERNATIONAL CLIENT INFORMATION AND MARKET DEVELOPMENT ASSISTANCE?

Collecting client information on potential international clients is complex and at times frustrating for sales professionals. Language, cultural, political, and even legal factors can impact upon the type of information available on potential clients in an international marketplace. Many of the same sources of market and client information cited previously in this section also provide information on international clients. The chamber of commerce Web site contains an international directory.

State and federal government organizations can be a significant source of data. The local department of commerce can be a great link to resources in the targeted countries and can help to facilitate potential partner relationships. Sales professionals who are able to develop these contacts can be positioned to receive updates on the economic or political activity of a region or a country. The small business administration centers across the country provide support services for smaller businesses exploring exporting or franchising opportunities.

The World Bank publishes information on a regular basis regarding economic trends and market growth on a regional and country-specific basis. Many state governments have export specialists who can provide insight into market trends and have developed in-country agents who are on retainer to facilitate export opportunities.

ARE YOUR SALES PROFESSIONALS AWARE OF INTERNATIONAL INDUSTRY TRENDS AND INNOVATIONS?

Product innovations are occurring at a tremendous pace around the world. Successful organizations in the international marketplace are nimble, innovative, and able to understand the unique characteristics and needs of international clients. Sales professionals operating in the international marketplace must become sensitive to cultural factors and make a concerted effort to learn about their foreign clients.

Developing an understanding of foreign countries takes an investment of both time and money as sales professionals must be trained in cultural traditions, at least a minimal level of language fluency, and have an understanding of the political realities of the country they are dealing with, whether it be in South America, Europe, or Asia.

Technology growth and innovation in the Asian countries is forcing competitors around the world to keep up or be forced out of business. Understanding the impact of the changing technology environment is critical for sales professionals as they establish relationships and create opportunities. Understanding the needs of international clients requires considerable research and concentration on industry knowledge, as the costs for developing relationships through face-to-face contact can be enormous and thousands of dollars can be quickly wasted on unsuccessful sales calls.

DO YOUR SALES PROFESSIONALS UNDERSTAND YOUR ORGANIZATION'S GLOBAL STRATEGY?

Many smaller organizations are joining the international marketplace that was once viewed solely as an arena for the global giants. Just as in the domestic market where smaller organizations can bring innovative ideas to the marketplace in a much shorter time frame, in the international marketplace smaller organizations can address the needs of narrower niche markets. Communication strategies are critical as sales professionals must evaluate the most effective methods for overcoming time differences and cultural expectations to meet client needs.

Sales professionals may take on very nontraditional roles in the management of international clients. Franchising, commissioning in-country sales agents, or accessing international markets via the Web with phone or face-to-face follow-up are all marketing strategies both large and small organizations are utilizing. When working with sales agents roles and responsibilities must be clearly defined and understood by all parties. Written agreements clarifying the relationship can be effective and in many cases are a must.

Critical Situation: Global Client Cultivation and Management— International Prospecting Challenges

Situation: In my role as manager of technology for a large Fortune 500 corporation, I am responsible not only for selling technology around the world but also for buying technology around the world. Our sales organization is segmented into territories with each territory being assigned a client manager we call a contract manager who is responsible for all the organizations and companies in that particular territory of the world. As a matter of course, we have profiled all the major clients or prospects in each part of the world and the assigned contract managers are responsible for selecting the potential clients that they will personally take responsibility for and also establishing agent relationships to cover those other prospects in their region that might be in need of our services. We require contract managers to supply information and organize events in their worldwide territories and coordinate all activities in those areas of the world. In addition to quarterly visits to each client around the world, we conduct an annual symposium of all clients, hosted at our headquarters with the symposium conducted by our technology experts. In addition to the clients, we include our network of agents whom we also provide with specific product training and knowledge while trying to establish an atmosphere of open communication. Our agents are motivated by what we consider to be a generous commission compensation structure whereby they receive 5 percent of the overall gross of any technical-services arrangement plus 15 percent of any equipment purchases by selected clients. We have a formalized agreement with our agents and depend on them to make daily contact and communication with clients and prospects in their region and to report those activities on a monthly basis. We ask that our international agents make five to ten face-to-face calls per week with clients and/or prospects. On a capital-employed basis, our division is the most profitable of our company.

Development Issues: To maintain quality client interactions and cultivate prospects routine communication is essential. For many organizations that may require not only face-to-face contact from their direct employees but also arrangements with agents and others to maintain or establish relationships. With fair and equitable treatment, development of agents can offer a cost-effective way to extend business relationships globally.

Action Tips:

• Search and network for trustworthy agents of interest to you and your business in various parts of the world.

• Conduct an annual symposium to orient, update, and train not only your sales professionals but your agents as well.

DOES YOUR ORGANIZATION SPONSOR PROGRAMS TO HELP FORECAST, PLAN, AND PROSPECT FOR CLIENTS?

Where should you start in helping sales professionals in your organization forecast, plan, and prospect for clients? Consult the following checklist of developmental strategies to build competence in this area, then use this plan to help build the competence of your sales professionals in enhancing ongoing client and stakeholder informational processes.

☐ Offer a fundamentals of marketing course.

☐ Generate a list of prospecting practices going on in your department today.

☐ Examine the demographic, ethnic, and cultural profile of your market segments and develop strategies to increase sales in selected niches.

☐ Ask all members of the sales organization if they feel they have equal access to you and to the information you share with them.

☐ In establishing hiring criteria, include planning experience as a hiring goal.

☐ Consider special developmental assignments for members of your sales organization, such as assigning them the task of forecasting trends in selected market segments and generating innovative ways of prospecting in that market segment.

☐ Ask your accounting department to conduct an introduction to costs and budgets session with your sales organization.

☐ Arrange a visit to your state's department of commerce to explore both domestic and international opportunities and sources of assistance.

A Sample Program Outline to Guide Forecasting, Planning, and Prospecting for Clients

Title: Knowledge of Clients and Business

Competency Dimension: Forecasting, planning, and prospecting for clients

Learning Objectives:
- Demonstrate how to network with, and seek information on, key groups and individuals
- Understand impact of different sources of information
- Demonstrate appropriate use of information to forecast, plan, and achieve goals
- Able to screen and prioritize clients

Potential Content Topics:
- Changing demographics
- Managing a sales territory
- Prospecting for clients
- Business planning and forecasting
- Business networking
- Fundamentals of market research
- Web searching
- Applied database management
- Basic forecasting, budgeting, and costs
- International business planning

14

Managing Calls, Time, and Sales Territory

Sales professionals may find it frustrating to maintain focus and direction in a hectic organization, as most of today's organizations are. They may experience considerable stress in managing multiple accounts, projects, and priorities. As middle management positions continue to be reduced, sales professionals find new responsibilities and accountabilities thrust on them. Moreover, mergers and acquisitions often force sales professionals to reexamine the organization's strategic direction and realign or restructure sales territories.

This chapter focuses on managing calls, time, and sales territory. To demonstrate this competency, sales professionals should

- work persistently toward goals
- organize, plan, schedule, and set priorities for sales calls to clients
- manage their own time and travel efficiently

What are the development needs of your sales professionals for managing calls, time, and sales territory? Consult Figure 14.1 to see how the respondents to our survey rated the relative importance of the behaviors associated with this competency. Then reflect on how you would rate sales professionals in your organization.

Figure 14.1
Behaviors Related to the Competency of Managing Calls, Time, and Sales Territory as Rated by Survey Respondents

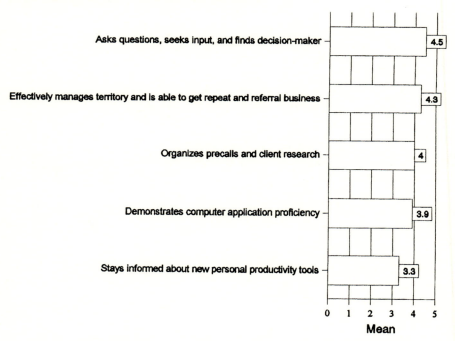

Source: From *A Survey about Sales Training Programs* by W. Rothwell, W. Donahue, and J. Park, 2001 (unpublished survey results), University Park, PA: Pennsylvania State University. Copyright 2001 by W. Rothwell, W. Donahue, and J. Park.

Now complete the following self-assessment and worksheet to organize your thinking about ways of building this competency among sales professionals in your organization.

Self-Assessment: Managing Calls, Time, and Sales Territory

Directions: With your sales organization in mind, place a number on the line in the left column below that matches your level of agreement with each statement. Then add up the numbers and score your assessment.

Disagree									Agree
1	2	3	4	5	6	7	8	9	10

_____Your sales professionals organize and manage their time effectively.
_____Your sales professionals manage their travel efficiently and effectively.
_____Your sales professionals effectively manage their use of e-mail.
_____Your sales professionals effectively use the phone as a sales and problem-solving tool.

_____All of your sales professionals are sensitive to the value of other people's time.

_____Your sales professionals manage multiple priorities effectively.

_____Your sales professionals understand how to participate in and lead effective meetings.

_____Your sales professionals are able to conduct meetings using the Web and video conferencing.

_____Your sales professionals understand productivity metrics and how to do a break-even analysis.

_____Your organization sponsors programs to help sales professionals manage calls, time, and sales territories.

_____Total

How Did You Score?

Here is the key to managing calls, time, and sales territory. Add up your responses to get your score.

91–100   Great job! Congratulations! Your organization is effectively working to manage client communications.

81–90   Keep up the good work! You've probably had considerable success. But by using some of the tips in this chapter, you could improve your success.

71–80   Help is needed! There's room for improvement. You'll find this chapter helpful.

0–70   Warning! Your sales organization probably has some challenges managing calls, time and sales territory. Read on!

A Worksheet to Organize Your Thinking About Managing Calls, Time, and Sales Territory

Directions: In your opinion, what problems or challenges does your sales organization face in managing calls, time, and sales territories? Use this worksheet to organize your thinking about how to answer this question.

Notes:

DO YOUR SALES PROFESSIONALS ORGANIZE AND MANAGE THEIR TIME EFFECTIVELY?

When sales professionals are asked about the biggest challenges they face the two that inevitably come up are interruptions and lack of time. Both of these challenges are severely impacted by the sales professional's ability to prioritize and manage events and activities. For sales professionals every minute of every day is a potential "sellable moment" that if not spent on a selling-related activity could mean a lost or delayed sale. Just ask any experienced sales professional and he or she will tell you that time wasters lurk around every corner just waiting for unsuspecting sales professionals trying to meet their goals.

Some of the common time wasters identified in the research and encountered in the authors' own experiences are contained in the following checklist.

☐ Unqualified leads

☐ Meeting with dead-end nondecision makers

☐ Meetings with clients, managers or other internal staff that were mismanaged

☐ Poor travel arrangements that resulted in a long layover or missed connection

☐ Crisis management—managers or clients ask for something that must be done immediately

☐ Drop-in visitors

☐ Nonwork related phone calls

☐ Can't get the client or colleague off the phone

☐ Junk mail

☐ Junk e-mail (SPAM)

☐ Insufficient resources to do something the right way, so it gets done multiple times

☐ Disorganization (lost or misplaced files)

☐ Double booking

☐ Others:

Ask your sales professionals to check those time wasters that they most frequently experience and add them to the list.

Each of these time wasters can frequently be related in some way to the sales professional's success in meeting goals. When looked at individually their impact upon the sales professional's time may appear insignificant. However, their cumulative effect can contribute to difficulties in meeting performance expectations and create excessive stress for sales professionals.

Dealing with interruptions, whether they be from drop-in visitors or unexpected phone calls, can free up time and reduce stress on busy sales professionals. The flow of drop-in visitors can be significantly influenced by the location of the sales professional's workspace or office and the flow of traffic through the area. The messages sent to the drop-in visitor during the initiation of the visit clearly set the tone and influence the length of the stay. A common mistake is to invite visitors in and to extend them the opportunity to be seated. This is a green light for the visitor to come in, get comfortable, and stay a while! It takes finesse and diplomacy to graciously steer the drop-in down the hall to another colleague. This can be especially challenging when the drop-in visitor is the sales professional's boss or another manager.

One strategy is to not let visitors sit down or get comfortable when they enter the sales professional's office or workspace. Standing up and moving toward the door to greet people is a fine courtesy only if it does not discourage them from sitting down. Conversations that are conducted standing up are much shorter then those that occur after the visitor has been seated. This strategy can be taken even further by not stopping inside your office once you stand up; rather continuing to walk out the door and down the hall or across the room to the coffee pot or the water fountain. This type of walking conversation can be limited to the length of the walk and then the drop-in visitor's focus can be shifted elsewhere.

Another strategy to reduce the drain on time of drop-in visitors is "Could we do this (later today, tomorrow morning, over lunch, and so forth) because right now I am in the middle of something I have to get completed," or some variation of this statement that reflects how the sales professional communicates and is comfortable with. The point of the strategy is taking control of the interaction so that it occurs at a time that is more appropriate and potentially less productive. For sales professionals who are morning people this type of conversation may fit best late in the day when other people are more inclined to end it promptly so they can beat rush-hour traffic or for those afternoon or evening people a discussion over coffee the next morning may be less disruptive and have a lesser impact on their most productive time. Regardless of when it is, the drop-in must be given an opportunity to continue the conversation at another time and the sales professional must be sensitive to not appearing rude or aloof. These are only two examples of some of the strategies that can be incorporated into the sales training program to help sales professionals effectively handle drop-in office visitors.

For sales professionals working out of their homes drop-in visitors could be kids home from school, a neighbor stopping by to borrow something, or a delivery person. Home office visitors can be a more difficult situation to address. The trend toward telecommuting and home offices continues to grow. Individuals who make this transition successfully are able to create quiet time and to separate themselves from household activities in an out-of-the-way portion of their home. Handling nonfamily drop-in visitors is another issue. The most obvious strategy used by many sales professionals is to ignore the doorbell rings, knocks, or phone calls. Others screen their calls with an answering machine and go as far as turning off or disconnecting their doorbells. Again, these are a few of the strategies available to sales professionals for addressing unplanned or drop-in visitors. Some traditional questions sales professionals can ask themselves when evaluating and prioritizing activities are as follows:

- How important is this activity to me personally and to my organization?
- How urgent is the completion of this activity and what is the real date it needs to be completed by?
- What would happen if I did not do this activity right away?
- Who does it matter to that I complete this activity or don't complete it?
- Is there someone else who I could delegate this activity to that could do it better, faster, or cheaper and allow me to focus on other more value-adding activities?
- Does this activity help me to meet my weekly, monthly, or annual goals?

Each question can serve as a filter that sales professionals can run activities through to determine if they should be focused on the completion of the activity, moving the activity aside until a later time, identifying options for moving the activity elsewhere through delegation or transfer and finally, if appropriate, ignoring the activity completely.

Critical Situation: Telesales Management—No Time Wasters Here

Situation: In my telesales role for a very large financial services organization we don't waste a minute. We try and implement the latest technology to gain new clients, manage existing clients, and improve overall productivity. Our organization is constantly moving to the latest technology and currently uses an intranet system whereby telesales representatives utilize computer systems with several specialized features. Our computer screen is split into four quadrants. The first quadrant represents the automatic dialing system. One of the features built into the automatic dialer system is, if it encounters a busy signal it will automatically dial a new number. It will also filter and screen answering machines and call a new number. Another embedded feature is the ability to cut and paste the names from prospects into the second quadrant that is our customer application program whereby basic data is collected on each of the prospects. If additional information is collected, it is entered into the second application quadrant as a comments section. The third quadrant is an on-line business information system that is centrally maintained in a database. This system incorporates information in two main areas: product information and special endorsements of those products. The fourth quadrant is a competitor information system. Embedded in this database-driven system is information on our top ten competitors in the industry. The database is centrally maintained and if we learn information about our competitors from customers we can enter it as a comments section. A fifth optional pull-down window is a basic mathematical tools window that includes such things as a calculator and quick comparison tables. Overall, our system continues to evolve and be improved. Over the past two years our telesales productivity increased over 100 percent.

Development Issues: Productivity enhancements significantly increase call management and effectiveness. Sales professionals must be receptive to implementing technological systems. Obviously adoption of new technologies requires flexibility and additional training and development.

Action Tips:

- Research telemarketing and telesales systems, and call management systems to increase prospecting effectiveness.
- Benchmark your prospecting and call-management activities with others in your industry.
- Establish templates and databases for collecting and consolidating prospect and client information.

DO YOUR SALES PROFESSIONALS MANAGE THEIR TRAVEL EFFICIENTLY AND EFFECTIVELY?

In the sales profession it is clear that time is definitely money. Days wasted traveling to a single sales call or trips made across the country to meet with a client who cancels at the last minute can be the downfall of new sales professionals. This type of nonproductive effort is a waste of time for the sales professional who could have been making other sales contacts and for the sales organization the financial cost of poorly planned and managed sales trips can be significant in car mileage expense, motel rooms, per diems, and airfare, plus other less obvious costs.

Critical Situation: Managing Territories—Annual Planning Calendar

Situation: Effectively managing time and territories is critical to our success. We have several plants located throughout the United States and our sales organization consists of eight territory sales managers, one national client manager, and four independent manufacturering agents who work on commission. Our products require a lot of personal interaction to make sure that design specifications for various projects incorporate our products. In order to maintain client relationships, we have established an annual travel planning calendar. We prioritize clients according to sales potential and plan frequency and types of ongoing contact, whereby our best customers are designated so that we visit them monthly, the next level of client, quarterly, and the third level, annually. The levels are somewhat subjective but essentially are based on dollar volume and potential. All of our sales professionals complete an annual planning calendar and we track their performance against the goals they set. We do understand that strict schedules change but on a monthly, quarterly, and annual basis it's easy for us to keep focused on which clients need more attention than others or deserve more attention than others and act accordingly. We treat our independent sales representatives as though they were part of our sales organization and include them in sales meetings which we conduct every other month at various locations. In addition to the annual face-to-face meeting schedule we also have planned our mailings and e-mailing on a scheduled basis so that each of our best clients gets something across the desk or computer screen at least once a month from us and others on a less frequent basis. The point is to make sure that our name and brand image are on their mind all the time. We must be doing something right, as our sales continue to escalate above industry averages.

Development Issues: Managing client relationships is a communications process characterized by multiple communication methods. The communication process is managed as a project within itself with assigned responsibilities.

Action Tips:

- Provide all sales professionals with "To-Do List" pads and ask them to prioritize demands on their time as well as track how they spend their time.
- Prioritize clients according to sales potential and plan frequency and types of ongoing contact.
- Ask sales professionals to create an annual travel-planning calendar to encourage thoughtful travel planning and appropriate frequency of face-to-face client interactions.
- Ask sales professionals to create a listing of tasks which are not time-effective for them to do and can be delegated.
- Establish an annual communications calendar to manage client relationships with multiple communication methods.
- Establish a newsletter for dissemination several times a year as well as dissemination of product information to be sent at the same mailing.

The challenge for sales professionals is coordinating their travel schedule to allow multiple appointments during day trips and when extended trips are required, tying together multicity stops that leverage airplane flights or driving time. Using maps and trip-planning systems can allow sales professionals to avoid overlapping trips and wasted overnight stays. The use of a Geographic Information System (GIS), a computer-based planning tool that combines graphics and database capabilities to analyze geographic sales territories and capabilities, is a growing trend with sales professionals. The more advanced systems can examine customer potential in relationship to demographic and geographic factors and provide the capability to realign sales territories and evaluate the cost of sales in relationship to travel time.

Combining client maintenance or cross-selling trips with prospecting new business calls is also an effective strategy for managing travel time and expense. Planning trips in advance that require air travel can result in significantly cheaper fares, however in today's changing environment this can also create problems when clients reschedule or cancel appointments.

DO YOUR SALES PROFESSIONALS MANAGE THEIR USE OF E-MAIL?

Literally billions of e-mails are sent and received each workday. E-mail can be a time-saving and highly effective tool for solving problems and staying in contact with current and potential clients. E-mail can also be a tremendous drain on the time and energy of busy sales professionals. The acceptance and use of e-mail varies greatly within organizations. There are managers and employees at all levels of organizations who have totally embraced e-mail as their communication channel of choice and find themselves using e-mail to communicate as much as 80 percent of the information they need to share with coworkers or clients. E-mails can be quickly sent to multiple receivers in seconds and replies generated equally as efficiently. Some individuals refuse to send or read e-mail and revert to having support staff print their e-mails for them to read and handwrite responses that are typed and sent, while others continue ignoring e-mail completely and are only dealing with information received via traditional mail channels. Ultimately whether client communication is conducted by e-mail, fax, or phone should be determined by what is most comfortable and efficient for the client.

One of the first strategies to consider in managing e-mail is any time an e-mail is sent it can be expected to generate at least one response and in many occasions this response factor can result in four or five responses or up to hundreds. By being more thoughtful in the formulation of e-mails to others the number of responses that will need to be read and potentially replied to by the sales professional can be reduced.

Many e-mail systems have an automatic response system that issues a notification alert sound ranging from a bell to a duck quacking each time an e-mail is downloaded. By deactivating this alert e-mail arrivals do not distract the sales professional and they can be read on an hourly or less frequent basis depending on the number of e-mails received daily and their importance. Just as phone calls can be returned at one predetermined time each day, whether it be morning or afternoon, to more effectively manage time e-mails can also be held until a specific time for responses.

One downside of e-mail is that with responses so easily generated careless or poorly thought-out responses can be quickly formulated with their negative impact felt long after the e-mail was sent and read by the other party. Letters and memos, whether they are created using a word processor or are handwritten, typically force the writer to organize their thoughts and think through the message or messages they are attempting to deliver. Just placing a message in written format creates the perception of added importance. With the immediacy of e-mail, much of the thoughtfulness and consideration of the impact of the communication can be easily forgotten. E-mail does not allow the reader to hear the writer's tone of voice or understand the mood when the message was sent and frequently it can be difficult to interpret where the writer is coming from with the message or if action is required of the reader. Individuals who might not be confrontational or aggressive in a face-to-face encounter with a subordinate or coworker are suddenly able to "flame" people with a nasty or mean-spirited e-mail and not be forced to look the person in the eye when sending the negative message. Some guidelines and issues to review with your sales professionals on sending e-mails are the following:

- Be cautious about delivering bad news or a mean or harsh message via e-mail. It is important to think about how you would handle this message if the person was sitting in your office. If you wouldn't have the confidence or the nerve to deliver the message face-to-face then don't sink to using e-mail. The bottom line is don't include anything in an e-mail that you wouldn't say to the person face to face.

- Remember that it is easy to forward an e-mail to other parties. Forwarded e-mails can be edited or parts cut out and replaced. Think through the impact of other people reading an e-mail before it is sent.

- Don't initiate a conflict via e-mail and don't try and resolve a conflict through e-mail. Phone conversations are a better alternative but even then it is much easier to be confrontational over the phone than face to face. When possible arrange a mutually acceptable meeting place to work through potentially sensitive situations that could result in conflict.

- If you receive a "nasty-gram" don't fire off a quick response. If you must write something immediately save it on your computer in draft form and hold the response for a day or two and then reread the message and think through the impact. In the meantime consider phoning the person or arranging for a meeting.

- Remember to notice who is copied on e-mail messages and recognize the impact of hitting the "reply to all" message. Also, most e-mail providers have a blind carbon function so it is easy to copy a manager or coworker on a message with the reader not being alerted to this.

- Don't overwhelm recipients with e-mail. First, only include those individuals who will be interested in the messages and find it relevant in the "to" field. Second, work to keep your messages high quality and well written with important points delivered in a clear, concise, and understandable format.

- Know your audience. Analytical readers will expect you to get to the point and to provide bulleted facts to support your position, while other personality types will be interested in how people feel about the decision and will be more willing to read a longer, more detailed message.

- For long or detailed messages that require a response on a task try including that information as an attachment to make it easier for the recipient to work with the document.

These are just a few key factors that should be considered when using e-mail to work with clients or coworkers. The technical aspect of using e-mail effectively should also be included in the sales training program. Creating multiple mailboxes and folders for filing of messages, creating filters that collect and route messages, and using mailing lists are all tools that exist on specific e-mail systems that should be developed on a company-specific basis.

DO YOUR SALES PROFESSIONALS USE THE PHONE AS A PROBLEM-SOLVING AND SALES TOOL?

Many times a simple, well-timed phone call to the right person can head off a potential disaster, solve a problem, or better yet close a sales deal. Having the ability to professionally conduct business over the phone is more than having a simple conversation. Recognizing when it is appropriate to pick up the phone and let clients know that their order has been delayed or that it was shipped and should be delivered that day are the type of value-adding activities that businesses are growing to expect from the sales professionals they work with. However, sales professionals can also quickly wear out their welcome with clients if they are continually calling without a clear purpose and agenda. Few people in today's world have the luxury of spare time they can spend chatting about the weather or other nonwork related issues. Sales professionals must recognize individual client needs regarding small talk and socializing and pick up on their signals when it is time to get down to business.

As described in an earlier chapter the effective use of voice mail can save time and in many cases help the sales professional to avoid playing phone tag. Sales professionals can enhance the effectiveness of their own voice mail by changing their message if they are going to be gone for prolonged periods of time and not be able to respond to messages. Voice mail messages should be professional and concise. Any attempts at humor or unprofessional messages are frequently a turn off for clients. When leaving voice mail messages for current or potential clients it is critical that they be left in a clear, friendly, and positive voice. Sales professionals whose message comes across in a positive professional manner are much more likely to have their calls returned. Messages that are weak or apologetic in their tone and message points become self-fulfilling and rarely warrant callbacks.

The phone can be a great tool for gathering information on client satisfaction and overall client acceptance of a product or service. Sales professionals with a well-prepared script can quickly get a sense for how their clients feel about the service they are receiving and pick up on any potential problems lurking on the horizon.

ARE YOUR SALES PROFESSIONALS SENSITIVE TO THE VALUE OF OTHER PEOPLE'S TIME?

Valuing the time of clients, managers, and other coworkers is indicative of seasoned and well-trained sales professionals. Experienced purchasing managers and others responsible for the purchase of products and services are routinely contacted on a weekly basis by dozens of potential vendors trying to sell them something. A challenge for the sales professional in establishing a relationship with this type of seasoned purchaser is how to balance the relationship side of developing the contact with concentrating on the identification of needs and problem solving.

Critical Situation: Managing Client Calls— Viewed as a Technical Expert

Situation: Early in my career, I walked into a new client's office and I had barely gotten seated when she started firing questions at me beginning with how long I had been with the company, to questioning my sales experience and the types of clients I had been working with. I tried on several occasions to focus the conversation on her needs and she just kept turning it back in to an interview of me. I even mentioned the pictures of the kids on her bookcase and how mine also played soccer. But she just blew right by that one and started asking me industry and product-related questions. I know my face was red while I tried to remain calm and composed. It was as if she was testing me to see if I knew what I was talking about and if she could trap me in some half-truth or a total mistake. Well, this went on for nearly thirty minutes as she seemed to toy with me and by that time I had decided this was one of those wasted calls that I could chalk up to my inexperience when she said to me, "So when can you have our order delivered here to this plant and to the one in Georgia?" Well, needless to say you could have knocked me right out of my chair with a feather. I sure couldn't figure that one out and never dreamed I would walk out of there with a sale. Then she went on to explain to me that she had an engineering degree and had spent fifteen years in technical sales before she became the purchasing manager. It was obvious that she was testing me to see what approach I would use in trying to sell her something and if I really did know anything about the business and could be trusted to deliver. Well, I must have passed the test because she has been one of my best clients for over five years and from time to time she still quizzes me on industry trends to see if I am staying current and keeping up with my homework on the business. It has built my confidence and challenges me to learn as much as I can about our products and the competitors' offerings as well. I now really enjoy meeting with her as I sense she values my expertise and professionalism.

Development Issues: Selling to people with sales experience and training can be tough. In many cases they have had the same or similar sales training and in many cases can almost anticipate what you will do next. In this case it also pointed out that there is no replacement for hard work when it comes to developing industry and product knowledge. Clients today are not just looking for someone to come in and give them a sales pitch. Clients are looking for sales professionals who are business experts and are able to offer potential solutions and work with them to meet their business needs and solve problems.

Action Tips:

- Learn as much as you can about your products and services and those of your competitors.
- Establish a list of client problems or opportunities for improvement that your products or services can help solve.

ARE YOUR SALES PROFESSIONALS ABLE TO MANAGE MULTIPLE PRIORITIES?

Sales is a complex and challenging profession that requires a diverse set of skills and knowledge. Effective sales professionals are able to quickly shift from task to task and refocus their energy while continuously moving several sales initiatives forward. Managing multiple priorities requires flexibility and resiliency. Sales professionals must be able to regroup and bounce back when they are faced with unsuccessful sales attempts and be able to not take rejection personally. Sales professionals are constantly faced with challenges and pressures to reach sales goals, satisfy internal expectations for follow-up reports and administrative details, and balance all of this (in many cases) with trying to maintain a family and life outside of work. Sales professionals must also be able to manage their own learning and personal development as they grow in their career. Developing a personal vision statement that guides personal decision making and serves as a framework for prioritization of activities and events can be a positive experience for many new sales professionals struggling with balancing work and personal activities. Creating goals at each level of an organization beginning with the overall organization and breaking them down to a departmental and individual level provides direction as to what is important for the organization and creates targets for performance to be measured against. There are many tools available to facilitate organizational and personal goal setting. The SMART framework mentioned in a previous chapter is one the authors have found effective.

Organizational skills and time-management techniques are keys to the successful management of multiple priorities. Maintaining either an electronic or traditional paper schedule, having access to important information when and where it is needed, and relying on support staff as appropriate are all necessary if a sales professional is to successfully meet all professional and personal goals. Some of these behaviors and skills may be reflective of an individual's personality and the natural inclination to be organized while other skills can be learned and maintained. Staying organized takes time, the proper tools, and the energy needed to focus on multiple activities in parallel. Effective sales professionals plan their weekly activities and document important information and needed actions. While computerized contact management systems help, it is important to recognize that no matter what system works for your organization, they are all based on basic planning principles. Use Figures 14.2 and 14.3 as planning tools. They may be adapted for most any sales organization.

DO YOUR SALES PROFESSIONALS UNDERSTAND HOW TO PARTICIPATE IN AND LEAD EFFECTIVE MEETINGS?

For meetings to add value to an organization they must be held for the right purpose and they must be held at the proper place and at the right time. Meetings are an effective technique for problem solving when multiple perspectives can help to identify higher-quality solutions, when team ownership in the solution will help increase the probability of successful implementation of the solution, when the potential solutions to the problem could impact most or all of the team members in attendance, and when there is a significant volume of work that cannot be completed by an individual member of the team. Meetings are ineffective and members of the team attending the meeting typically struggle when there is not a clear understanding of the purpose of the meeting. Meetings that are strictly held for the sake of meeting and because of historical reasons and where the team lacks a common and recognized purpose for the meeting rarely add value to the organization or to the individual members. This type of meeting can be discouraging to members of the team and experience problems with attendance and participation.

Figure 14.2
Worksheet: Weekly Planner

To: _____

Sales Professional: _____   Week of: _____

Day / Date	Client or Prospect	Location	Purpose of Contact	Type of Call*
Monday _____ _____ _____ _____ _____				
Tuesday _____ _____ _____ _____ _____				
Wednesday _____ _____ _____ _____ _____				
Thursday _____ _____ _____ _____ _____				
Friday _____ _____ _____ _____				
Central Support Needed:				

*P = Personal Visit; T = Telephone Call; E = e-mail

234

Figure 14.3
Worksheet: Contact Record Card

Name of Organization	Phone	Call back dates	
	Fax		
Location / Address	Email		

Contact People	Phone	Fax	Email

Products and Services of this Organization

Record of Products Furnished to this Organization

Date	Date

Record of Visits

Date	Contact	Purpose/Goal	Actions Required

The proper scheduling of meetings can have a strong impact on attendance and participation. It is rarely possible to schedule a meeting that perfectly suits all members of the team. However, planning meetings at times that are least burdensome to the majority of the team members is critical. Meeting times should not conflict with particularly heavy client contact times or other regularly scheduled meetings. An agenda should be created for each meeting that at least guides the start and stop times of the meeting and provides a framework for the amount of time devoted to the activities or issues identified as the focus of the meeting. Building in some open time for new items, unfinished business, or general discussion is also important.

When identifying meeting space it is important that the size of the space reflect the membership of the team. Cramped or crowded meeting space can create unnecessary distractions and in some cases even contribute to disagreements or conflicts. Access to necessary equipment, data, or network lines and even restrooms should be considered when selecting space. Team members must also be realistic in recognizing the realities of an organization's facilities and the need for space by other groups.

Each meeting requires a team leader to convene the meeting and clarify the purpose of the meeting. In some cases this person also plays the role of facilitator while in other more formal settings the leader is responsible for content issues and providing insight into the mission for the group. The facilitator's role is process oriented. The facilitator should be the gatekeeper for the meeting, attempting to draw all participants into the meeting, summarizing key points and providing feedback, managing the agenda for time and focus, paying attention to group dynamics, and keeping the group focused on its core purpose. In some cases the facilitator also serves as the timekeeper or a volunteer from the team serves in this role.

The team leader should step forward at the conclusion of each meeting to summarize the activity and establish the time, location, and tentative agenda for the next meeting. A scribe should be appointed on a rotating basis or a volunteer may step forward to take on this responsibility for an extended period of time. The scribe records the notes or minutes of each meeting and is responsible for preparing them for distribution to all team members by the leader.

Meeting participants have an obligation to the organization and to other members to participate and contribute to the best of their ability. Each participant must take ownership in the success of the meeting and take personal responsibility for sharing ideas and pertinent information. Active listening, encouraging other participants, being prepared, and completing assignments are all important duties each participant in the team must accept. Meeting participants should also strive to resolve any disagreements or conflicts within the confines of the team meeting. Carrying grudges or hidden agendas are unproductive and potentially damaging activities. Team leaders and facilitators should work to have all team members take ownership in all recommendations and decisions and provide visible support.

For sales professionals the ability to lead and participate in effective meetings can add value to the entire organization. Meeting-management skills can also be transferred over to larger client-sales meetings.

Critical Situation: Participating in Client Meetings— Contributing to Performance Improvement

Situation: Many of our sales professionals are trained facilitators and experienced participants in all types of teams and committees. One of the value-adding services we provide to our clients is we offer to participate in and sometimes help out with the facilitation of their performance-improvement work teams. These are multidisciplinary teams that can have doctors, nutritionists, bankers, and accountants on them. The different backgrounds certainly add spice to the meetings in bringing such diverse experiences and interests. At the beginning of almost every one of the teams I have helped with you can see everyone jockeying around for position and trying to figure out what everyone else is trying to accomplish. But after a few meetings people usually get settled in and start to trust each other and then we can really help the client out with solving problems, working out difficult situations, and analyzing opportunities. We participate in these meetings because they can really help the client and in the long run if they are successful we are successful. The days of just going in and giving a sales pitch and dumping a bunch of products on someone are gone. Everyone is looking at salespeople and saying "How can you help us be profitable?" and "What are the value-added services your organization can provide beyond your product?"

Development Issues: Skills that on the surface may appear unimportant for sales professionals can surface as valuable assets and allow sales professionals to create a strong nontraditional value proposition for their clients. By participating in advisory team meetings this sales professional is able to confirm his or her larger scale value to the client beyond just being able to provide a product or service to meet a need that any number of competitors could fulfill. Relationships are important in the sales process but many clients are focused on how you and your product add value to their organization.

Action Tips:
- Learn and practice team facilitation skills. Recognize the many different ways of creating value-added services for clients.
- Volunteer to participate in client performance or process-improvement meetings.
- Practice preparing agendas for client meetings and providing summary reports to your sales organization and clients.

ARE YOUR SALES PROFESSIONALS ABLE TO CONDUCT MEETINGS USING THE WEB AND VIDEO CONFERENCING?

The use of video conferencing for the delivery of educational events, company meetings, or client contacts began over ten years ago. Initially much of the technology was complex and expensive, with the quality of the video grainy and delays of the audio transmission of a second or two common. Many universities were early adopters looking at the technology as a mechanism to reach location-bound students. Larger corporations also looked at video conferencing as a mechanism for linking employees distributed across the world. The cost of video conferencing technology has dropped significantly in the last few years and the quality of both the video and audio has improved dramatically. Video capabilities available through the Web are seeing constant innovation as lower-cost solutions are appearing through a variety of vendors.

Video conferencing is an effective medium for reaching large numbers of people to deliver a personal message and to accept questions and have a discussion. In a training setting, video conferencing is working to support other Web-based learning activities. On-line learning continues to be one of the hottest issues in discussions on the delivery of training.

Using video conferencing, whether it is through the Web or a traditional phone connection, to interface with a potential or current client, can be positive or it can quickly destroy the chance of a sale. As emphasized in earlier chapters premeeting planning and preparation are critical in face-to-face encounters and equally (if not more important) for non–face-to-face encounters with clients. Sales professionals should not attempt any type of real-time meetings with clients until they are comfortable with the technology and have practiced using the technology with internal colleagues. If the technology is a distraction or becomes the focus of the meeting then the sales professional can quickly be perceived as wasting the potential client's time.

Use the following checklist to consider when you evaluate using video conferencing for client meetings.

☐ Is the client comfortable at their end with the technology and will they have the technical support they need?

☐ Is it clear to both parties that using video conferencing is the most efficient way to have the meeting?

☐ Is there a clear purpose and agenda for the meeting that meets the needs of the client and the sales professional?

☐ Does the sales professional have a script or plan to guide their presentation and have they rehearsed?

☐ Is the sales professional up to speed on the technology and is the technology ready to go for the meeting?

☐ Has the room being used for the meeting been reserved and is it cleared of distractions?

☐ If the meeting goes across time zones has it been clearly established when the meeting would begin?

☐ Does the client have all of the information needed for the meeting well in advance?

☐ If graphics and support materials are being used have they been tested for readability?

☐ Do sales professionals understand how they appear on video and the impact of certain clothing colors on their appearance?

❑ Does the sales professional understand how hand movements and facial expressions can distract the audience from the presentation?

❑ Does the sales professional understand how off-camera discussions and sidebars can be distracting and offend clients?

Video conferencing can be a time- and money-saving way for sales professionals to make contact with potential clients or stay in contact with current clients. In cases where the clients may be international or in remote parts of the United States video conferencing can allow sales professionals to move beyond telephone conference calls and bring a more personal touch to the relationship. The client's potential value to the organization should ultimately be a key driving factor in determining if video conferencing is an adequate format for the sales call or if a face-to-face call is warranted. For sales organizations that utilize video conferencing in their sales contact process, ongoing training should be included as a part of the sales training program.

DO YOUR SALES PROFESSIONALS UNDERSTAND PRODUCTIVITY METRICS AND THE CONCEPT OF BREAK-EVEN ANALYSIS?

By understanding productivity metrics and the concept of break-even point analysis sales professionals can appreciate the importance of controlling expenses for each product or service they sell and the impact upon organizational profitability. The break-even point is the level of sales needed by the organization to balance out and cover operating expenses. Break-even is the level of financial activity where the organization is not losing money or making a profit. By understanding where the break-even point is organizations can then determine what level of sales they need to meet profitability goals.

To determine the break-even point organizations must first analyze their expenses and break them down into fixed costs (expenses that do not change in connection with sales volume such as loan payments and rent) and variable costs (expenses that change based on the amount of sales volume such as the cost of raw materials or sales bonuses). There are also some expenses that don't fit neatly in either category and that is when it may be appropriate to turn to the organization's accountant for insight into how these costs should be assigned.

Once the total amount of expenses has been broken down into the appropriate fixed or variable category, the ratio of variable expenses per dollar of sales volume can be determined (total sales ÷ variable expenses), then the contribution margin is determined. The contribution margin is the amount of each sales dollar left after variable expenses to cover fixed costs and profit for the owners or stockholders.

By understanding how a break-even analysis is conducted sales professionals can better grasp why sales volumes must be established at certain levels.

Sales goals should be created from a realistic analysis of the organization's potential markets and reflect the financial realities of the break-even analysis. Sales professionals who understand the impact of variable expenses on the calculation of break-even can be more inclined to participate in their control and reduction. Information pertaining to profit volume can be expressed graphically. A common graph used to determine profit volume is the two-variable graph. The two-variable graph consists of a horizontal X axis and a vertical Y axis. The Y axis represents sales and expenses in dollars. The X axis shows the number of units sold. In the two-variable graph, the break-even point (BEP) is determined where the "total sales" and "total expenses" lines intersect. The "total expenses" line begins at the "fixed expenses," whereas the "total sales" line begins at zero, which is the number of sales. Until they intersect at the break-even point, the "total expense" line is above the "total sales" line; thus, the area between the two lines below or left of the BEP represents loss. The area between the two lines above or right of the BEP represents profit.

Obviously productivity metrics vary from organization to organization. Ask your accounting and/or finance group to prepare an overview seminar for your sales organization focused on the metrics important to your organization. The following is a list of common tools for measuring sales productivity.

Sales Time Productivity = Dollar Sales Volume ÷ Time Period

Sales Call Productivity = Dollar Sales Volume ÷ Number of Calls

Average Sales Order Size = Dollar Sales Volume ÷ Number of Orders

Average Sales Call Cost = Selling Expense ÷ Number of Calls

Average Sales Order Cost = Selling Expense ÷ Number of Orders

Average Sales Call Rate = Number of Calls ÷ Actual Sales Days

Sales Call Attainment Rate = Planned Calls ÷ Completed Calls

Sales Call Success Rate = Number of Calls ÷ Number of Orders

Sales Account Cost Ratio = Selling Expense ÷ Number of Active Accounts

Average Travel Mile Rate = Travel Miles ÷ Number of Calls

Average Travel Time Rate = Travel Time ÷ Number of Calls

Critical Situation: Managing Relationships—Performance Metrics

Situation: As coowner of a franchise retail business located in a regional mall, prospecting and managing customer relationships are responsibilities expected of our sales professionals. A large portion of our sales are with repeat customers, therefore we try to keep them satisfied and grow the relationships. Performance realities and the success of our salespeople is sometimes complicated since a lot depends on the time of day, the particular day of the week, and, of course, seasonal fluctuations. This makes it difficult to track the true performance of various salespeople. Therefore, in order to level the playing field we have developed a number of measures to track performance. One metric we implemented is to track dollar sales per hour segmented by three different product categories. As part of our sales-management process a second metric that we track is multiple sales per customer. This indicates whether in fact sales professionals are offering multiple products during the sales encounter. In addition, a third metric we track is referrals. We ask existing customers for referrals as part of our normal selling process and the number of referrals per hour and per month is documented. This too, is a method of prospecting for new customers. Obviously when our store is busy, dollar sales per hour should be high and those sales activities take precedence. However, we also track as a fourth metric "number of follow-up phone calls" our salespeople make per hour and per month as an added responsibility of the salesperson. We have a sliding-scale bonus system whereby the higher dollar per sales per hour the higher the bonus, so there is definitely an incentive for our salespeople to achieve sales goals while at the same time working to cultivate new business and maintain important relationships with existing customers. We offer various special rewards and incentives for salespeople with the best customer relationship performance.

As another customer relationship and prospecting approach, we expect salespeople to prepare informal networking presentations and ask that they conduct miniseminars once per month with targeted audiences. We give a flat bonus for each seminar conducted and a special reward for those with the highest number of presentations per month. We report sales performance weekly and salespeople know where they stand in relation to their team members.

Development Issues: Up-selling and asking for referrals is an effective method of growing client relationships as well as an effective prospecting approach when integrated into the normal selling process. Training and observation combined with ongoing coaching is effective. In addition, a mentoring arrangement can naturally be established when sales professionals know where they stand and have the opportunity to observe superior sales performance.

Action Tips:
- Ask exemplary salespeople to share their effective best practices and serve as mentors.
- Implement metrics that encourage add-on sales and capturing of referrals.

DOES YOUR ORGANIZATION SPONSOR PROGRAMS TO HELP SALES PROFESSIONALS MANAGE CALLS, TIME, AND SALES TERRITORIES?

Where should you start in helping sales professionals manage calls, time, and sales territories? Consult the following checklist of developmental strategies to build competence in this area. Then use the sample outline to help build the competence of your sales professionals in this area.

❐ Maintain a "To Do" list either in written or electronic form and distribute to sales professionals.

❐ Prioritize clients according to sales potential and plan frequency and types of ongoing contact.

☐ Create an annual travel planning calendar to encourage thoughtful travel planning and appropriate frequency of face-to-face client interactions.

☐ Make friends with your local librarian to help identify sources of information related to prospecting and forecasting activities.

☐ Establish a format or template for preparation of sales forecasts and budgets.

☐ Communicate the methods, procedures, and organization-specific policies related to travel and required reporting.

☐ Conduct an annual informational session between your sales professionals and accounting and/or finance.

A Sample Program Outline to Guide Managing Calls, Time, and Sales Territory

Title: Knowledge of Clients and Business

Competency Dimension: Managing calls, time, and sales territory

Learning Objectives:
- Demonstrate setting sales goals
- Practice organizing and planning schedules
- Demonstrate process for setting priorities for sales calls to clients
- Able to manage own time and travel efficiently

Potential Content Topics:
- Essentials of sales
- Time and territory management
- Managing multiple priorities
- Time management
- Managing the telephone and e-mail
- Managing meetings
- Understanding risk priority
- Overview of financial management
- Budgeting, costing, and break-even analysis
- Finance for the nonfinancial manager
- Understanding costs and budgets

15

Providing Service and Managing Client Relationships

Salespeople face increased competition as well as growing expectations for the added value they can bring to their clients. Providing service and managing client relationships have become critical to the long-term success of sales professionals. Sales professionals are on the front lines to establish and maintain a reputation for offering exemplary customer service. Today most organizations are looking for a competitive advantage, and many find it by improving operational processes or efficiencies in delivering services. Sales quality includes effective customer service that is linked to the sales process. Important foundations for taking client management actions stem from making it easy to do business with the organization, regularly assessing and acting on client satisfaction levels, and determining why clients stay or leave.

This chapter focuses on providing service and managing client relationships. To demonstrate that competency effectively, sales professionals should

- actively seek internal and external client input
- ensure client needs are met
- continuously seek to improve the quality of services, products, and processes
- provide follow-up in a professional manner

What are the development needs of your sales professionals for providing service and managing client relationships? See Figure 15.1 to see how the respondents to our survey rated the relative importance of the behaviors associated with this competency. Then reflect on how you would rate sales professionals in your organization.

Now fill out the self-assessment as it applies to you and your organization.

Self-Assessment:
Providing Service and Managing Client Relationships

Directions: With your sales organization in mind, place a number on the line in the left column below that matches your level of agreement with each statement. Then add up the numbers and score your assessment.

Disagree									Agree
1	2	3	4	5	6	7	8	9	10

____Your sales professionals understand the need for a total team effort to provide high-quality service to clients.

____Everyone in your organization focuses on creating positive client interactions.

____Everyone in your organization focuses on listening to and understanding client needs.

____All the members of your sales organization understand the importance of positive and courteous face-to-face and phone communication.

____Everyone in your organization understands the impact of dissatisfied clients.

____Your sales professionals and other members of your organization know how to handle dissatisfied clients.

____Your organization's performance management system includes customer or client service as a performance factor.

____Your sales professionals are able to deal with change in a positive manner.

____All of your sales professionals demonstrate a base level of computer literacy appropriate to your organization.

____Your organization sponsors programs to help provide service and manage client relationships.

____Total

How Did You Score?

Here is the key to providing service and managing client relationships. Add up your responses to get your score.

91–100 Great job! Congratulations! Your organization is effectively working to provide service and manage client relationships.

81–90 Keep up the good work! You've probably had considerable success. But by using some of the tips in this chapter, you could improve your success.

71–80 Help is needed! There's room for improvement. You'll find this chapter helpful.

0–70 Warning! Your sales organization probably has some confusion. Read on!

Once you have completed the self-assessment, use the following worksheet to organize your thinking about ways of building this competency among sales professionals in your organization.

Figure 15.1
Behaviors Related to the Competency of Providing Service and Managing Client Relationships as Rated by Survey Respondents

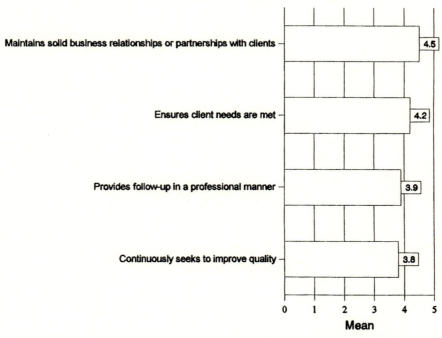

Source: From *A Survey about Sales Training Programs* by W. Rothwell, W. Donahue, and J. Park, 2001 (unpublished survey results), University Park, PA: Pennsylvania State University. Copyright 2001 by W. Rothwell, W. Donahue, and J. Park.

A Worksheet to Organize Your Thinking about Providing Service and Managing Client Relationships

Directions: In your opinion, what problems or challenges does your sales organization face in providing service and managing client relationships? Use this worksheet to organize your thinking about how to answer this question.

Notes:

DO YOUR SALES PROFESSIONALS UNDERSTAND
THE NEED FOR A TOTAL TEAM EFFORT TO PROVIDE
HIGH QUALITY SERVICE TO CLIENTS?

High-quality customer service requires a team effort. In high-performing organizations it is clear that customer service is everyone's job and that the delivery of high-quality customer service creates long-lasting sustainable relationships that benefit both the client and the organization providing the product or service. Clients are searching for vendors or suppliers who provide more than a product; they are looking for a relationship that provides value through the support and service that goes with the product. Organizations across the country and around the world are asking themselves the question "How can we provide service and deliver value that goes beyond that of our competition?" High-quality customer service means understanding what business issues are important to the client and being an expert in product and industry knowledge. Moving the concept of quality service from the discussion stage to an ongoing reality as part of the organization's culture requires that the organization develop a clear vision and shared understanding of how everyone in the organization needs to work together to identify and meet the needs of each client.

Excellent customer service teams are able to make clients feel special and to identify what clients really needs to help them succeed. It is easy to forget that the reason businesses exist is because of their customers and the purchases they make. Clients can quickly pick up on when there is tension or dissatisfaction among sales professionals and others involved in client contact efforts. Teams that interact with each other as if they were the customers of the other members of the team develop a positive and professional environment that sends a clear message to clients that we are here to work with you to deliver seamless service and support.

Seemingly small details such as how a coworker's absence from the work unit is explained can send a positive or negative message to a client. For example, "She's left work early again," versus, "She's out of the office until tomorrow, can I leave her a message that you called and have her call you back first thing in the morning?" Or an example of how the wrong delivery of information to a client can create problems: "I know they were having some problems with your project, my guess is they will be lucky to get it done on time," versus, "I know they have been working hard on your project, let me have Sue get back to you with an update." Respecting the privacy of coworkers and not providing inaccurate or poorly timed information on a project are parts of being a professional and go a long way toward creating a trusting and positive environment among coworkers. The following is a checklist of key activities your sales professionals need to avoid. As an awareness activity, ask them to review the list and add any additional activities your team should refrain from doing.

☐ Discussing organizational or team problems in public areas where coworkers or clients could overhear the conversation

☐ Speaking negatively about other team members or blaming problems on specific team members to a client

☐ Providing incomplete or inaccurate client information to other team members

☐ Conducting personal conversations in front of a client or using the phone for personal conversations while a client waits

☐ Becoming involved in disagreements or conflicts with other team members in front of a client

☐ Others:

All teams go through cycles. At times, everything is running smoothly. At other times, everything and everyone are stressed out.

Consider the following situation. Note the developmental issues and action tips provided at the end of that situation as key points for helping sales professionals cultivate their talents.

Critical Situation: Customer Service—Corporate Curriculum

Situation: As a large retail sales organization we developed our own corporate university. Most of the curriculum is focused on how to serve our clients better. Good client service starts by first hiring the right people. First of all we screen potential sales representatives with a personality profile. Our process begins when a particular recruit wants to fill out an application. We first have her sit at a terminal and complete some basic information as well as a series of personality profile-focused questions. Then, depending on how the particular person scored and other information, we would invite them to come back for an interview. If hired, all new employees go through a one-day orientation program focused on our store operations as they relate to providing exceptional service. This customer service activity incorporates a number of different components. We have a specific training area designated in each of our store locations and while some stores vary on the products and services offered there are four basic components offered in all of them. We have our stores segmented into four basic client service processes: Hard lines; soft lines; front; back. For each of these areas we have a specific CD and connection with our intranet to offer one-hour orientation sessions on each area. Each CD or intranet course incorporates video vignettes of particular client service issues and appropriate responses as well as testing features at the end of each session, whereby new employees would first complete the CD module then would spend an hour on the floor applying or observing what they had learned. Next we would follow to the next section of the store, complete the CD on the orientation to the operations methods and procedures and again, hands-on training and orientation at the store level. We would continue this throughout the day, covering the four basic sections of the store. Obviously, some stores have special features such as a snack bar, drug store, and so forth. For these particular areas we have additional CDs covering them. After the initial orientation, over the next two-week period we ask new hires to view a specific targeted CD on a topic list each day so that they can become more fully integrated into our system. Such topical areas include safety, theft, Americans with disabilities, sexual harassment, as well as a number of specific department related courses such as how to inspect food products. Our superior customer service has not occurred by accident. We have a process in place to try and hire the right people and train them appropriately in our expected methods and procedures.

Development Issues: In order to hire and recruit the people right for your organization, you must first look at the skills and competencies that are important to that particular job function. Then outline what specific duties and tasks they are to perform and design appropriate training to accomplish your goal.

Action Tips:
• Create customized job profiles of critical jobs and processes in your organization.
• Create an orientation curriculum for each major job category.

DOES EVERYONE IN YOUR ORGANIZATION FOCUS ON CREATING POSITIVE CLIENT INTERACTIONS?

Without clients few organizations would exist. However, many organizations fail to acknowledge or recognize this factor and it is easy to slip into an atmosphere where employees have the feeling that clients are an intrusion or an inconvenience. The importance of positive client interactions can be taken for granted.

One way to help ensure that client interactions are consistently positive is to establish a set of standards or guidelines that frames up how positive interactions are defined and what they look like. Creating a framework for client interactions reduces the opportunity for misunderstandings on how quality client interactions are defined and reduces the chance that an individual employee's moods or own interpretation comes into play. Standards are not a set of rules that are used by managers to punish employees; rather standards should be the benchmark for the level of service the organization's clients expect. Client interactions occur rapidly and there is little margin for error. Clients' perceptions of how they are being treated occurs within seconds and if that first impression is negative it will be hard to overcome. Many customer-focused organizations have established standard operating procedures to guide their performance. A checklist of selected standard operating procedures is offered:

☐ A person, not a machine, will answer all phones.
☐ All phones will be answered within three rings.
☐ No one will be placed on hold for more that twenty seconds.
☐ Offices should be open and covered during all hours of operation.
☐ All voice mail messages should receive a reply within twenty-four hours.
☐ The technical support line will be covered twenty-four hours per day, seven days a week.
☐ Others:

Please ask your sales professionals to review the list and add additional procedures or guidelines your organization should consider adopting.

Standard operating procedures or guidelines need to be related to key business areas that are important to the organization's clients and be clearly understood by everyone in the organization. Creating standards that are unrealistic or are not followed by everyone in the organization is meaningless. When analyzing the organization to determine where and when standards could be helpful some questions to ask are

- What factors about our organization are most important to our clients?
- What are the key measures of success for our organization?
- In what customer-contact areas do we have employee turnover issues?
- What type of rewards do our employees receive for outstanding customer service?
- For what products or services do we receive the most client compliments?

Creating meaningful standards related to client interactions can take time and effort and, if not carefully thought through and designed, create negative feelings with employees and have little or no positive impact on the organization's ability to serve their clients. For standards to have a positive impact on client interactions they must be focused on areas of the organization that are important to clients and have an impact on whether they remain clients. For standards to improve customer service they must become ingrained into the organization's culture and measured in some way as part of the performance management system. Employees who meet or exceed service standards must be recognized and rewarded.

DOES EVERYONE IN YOUR ORGANIZATION FOCUS ON LISTENING TO AND UNDERSTANDING CLIENT NEEDS?

Allowing clients to vent their frustrations and provide feedback on a problem does not mean the sales professional is actively listening and trying to understand the client. Listening is not just pausing from talking to take a rest while the other people involved in the conversation take their turn to talk. Listening is the foundation of all successful sales calls and critical to the resolution of any customer complaints. If the sales professional has not heard and understood the client's problem or complaint then the likelihood of being able to resolve the problem is minimal.

Listening to and understanding clients can be difficult and challenging. Clients can present distorted, incomplete, and inaccurate information about an issue and it is up to the sales professional to sort through the information and ask follow-up questions that allow them to get to the root cause of the problem. Product and process knowledge is also critical in the understanding of client needs and problems. Sales professionals must have an accurate understanding of the product or process being described by the client if they are to understand the need and work with the client to resolve the situation. The sales professional must also have an understanding of the client's business and the application of the product or service prompting the discussion. The sales professional or customer contact person's focus must be on the client and they must work to understand the situation from the client's perspective. Listening is a participative activity that requires skill and practice.

Client needs are changing and fluid in nature. What is perceived as outstanding customer service today can quickly become the expected and taken for granted. Client needs must be understood and appropriate responses created by sales professionals and other client support personnel in an efficient and timely manner.

Critical Situation: Client Service—Thank You Notes Can Help

Situation: I missed it! I don't know how it happened, maybe I was daydreaming, maybe I was just tired or I had slipped into my old habit of thinking about what I was going to say next and I zoned out. Whatever happened, the meeting ended and he thought he had provided me with more than enough information to solve his problems and allow us to keep the competition on the outside looking in. But as I drove home I realized I didn't have a clue about what he expected different from us. I went back and reviewed all of the questions I had prepared and realized that somehow I had gotten off track and after one or two questions the client started telling stories and I fell into a passive listening mode. In the past it has always been the same old thing only packaged a little bit differently. I could tell from the tone of his voice when we wrapped up the conversation that this was different and we needed to think this through and respond appropriately. Well, it was embarrassing but I didn't seem to have any choice. I gave him a call and told him I was still a little unclear about his expectations and could we go through the project again. Needless to say he wasn't very happy and he was pretty short in his descriptions but I got him to go through it again over the phone and this time I asked all the right questions and got a real good handle on what his needs were and how they were changing. As an impulse I decided to write a "thank you" card to the client for being so understanding. I can't believe the impact that note has had on our relationship. In several subsequent meetings he has referred to how nice it was to receive the note from me. Needless to say, I now regularly send out such notes and set aside a half hour each week devoted to thanking those that deserve some special recognition.

Development Issues: Identifying and understanding client needs is not easy but essential to developing long-term relationships. It is easy to become complacent or distracted and not focus on the client. Successful sales professionals recognize the importance of understanding needs and developing a disciplined systematic approach for understanding needs. Sales professionals who are careless about identifying needs will face difficulties in developing long-term client relationships.

Action Tips:
- Establish a routine process for obtaining input from clients and other stakeholders relating to the performance of your sales professionals.
- Treat lack of client input as warning signs.

- Provide all sales professionals with professionally printed "thank you" cards and ask that they set aside time to write several each week.

DO ALL THE MEMBERS OF YOUR SALES ORGANIZATION UNDERSTAND THE IMPORTANCE OF POSITIVE AND COURTEOUS FACE-TO-FACE AND PHONE COMMUNICATION?

There are several common-sense types of behaviors that when used go a long way toward making a positive first impression. However, based on personal observations and discussions with numerous groups it is apparent that there is a problem in many organizations with understanding the importance of a positive first encounter.

It is critical that every time clients come in to an office or any place of business that they be greeted with a smile and an appropriate greeting, "Good morning" or "Good afternoon," followed with the employee giving the client his or her name and asking the critical question, "How may I help you?" First impressions are critical and the client will quickly create a perception of the organization based on this initial contact. Factors such as how the person making the initial contact is dressed, his or her friendliness, professionalism, and ability to provide appropriate information and cleanliness of work area are all taken into consideration. Each of these customer service factors contributes to the clients' first impression. Sales professionals set the tone for positive customer service in their organizations. By understanding the impact they have and the importance of modeling positive and appropriate behaviors sales professionals can set the tone for the entire customer contact team. Excellent customer service positions an organization in a positive manner against the competition even if there is little or no difference in the products or services they deliver.

In many ways effective telephone communications is similar to effective face-to-face communications. When answering the phone, sales professionals or customer service persons should always identify themselves to the client and then follow up with a positive and pleasant "How may I help you?" There is considerable evidence that suggests that people who smile when they are talking on the phone come across as much more positive and customer friendly. First impressions are again critical in the interaction with the client. Answering the phone promptly and being able to use the features on the phone such as the hold button and the transfer key can help prevent potential problems. Clients will usually forgive what they believe is an honest mistake or miscommunication, but when it is accompanied by rudeness or a perceived lack of caring clients have little patience.

Critical Situation: Customer Service—They Know My Name

Situation: As a salesperson when I walk into places like retail stores or banks I am always watching and listening to how people deal with customers and how they try to sell things. I mean, let's face it; some banks used to have a history of giving mediocre customer service. On the other hand some of the larger retail chains have really focused on taking customer service to a new level and I believe it has helped them with their bottom lines. I am sure everyone has stories like this one but when you look at positive and negative customer experiences this example really makes you wonder. I stopped in early one morning at a branch office of a large bank. When I entered the lobby it was empty and there were no tellers at the windows. I looked around and saw three bank employees standing in front of a computer pointing and laughing. It was as if I was invisible. After what seemed like several minutes to me they kept watching the game and laughing. Finally I coughed a couple of times to get their attention and a young women came over to me and glared at me and asked if she could help me. Well, her attitude just added to my anger and after a couple of minutes I said "No, on second thought you can't help me" and left the bank. The next day I closed my accounts and transferred my funds to another bank. I am sure that the bank didn't miss my small account. But I have made sure that I have told hundreds of other people about the bad customer service they have at that bank. Interestingly, the atmosphere at my new bank is completely the opposite. Obviously the importance of customer service has been stressed to them and is evident in everything they do. Every time I enter the bank one particular teller greets me by name.

Development Issues: Every business has a slip-up from time to time when something happens and a customer is not happy about the service received or the product purchased. However, the truly outstanding organizations are able to recover from such incidents in ways that leave customers' confidence in these organizations unshaken. However, if those slip-ups are not settled with the client in a favorable way, the client will be lost and, as in this case, will tell many people about the unsatisfactory experience.

Action Tips:
- Ask past clients why they stopped using your products or services.
- Ask your sales professionals what policies or procedures within your organization get in the way of serving clients.

DOES EVERYONE IN YOUR ORGANIZATION UNDERSTAND THE IMPACT OF DISSATISFIED CLIENTS?

There have been a variety of studies conducted that examined the number of people a dissatisfied client tells about their negative experience when purchasing a product or service—10 is a number that appears frequently. For example, in a retail store where every dissatisfied or angry customer that walks out the door tells an average of 10 other people about the negative experience, how significant is the impact of 5 unhappy customers per week? If the retail store is open fifty weeks per year that could mean there are 250 unhappy customers every year and if that group each tells 10 people 2,500 people during the course of one year will have heard negative or uncomplimentary comments about the store. Over the course of five years that group of people who have been contacted becomes 12,500. For comparison purposes, how much does the store spend on advertising each month, and how many new customers does it generate? What could be the lost opportunity cost in having 2,500 potential customers hear negative comments about the store each year and not consider even coming in to find out for themselves?

In business-to-business marketing and selling the impact can be debated. However, it is clear that the negative impact of a dissatisfied client does not end with only losing that client's current and future business. It is much more complex and the lost opportunities are much more significant. Being able to quantify the cost of losing clients can emphasize to employees the cost in real dollars of losing clients. Some questions to consider are

- How many dissatisfied clients do we have each week? Each month? Each year?
- What does it cost the organization to generate each new client?
- What does it cost to solve the typical customer complaints so they are positive about the experience?

A positive or outstanding client recovery from a negative situation can create a fan for life. In many cases a dissatisfied customer who has a problem resolved in a positive manner will share the story freely and become a long-term client.

Critical Situation: Customer Service—
Make Good on Promises or Pay the Consequences

Situation: I try to learn from other sales organizations as much as I can. One story I like to relate to sales professionals is the need to make good on promises or you will pay the price. My family wanted a new van and of course every member had something a little different in mind. My oldest son is quite the salesperson himself and managed to talk me into purchasing a van that was loaded to the hilt with features that were attractive to him and other members of the family, but not to me. He managed to overcome every objection I could deliver and the rest is history. However, upon signing the papers I mentioned to the owner of this very large car dealership that my son was the one to credit for the purchase, not me. The owner thanked my son and then asked, "Do you like college football games?" My son replied "yes," and the owner explained that he had season football tickets to the Penn State games and offered him tickets to a game of his choice. My son said he would call him the next day to reserve which game we wanted to attend. The next day he tried calling the owner of the dealership only to be met with "The owner is unavailable." Repeated calls met with the same response, so he sent a "thank you" note to the owner incorporating which game we wanted to attend. The owner never replied and never made good on his promises of the tickets. Needless to say, my son has never had a good word to say about the dealership and takes every opportunity to tell anyone in the market for a car not to shop at the dealership. Six years have since passed and I know my son has told hundreds of prospective buyers of his negative experience.

Development Issues: Good customer service is not rocket science. The golden rule applies, "Treat others the way you want to be treated." Establishing a consistent process for providing customer service and only promising what you can deliver is a good rule to follow.

Action Tips:

- Make good on all promises.
- Tickets to sporting or other events are a good mechanism to build customer relationships and allegiance.
- Treat others the way you want to be treated.
- You only get one chance to make a favorable first impression.

DO YOUR SALES PROFESSIONALS AND OTHER MEMBERS OF YOUR ORGANIZATION KNOW HOW TO HANDLE DISSATISFIED CLIENTS?

Angry and dissatisfied clients can be a difficult challenge that requires sales professionals or other members of the organization to be patient and to have control of their emotions. As we discussed earlier in the section on managing conflict it is critical that the sales professional listen and work through the problem with clients to develop a solution that satisfies their needs and, if possible, salvages the relationship.

Sales professionals must be constantly aware of not getting involved in the "blame game" where they blame themselves or blame others for the events causing the client to be upset or dissatisfied. Blaming statements such as "I wasn't working when it happened," "That's not my job," or "I didn't know I was supposed to do that" are nonproductive, unprofessional, and a waste of the client's time. Clients are not interested in excuses, whose fault it was, or all of the reasons why they did not receive the product or service they expected. Their biggest concern is what the sales professional will do to recover from the situation and solve the problem. Turning a negative into a positive should be the goal of the sales professional when working to resolve a dissatisfied client situation. Although clients may realize they cannot have everything they want, that does not prevent them from being upset or angry when they have to compromise. Presenting clients with alternatives and then allowing them to make a choice is one strategy that involves clients in the problem-solving process and allows them to have a sense that they have control of the situation. Some examples of phrases that can be used in that type of situation are "Would either of these solutions meet your needs?" "X is an alternative that others have found effective." "We can't do A, but we could B or you could try C." These are a few sample phrases that can be provided to sales professionals in a training program.

If "no" is the only alternative the sales professional has with the client, then how it is presented to the client can determine the future status of the relationship. A "no" that is not explained or is delivered in an uncertain or unprofessional manner will most likely assure that the sales relationship has ended. However, a "no" that is delivered in a professional manner with a reasonable explanation can be accepted and viewed as a limitation of the sales professional's organization, not a personal attack on the client. Blaming the "no" on a policy or either verbally or nonverbally giving the client the impression that the request was ridiculous or stupid will quickly end a relationship and guarantee no chance for future opportunities. In the case of a "no" it is critical that the "no" be clearly communicated so there is no chance of miscommunication or any false hope of a different response given to the client unless there is a possibility that the decision could be overturned. Stretching the decision out or giving the client false hope only increases the likelihood that the client will be upset with the answer. Promising more than you can deliver can be harmful. It is critical that the sales professional not commit to a solution that is beyond what the organization can or will provide. Promises made to the client should be delivered on.

In difficult situations with unhappy clients, the sales professional should strive to avoid becoming defensive, rather to look at the situation as an opportunity to solve a problem for the client. This is an opportunity for sales professionals to display professionalism and convey their self-confidence and ability to solve problems and provide value to clients beyond the product or service they purchased.

DOES YOUR ORGANIZATION'S PERFORMANCE MANAGEMENT SYSTEM INCLUDE CUSTOMER OR CLIENT SERVICE AS A PERFORMANCE FACTOR?

Most successful organizations, regardless of their size or type of business, have a performance-management system that allows managers and others in leadership roles to provide systematic performance feedback to their employees on a regular basis. Performance feedback can serve to motivate employees, improve job satisfaction, and clarify expectations about the required level of performance in their position.

The following is a checklist of typical factors included as measures of effectiveness in a performance-management system for sales professionals. Add other important measures that should be used to measure the performance of your sales professionals.

❏ Total sales generated
❏ Expenses-to-sales ratio
❏ Number of client contacts
❏ Quality of client communications
❏ Knowledge and adherence to company policies
❏ Safety
❏ Participation in teams
❏ Information sharing
❏ Client satisfaction survey results
❏ Others:

Performance-management systems should communicate very clear messages to sales professionals as to what the organization values and what is important in terms of how they will be recognized and rewarded. Incorporating performance standards into the evaluation process on client communications and client service communicates the importance of these factors to the success of the organization. Managers at all levels throughout the organization must have a true commitment to performance management for it to work. Performance reviews should occur on a regular basis.

During the initial stages of their involvement in the sales development program new sales professionals should receive detailed performance feedback on a monthly basis for the first six months to one year. Upon completion of this probationary period formal reviews should occur annually with informal performance feedback provided on a more frequent basis as appropriate.

ARE YOUR SALES PROFESSIONALS ABLE TO DEAL WITH CHANGE IN A POSITIVE MANNER?

Sales organizations are reinventing themselves on a regular basis. New approaches to the use of technology, changing expectations regarding performance, new and innovative ways to approach selling, increasing customer expectations, and changing corporate cultures that redefine organizational relationships are some of the developments occurring across the corporate landscape that sales professionals must deal with on a regular basis. Sales professionals must be able to adapt to these changes more as they deal with ambiguity within their own organizations and in their relationships with clients. Sales professionals must expect to be frustrated, stressed, and at times overcommitted as they push to meet and exceed their personal and organizational goals. How they are able to handle these situations and their resiliency in bouncing back from them can be influenced by the training and coaching they receive from their sales managers.

Patience is a behavior frequently linked with the ability to deal with change or adapt to a new position or responsibility. Developing patience and the ability to refrain from snap judgments or overreactions to a situation requires a careful examination of personal strengths, weaknesses, and values, and the acceptance of feedback from others. By recognizing when they are inclined to lose their patience and become upset or angry sales professionals can be proactive in their attempts to redirect this energy and turn it in a positive direction. One strategy is the use of self-statements such as "This is important, I need to take the time to listen and understand," or "This is not that important, it will be over soon." Self-talk can help the sales professional to be more accepting of the situation and to focus on the positive and not the negative. Sales professionals can also work to better understand a situation and why it may be more important to others than it is to them by forcing themselves to hold judgment on the situation and by using open-ended questions to encourage other people to explain their perspective and share their concerns or reservations. By avoiding an either–or perspective a situation can be turned from a win–lose event into a change that is given the opportunity to be adopted and succeed and, if need be, adapted or rethought during its implementation.

Sales professionals differ in what types of changes they are comfortable with and which ones create stress or anxiety. For some sales professionals adopting new technology causes stress; others struggle with changes in leadership or management while others may have difficulty with changes in market territory or market segments. By recognizing what types of change cause stress or have a negative impact on their performance sales professionals can identify strategies for more effectively influencing or adapting to the change. By objectively evaluating why the type of change causes problems the sales professional can look for ways to better adapt to the change either through training or coaching.

Sales managers frequently influence how well sales professionals accept change. A lack of understanding or clarity about a change can lead to inaction or resistance. Clear explanations of why a change must occur and the potential impact of the organization not changing can help to reduce uncertainty or resistance.

DO ALL OF YOUR SALES PROFESSIONALS DEMONSTRATE A BASE LEVEL OF COMPUTER LITERACY APPROPRIATE TO YOUR ORGANIZATION?

Dinosaurs still exist! There are still hold-outs in organizations that refuse to use e-mail or sit down in front of a computer to work on a budget spreadsheet or to create a memo. However, they are becoming fewer and fewer as each year goes by. Corporate culture and industry expectations have had a significant influence on the use of technology in organizations. The traditional secretarial support once provided by organizations for sales professionals is dying or gone in many organizations. Administrative support personnel are involved in duties such as collecting and analyzing client data or providing other types of postsales client support and follow-up. Many sales professionals are on their own and have little administrative support.

It is tempting to jump on board with every new piece of technology that is brought to market. However, early innovation can have its challenges. Innovative new technology typically has had a short life span before the second or third generations appear on the market in more streamlined forms and significantly less cost. The use of Personal Digital Assistants (PDAs) has increased rapidly over the past couple of years. The capabilities of the technology are changing on an almost continuous basis. Beginning primarily as a calendar tool and a database for phone numbers, addresses, and so forth, as well as brief notes that could be synchronized with a laptop or desktop computer, the PDAs are being transformed into tools capable of delivering more complex computer functions packaged with communications capabilities such as a phone, pager, or e-mail tool. Organizational applications and culture should drive the technology competencies required of sales professionals.

What productivity tools make sense for your organization? Ask your sales professionals to identify those tools that can make them more effective. Instead of making the typical mistake of purchasing the latest and greatest, establish pilot initiatives and try before you buy.

DOES YOUR ORGANIZATION SPONSOR PROGRAMS TO HELP PROVIDE SERVICE AND MANAGE CLIENT RELATIONSHIPS?

Where should you start in your quest to help sales professionals in your organization to help provide service and manage client relationships? Consult the following checklist of developmental strategies to build competence in this area.

☐ Survey your clients and try to understand their points of view.

☐ Demonstrate interest in your clients by using active-listening techniques and responding positively.

☐ Help clients deal realistically with business opportunities and help them translate ideas into specific project plans.

☐ Enjoy the diversity of dispositions of your clients; capitalize on the diversity by thinking of ways in which each individual's unique talents and preferences can be drawn into the sales process.

☐ Take time to speak informally with clients. Show an interest in their families, goals, hobbies, and concerns. Share some of your personal interests with them.

☐ Create occasions to celebrate client achievements and to enjoy each other's company.

Now use this plan to help build the competence of your sales professionals in enhancing ongoing client and stakeholder informational processes.

A Sample Program Outline to Guide Providing Service and Managing Client Relationships

Title: Knowledge of Clients and Business

Competency Dimension: Providing service and managing client relationships

Learning Objectives:
• Demonstrate ability to actively seek internal and external client input.
• Document how client needs are met.

- Describe the process needed to continuously improve quality of products and services.
- Describe how to provide follow-up in a professional manner.

Potential Content Topics:
- Managing client relationships
- Customer service
- Job redesign and rotation for superior client service
- Determine the needs and motivations of others
- Interpersonal communication, awareness, and effectiveness
- Effective call management
- Managing change
- Managing with information technology
- Continuous service improvement

16

Developing New Products and Services and Managing Projects

Let's face it. Too often the sales function is relegated to low-level status. As a result, valuable client knowledge gleaned by salespeople has no channel to be fed back to market researchers, product developers, and market strategists. This valuable information can be lost unless a systematic process is established to collect and analyze it. Likewise, client complaints may serve as valuable opportunities for improvement and innovation, but the information is also lost without a systematic way to feed it back to key decision makers.

This chapter focuses on forging effective links between sales professionals and those responsible for developing new products and services. The chapter also examines the need for salespeople to manage projects effectively. The chapter reviews how sales professionals may apply important tools and concepts used in solving problems and managing projects.

To demonstrate the competency of developing new products and services and managing project, sales professionals should be able to

- develop insights and innovative solutions for developing new business
- foster creativity and new product development ideas among others
- coordinate and manage projects to achieve objectives

What are the development needs of your sales professionals for developing new products, services, and managing projects? Consult Figure 16.1 to see how the respondents to our survey rated the relative importance of the behaviors associated with this competency. Then reflect on how you would rate sales professionals in your organization.

When you finish looking at Figure 16.1, complete the self-assessment as it applies to you and your organization. Once you have completed the self-assessment, use the worksheet appearing in Figure 16.3 to organize your thinking about ways of building this competency among sales professionals in your organization.

Self-Assessment: Developing New Products, Services, and Managing Projects

Directions: With your sales organization in mind, place a number on the line in the left column below that matches your level of agreement with each statement. Then add up the numbers and score your assessment.

Disagree									Agree
1	2	3	4	5	6	7	8	9	10

_____Your organization has a process in place to collect client feedback on the need for new or adapted products or services.

_____Your sales professionals understand the importance of documenting new or different client needs that existing products or services do not meet.

_____All of your sales professionals understand the importance and cost of new-product development.

_____Your sales professionals are aware of the legal issues involved with new product development.

_____Your organization has a set of ethical standards for your sales professionals.

_____Your sales professionals understand their ethical commitment to clients.

_____All of your sales professionals collect and share information on new-product development activities of competitors.

_____Your sales professionals understand the steps in the project-management process and how project management is used within your organization.

_____Sales professionals in your organization understand and are able to use common project-management tools when managing teams or leading projects.

_____Your organization sponsors programs for developing new products, services, and managing projects.

_____Total

How Did You Score?

Here is the key to developing new products, services, and managing projects. Add up your responses to get your score.

91–100   Great job! Congratulations! Your organization is effectively working to develop new products and services and to manage projects.

81–90   Keep up the good work! You've probably had considerable success. But by using some of the tips in this chapter, you could improve your success.

71–80   Help is needed! There's room for improvement. You'll find this chapter helpful.

Figure 16.1
Behaviors Related to the Competency of Developing New Products,
Services, and Managing Projects as Rated by Survey Respondents

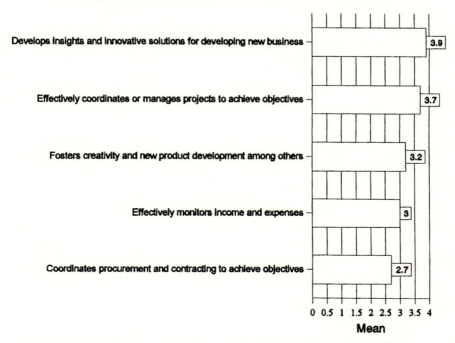

Source: From *A Survey about Sales Training Programs* by W. Rothwell, W. Donahue, and J. Park, 2001 (unpublished survey results), University Park, PA: Pennsylvania State University. Copyright 2001 by W. Rothwell, W. Donahue, and J. Park.

0–70   Warning! Your sales organization probably has some problems. Read on!

A Worksheet to Organize Your Thinking about Developing New Products, Services, and Managing Projects

Directions: In your opinion, what problems or challenges does your sale organization face in developing new products, services, and managing projects? Use this worksheet to organize your thinking about how to answer this question.

Notes:

DOES YOUR ORGANIZATION HAVE A PROCESS IN PLACE TO COLLECT CLIENT FEEDBACK ON THE NEED FOR NEW OR ADAPTED PRODUCTS OR SERVICES?

Sales professionals can be the catalysts for product or service changes in organizations. As the front-line contact with clients, sales professionals are uniquely positioned to be the eyes and ears of their organization. However, in many organizations this resource for product development ideas is underutilized or called upon on a very limited basis, as there is not a formal process in place to support information collection and review. The cost of developing new clients versus retaining existing clients was discussed in an earlier section of the book. Organizations that are able to identify and understand the impor- tance of working with current clients to meet new or developing needs can be out in front with new-product development. Careful analysis of data is re- quired to make decisions regarding the cost versus benefit of developing new products to address changing customer needs. But, if organizations do not work with sales professionals to formally collect and analyze the client-needs data, then they will not have the option to make choices about the financial viability of meeting a need. The organization will not know the need exists and the potential opportunity will be missed.

New-product client feedback forms could contain a checklist of information:

- ☐ A statement of the problem to be solved
- ☐ A description of the clients' perception of the need
- ☐ A description of how the new product could meet the need
- ☐ Potential features of the new product
- ☐ Other potential markets for the product, or organizations that could have similar needs
- ☐ How large the market could be for the product (primary and secondary markets)
- ☐ The existence of any similar products or competitors
- ☐ Approximate prices that the customer would pay for the product
- ☐ Potential distribution channels
- ☐ Others:

You may wish to add any other factors that you believe to be relevant for measuring the performance of sales professionals in your organization.

By providing the type of information outlined in the client feedback form sales professionals can influence and potentially speed up the new-product development process. Ultimately decisions must be made by managers in the organization about the potential new product's fit with the organization from a people, product, and a process perspective.

Critical Situation: New Product Development—The Big Ones

Situation: In my over thirty years of sales experience, I've had my share of opportunities. As I reflect on those opportunities, I realized that many times I was chasing the big ones, the big clients, the multimillion-dollar sales. And usually as a part of those activities—in attempting to maximize my face-to-face trips and visits—I would schedule those visits to the big clients first and fill in with other prospects, leading me down numerous back roads to dimly lighted, unassuming buildings or offices; most of which turned up as dead-end leads. However, in aggregate as I look over my thirty year history, few of the big clients actually produced big results. In fact, their playing musical chairs either in corporate takeovers or in restructurings was very frustrating. It seems that by the time you develop relationships within a big client they leave and the relationships are gone and you have to start all over again. However, the big ones for me were really some of those trips down the back roads. As I reflect on my successful sales, I can point to half-a-dozen major clients that I've secured for our organization all of which were entrepreneurial folks who I helped to meet their needs and fulfill or solve a problem that they had. All of these problems were in essence miniprojects to me, and I considered them fun. Using a typical project-management format, this involved defining the scope of what it was that they really wanted to do, looking for alternative solutions, gathering data and information on their particular need and situation, working with them to analyze the details and facts, developing alternative methods and processes for which we outlined what resources would be needed, and finally recommending which course of direction to follow and execute. Of course, in dealing with these folks there's no bureaucracy. We knew who the decision maker was and they made decisions that resulted in not only successful projects for them but sustained business for me. I mentioned that all these folks were entrepreneurial; but that doesn't mean that they are entrepreneurs who own their own companies—they could be purchasing agents or technical people within organizations but in all cases, they are the people making the decision on whether the project goes or doesn't go.

Development Issues: A key in managing client relationships is to determine the decision maker. Once the decision maker is ascertained, frame up his or her request into miniprojects and follow a formalized project management process. The objectivity of this should clearly outline the needed resources and scope of your activities as well as the resources needed by clients to produce the results and performance they desire.

Action Tips:
- Encourage sales professionals to develop friendships within client organizations that serve as listening ports as to what is happening.
- Follow a formalized project management process and establish templates in your organization to aid your sales professionals.

DO YOUR SALES PROFESSIONALS UNDERSTAND THE IMPORTANCE OF DOCUMENTING NEW OR DIFFERENT CLIENT NEEDS THAT EXISTING PRODUCTS OR SERVICES DO NOT MEET?

Taking ideas from the discussion stage to the development and delivery stage requires time and focus regardless of the size of the organization. In some cases, small organizations may be more nimble and able to respond more quickly to client needs than larger, more structured organizations. Sales professionals in smaller organizations can have the ability to walk in to the owner of the company and present opportunities and ideas.

Ideas for new products collected from clients can be broken down into needs, wants, and critical factors. The critical factors should be the key elements for new-product development. The needs are the factors that clients perceive they can't live without and will influence buying decisions, while the wants can be those fringe issues that aren't essential to the buying decision but fulfilling them can certainly influence decisions when all other factors are basically the same. Sales professionals can provide valuable insight that can help organizations to avoid building in product features that will not have any type of significant impact on buying decisions. It is essential that the new-product development team continue to go back to the critical factors, needs, and wants on a regular basis to validate the alignment between team efforts and the factors that were identified by the client. Sometimes simply repackaging or repositioning existing products will fit the bill. Independent focus groups can often help in looking at existing products in new and innovative ways.

Critical Situation: Developing New Products—
Inspiring Innovations

Situation: New-product development can be misunderstood and a big drain on an organization. I have seen several cases where a research and development project has led a management team down a primrose path. To me, as a person in charge of sales I like to think of it as innovations. Innovations are enhancing existing products and services in ways that allow you to capitalize on investments you've already made. I've found this to be very successful when working with companies and organizations whereby I take each of our existing products, look how we might change it and reconfigure it and present it to a new market area. In addition, we've looked at how to combine existing products and package them in multiple ways, in essence creating a whole new product. For example, walk around any wholesale-club store and you'll find that the existing products have been reconfigured in new ways to create essentially a whole new market and industry. The same is true for the financial services industry where you package multiple products together or in the real estate business where you package not only the sale of a home but the insurance that goes along with it. In order to generate ideas for developing new products we conduct focus groups with consumers and end users. It's very interesting; in a formalized focus group in which you're behind a one-way glass mirror and the folks giving input can't see you, they give input about your products and services and what might be done differently. It opens you to a whole new world of product development and opportunities for the future. We select our focus groups very carefully, balancing a blend of existing clients or customers with people on the fringe who could be potential users or people in related industries. We've been very successful.

Development Issues: Use focus groups to stimulate out-of-the-box thinking and look for enhancements or innovations that can adapt or change existing products for new product applications. Instill upon your sales professionals that no idea is a bad idea. Subscribe to the philosophy that for brainstorming, it's quantity not quality. You'll sift down the quality at a future date.

Action Tips:

- Conduct brainstorming sessions with your sales professionals for innovative ideas.
- Conduct focus groups of your clients and external constituents to give you an honest impression of your products and services and ideas for repositioning them in new markets.
- Repackage your products into multiple formats targeted at new markets.

DO YOUR SALES PROFESSIONALS UNDERSTAND THE IMPORTANCE AND COST OF NEW-PRODUCT DEVELOPMENT?

New and recreated products and services continue to appear and reappear on an ongoing basis. Businesses that are successful at bringing new products to market are able to analyze potential product markets and deliver the new concept to the marketplace in a timely manner. When mistakes occur and products don't perform to expectations they understand when to pull or re-think a product and examine what they can learn from the experience. Sales professionals continue to be an integral part of this process as they stay close to the customer and share their feedback. Early adopters deliver clear signals about their likes or dislikes of new products. Sales professionals are able to provide real-time market information that can allow new products to be adapted or changed to meet the demands of the marketplace.

Sales professionals typically do what they like and what they are rewarded and recognized for. If collecting and sharing client needs for new products is not recognized by the organization as an important task and responsibility for sales professionals then it will not happen. Sales professionals will channel their efforts in other directions that are rewarded.

Critical Situation: Developing New Products— Down the Primrose Path?

Situation: It seemed like the right thing to do at the time. But don't so many ideas that turn out as bad ones start out as good ones and then just unravel? We have been in business for about ten years and have really carved out two market niches that keep us busy and have really made us a fairly profitable little business. We have two salespeople out on the road plus the two of us who are the owners who also have always been involved in selling. The one salesperson is a real success and she has helped us to double our business in the past two years. Well, a few weeks ago she came in to my office with a big box and said "You've got to see this; it is just unbelievable what it will do." She was right. One of the big companies in our industry had come out with a version that did twice what our product could do. I couldn't believe it and as the engineer in the company I couldn't understand why we couldn't adapt our product to do everything that the new one could. I got started that day and twelve weeks later after days of little sleep and hundreds of hours of my time and the rest of the manufacturing department's we had a sleek new product that had all the features of the new one the sales professional had shared. There was one problem. No one bought the new product; they preferred the older, more simple model that we had been selling for years. When we asked them why they weren't buying the new product they told us "We like the new features but they are a lot more than we really need or are willing to pay for."

Development Issues: Sales professionals are always looking for that additional feature or product to meet their client needs. New-product development is a costly enterprise that can bankrupt a small organization if thorough market analysis and research is not conducted to confirm that developing the new product is the right thing to do and that sales of the product will be sustainable enough to warrant the investment and provide a return on investment.

Action Tips:

- Ask your clients for feedback before investing a lot in new-product development.
- Set challenging but realistic new-product development goals and deadlines.
- Document the scope and desired outcome of individual projects.
- Consider the strengths of each of your sales professionals and assign them to selected new-product development projects.

ARE YOUR SALES PROFESSIONALS AWARE OF THE LEGAL ISSUES INVOLVED WITH NEW-PRODUCT DEVELOPMENT?

There are many legal issues to be considered during the development or adaptation of new products and services. Sales professionals must be aware of the importance and impact of copyright, trademarks, and brand laws when reviewing printed materials or Web sites. In dealing with ideas or inventions patent issues must be considered. Patent laws govern how a new invention might be related to or infringe upon an existing idea that has been patented. Patent laws are constantly changing and individual cases are interpreted differently. Patent searches can be complex and time consuming. However, failure to examine similar processes or practices can result in significant delays as the result of court hearings or appeals.

Organizations must be aware of how they will respond to ideas or inventions created by employees. Legal counsel should guide policies regarding royalties or flat payment for ideas to employees. For example, with the rapid changes in technology and the biomedicine field there has been extensive litigation regarding intellectual property rights and the ownership of concepts and ideas. Sales professionals must be cautious in their collection and sharing of new ideas or concepts from clients. Discussions around these issues regarding rights and ownership should be referred to an internal contracts office or company legal counsel. Incorporating information on the legal aspects of new-product development into the sales development program can help to reduce opportunities for litigation. Consider asking your organization's legal council to conduct a miniseminar for your sales professionals on the legal aspects related to new-product development.

DOES YOUR ORGANIZATION HAVE A SET OF ETHICAL STANDARDS FOR YOUR SALES PROFESSIONALS?

Sales professionals are regularly presented with situations where they must make decisions with ethical implications. Ethics are the values and behaviors that guide a sales professional's decision making and client interactions. Much of an organization's position in the marketplace and its reputation in its community are determined by the types of decisions sales professionals make. Organizations that are guided by the principle of doing what is right regardless of what is most financially attractive are in a position to maintain a positive and trusted public image. However, it is not always an either–or situation where a business turns down an opportunity because of a potential ethical dilemma. In competitive situations where an organization's future is in jeopardy sales professionals and managers come under intense pressure to produce results and behaviors that at one time would not have been considered an option are suddenly considered. Unreasonable sales goals or pressure to make a profit can force sales professionals to lose sight of what is unethical behavior. In cases like this organizations may in fact knowingly or unknowingly condone unethical behavior by choosing to overlook or ignore the questionable behaviors completely.

Sales professionals must be trained to identify ethical situations where their decisions could have a significant impact upon the organization and its reputation and image. Many ethical situations are not clear right or wrong situations; rather, they are gray areas that could have impact beyond the immediate organization and affect stakeholders and clients.

Many organizations are establishing a set of ethical standards that provides a framework for decision making and serves to guide how employees react in specific situations. A code of ethics is a written set of expectations that describe the standards of behavior and ethical principles that guide day-to-day decision making and activities. The code of ethics should be developed to provide a set of guidelines that reflects the organization's environment and addresses the most common types of ethical dilemmas company employees could regularly face. The code of ethics should clearly communicate what is acceptable and unacceptable behavior. For a code of ethics to have an impact the code must be communicated and explained to all employees and modeled by the top-level managers and executives in the organization. In the case of ethical violations, organizations must be willing to take the appropriate disciplinary action. If the ethics code is only applied to specific situations or people then the ethics code exists only on paper and does not have any impact on the day-to-day decisions made in the organization. One leading business executive summed it up to his employees like this: "If you do something illegal or unethical, you are on your own!"

The following is a checklist that provides ethical questions to consider for your sales organization. Please add any other important factors that should by used for your sales professionals.

☐ Is the action legal according to the laws of the country you are operating in?

☐ If information about the activity appeared in the media would you be embarrassed and the organization's reputation damaged?

☐ Would this activity be something you would be proud to tell your family about?

☐ Would the president or owner of the company support you if he or she knew about the activity?

☐ Is what you say or write truthful and accurate to the best of your knowledge?

☐ Did you provide the complete story, even if some of the important details were not asked for?

☐ Could the decision endanger any employee's and/or client's safety or well being?

☐ What other issues, if any, should be considered to determine if the proposed action is ethical? (List them.)

DO YOUR SALES PROFESSIONALS UNDERSTAND THEIR ETHICAL COMMITMENT TO CLIENTS?

True sales professionals are able to balance the pressures of making the sale with the right thing to do for their customer. Sales professionals must recognize when there is a mismatch between the product they are selling and the needs of potential clients and be able to provide truthful, complete, and accurate information to clients so they can make the decision based on the complete package of information available. Sales made under circumstances where incomplete or inaccurate product information is communicated to the client can be considered unethical and in many cases lead to future client complaints or prevent any opportunity for a follow-up sale.

Sales professionals are client champions within the organization. In this role as client champion or advocate it is the sales professional's responsibility to facilitate and in some cases become directly involved in the completion of the series of projects that need to be completed in order to produce the product or provide the service that was purchased. Sales professionals can be caught in the middle as they work to negotiate sales terms that are in the best interest of the organization and allow for an appropriate profit margin while also striving to meet the clients' needs and gain their trust.

Critical Situation: Ethical Standards— Produce Results in the Long Term

Situation: Sometimes I think I am too honest, and early on in my sales career I thought that slowed me down a bit. But, interestingly enough, I own my own agency now and quite frankly am doing very well; and some of those other guys who did some questionable stuff when we first started are out of the business. As an independent agent I have to collect information and complete an application and send it to the company for review and then they provide me with the price and coverage quotation. Well, for some agents it is not so much a matter of lying as it is just not asking all of the questions they should or maybe forgetting to put everything down (unintentionally, of course) on the application they submit and this can make a potential client look a lot better than they really are. A lot of the agents that do that feel like if the underwriter doesn't ask the right questions they aren't going to volunteer information. That type of stuff catches up with you and after a while the underwriters at the company will start not trusting you, and they will begin double-checking everything you do and sending risk management people to check on everything. If you do get a piece of business by letting stuff out, it almost always catches up to you in a year or two and either the company finds out and increases the premiums and the person shops the account, or their loss history surfaces and they have more claims and they cost you your bonus because of high-claims experience.

Development Issues: There is a fine line between ethical and unethical behavior and many times it is a judgment call based on an individual's own interpretation of a situation. Allowing the pressure to produce sales to influence decisions can allow sales professionals to benefit short term but in many cases questionable actions can have a long-term impact on an organization's reputation and status in its industry.

Action Tips:

- Ask your legal counsel to conduct a miniseminar related to ethical standards and document the questions your sales professionals ask and the responses given.
- Remind sales professionals that it is sometimes better to walk away from situations they are not comfortable with. However, don't burn bridges; try to leave the door open for future discussions if the situation changes.
- Ethical actions may prevent a sales professional from making a sale, but in the long run they will be better off.

DO YOUR SALES PROFESSIONALS COLLECT AND SHARE INFORMATION ON NEW-PRODUCT DEVELOPMENT ACTIVITIES OF COMPETITORS?

The important role sales professionals play in the area of competitive intelligence was discussed in an earlier chapter. Collecting samples or detailed information regarding the capabilities and other specifications of new products developed by the competition can provide valuable ideas and information that can be useful in research and development projects. It is worth noting that all activities in this area of competitive intelligence should be conducted within the scope of what is legal and ethical. All new-product information should be collected in an appropriate manner. The collection and sharing of information about competitor's products should be addressed in the sales training program, and parameters must be established that provide a framework for acceptable behaviors.

New-product development teams can be exciting and demanding. Sales professionals bring a unique perspective to the development of new products. Ultimately sales professionals provide a real-time link to the client's perspective. The challenge for most organizations is balancing the use of their sales professionals' time, recognizing that time spent in new-product development is time not spent selling and anytime a sales professional is not involved in an activity related to selling or servicing a client there is a lost-opportunity cost.

DO YOUR SALES PROFESSIONALS UNDERSTAND THE STEPS IN THE PROJECT-MANAGEMENT PROCESS AND HOW PROJECT MANAGEMENT IS USED WITHIN YOUR ORGANIZATION?

A project is a specific activity within an organization that has a starting and ending point, a formal or informal budget that defines cost parameters, a time frame for completion, and quality standards or expectations. Project management focuses on the completion of a specific project. Projects can be managed by a single project manager, or depending upon the complexity and duration of the project it may require multiple project managers. The discipline of project management is focused on bringing together the necessary human resources, facilities, tools, equipment, and information to complete the project within the designated time frame and financial guidelines. Project-management concepts are currently being applied in a wide range of organizations from manufacturing and construction to service industries like insurance and food service. For sales professionals many of the activities they are involved in lend themselves to the use of project-management tools to help ensure that the project moves forward until its completion.

Projects move through a series of events and activities on a predictable basis that allow project managers to plan accordingly and use a set of tools at each point along the way to monitor and track progress. As projects go through their life cycle they can be broken down into five distinct phases:

1. initiation
2. planning
3. execution
4. control
5. closeout

In the initial phase of project management the project team must come to a clear understanding of what the project is and what the end result of the project will be. In some cases projects are very tightly defined and the project manager can quickly guide the team through the creation of the project definition and frame up the objectives. In other cases the project team may be assembled to focus on the identification of a solution for a loosely defined problem within the organization. When working on a loosely defined problem it is critical for the project team to analyze the problem to make sure the team is addressing the root cause or causes of the problem versus attacking symptoms. Prior to moving into the formal planning phase of the project it may be useful to do a pilot study, conduct research, or run a simulation to test the feasibility. The project sponsor(s) must be involved and confirm the definition and scope of the project.

Once the decision is made to move forward with the project a formalized plan should be developed to guide the activities required to take place for the successful completion of the project. At this point the project team should be assembled. The team should be created with consideration for who will be impacted by the project and the need for any type of special skills or knowledge. Integrating team members from stakeholder organizations can help to ensure participation and buy-in for the project. Plans for how project status will be communicated to stakeholders and team members should be established. During the planning phase the various tasks and subtasks required for the completion of the project must be identified and communicated to individual team members or subgroups of the team. A work breakdown structure is a project-management tool used to identify tasks and their subtasks and to examine who would be the appropriate person for the task and the level of responsibility. The work breakdown structure provides the project-management team with the opportunity to scrutinize the project to insure that tasks are not missed or overlooked.

As the plan for the project unfolds it is logical that the next step in the process is the execution phase. Identification of roles and responsibilities and core processes to get the project completed is essential. Estimating the time required for the completion of each task, its potential impact on other tasks, and the sequence or flow in which the tasks must be completed are all part of this phase. By examining the critical path for each task potential opportunities to save time and money can be identified. At this step in the project-management process past individual and organizational experiences provide valuable input for estimating completion times. As each task is broken down and examined, detailed cost budgets can be created and tasks identified where project delays could occur and cause overruns in salaries and other variable expenses. Other components of the execution phase include working with the client or project sponsor to make any necessary adjustments.

Once the project is being executed it is also necessary to control the project. During the control phase the project manager must take an active role in comparing and communicating actual progress on the project to the standards established in the planning phase. As the project execution and implementation occurs the project manager must focus on the technical aspects of the project as well as the human side of managing a team. In some cases project variances occur and performance is off target from the plan. When this occurs progress must be communicated to all stakeholders. In large complex projects minor variances can be expected; it is important for the project manager and the team to monitor these variances and determine if they will have an impact upon the final project delivery schedule.

The final phase in the project is closeout. The client must formally acknowledge that the project fulfilled all performance criteria and quality standards. Any changes that occurred during the execution or implementation of the project must be acknowledged and signed off on by the appropriate parties. Once all of the final details of the project have been resolved the project manager and the members of the project team should formally review the project for lessons learned and areas for adaptation or change that could benefit future projects. Documentation of the lessons learned can be formalized in a database that is accessible for future projects.

Sales professionals manage a wide variety of projects from the simple to the complex depending on their type of organization. Understanding and applying the basic components of the project-management process can help them to be more effective in their day-to-day sales activities and when they are called upon to lead or participate in project teams.

DO YOUR SALES PROFESSIONALS UNDERSTAND AND ARE THEY ABLE TO USE COMMON PROJECT-MANAGEMENT TOOLS WHEN MANAGING TEAMS OR LEADING PROJECTS?

Project-management tools have many applications beyond their use in larger scale projects. There are a variety of tools available to sales professionals to help them track a wide variety of small and large scale projects. The scope of this book does not permit us to provide detailed information on project-management tools. Incorporating basic project-management training into the sales training program prepares sales professionals to add value to their own organization and participate more effectively in cross-functional teams. The following set of brief descriptions provides an introduction to many of the more popular and readily used project-management tools.

The first tool, the work breakdown structure, allows the project manager to identify each task in the project and its consequent subtasks. The work breakdown structure allows the project manager to coordinate tasks and the team members who will be responsible on a primary or secondary basis for their completion. One way to break down a project is to brainstorm the activities that are needed to accomplish the project objective(s). These activities may then be organized into subcategories and prioritized to the levels needed.

Gantt Charts are simple horizontal bar charts that graph out the estimated times to complete each task in a project and compares that to the actual progress. The Gantt Chart graphically points out to project managers where tasks overlap and the potential need for additional people or equipment. The project activities and tasks are listed in the left column, and the estimated start dates are also identified. Bars indicate the length of the activities as well as the relationship between those activities.

A network (deterministic and probabilistic) diagram is a planning tool and method that lists a project's activities, their estimated duration, and the relationship of the activities. Two network-planning techniques—the program evaluation and review technique (PERT) and the critical path method (CPM)—were developed in the 1950s. Since that time other forms of network-planning have been developed. Figure 16.2 presents a simplified illustration of a CPM diagram. All network-planning techniques rely on a network diagram to de-pict how activities are interrelated and the flow of events. To emphasize the point, project management tools are useful to simplify depictions of events and thereby make them more easily manageable.

Action planning worksheets are simple yet effective tools to help organize and communicate the costs, resources, and timing of key project requirements. Figure 16.3 illustrates the typical layout of action planning worksheets.

These are some of the more commonly used project-management tools. There are several software packages available for each of these tools that can allow users, once they get past the initial learning curve, to create charts and graphs more quickly and in more detail than would otherwise be the case.

Critical Situation: New Product Development—Managing Projects

Situation: In my role as a national account manager in charge of a number of major clients, I've learned over the years that you can spend as much time with a thousand-dollar client as you can with a million-dollar client and no matter which, the success depends on personal relationships. Organizations don't buy, people do. It's important to realize the bigger the client, typically, the more bureaucracy they have to deal with and are thereby less flexible in what they can do. I try and use this to my advantage. One particular million-dollar client had a concept for a new product. Within that organi-zation many people were involved in the project and it required many decision points. As a normal course of business, I asked my contact what it is in the ideal world that they would like to see happen. In this open discussion they describe and essentially outline

Figure 16.2
Network or CPM Diagram

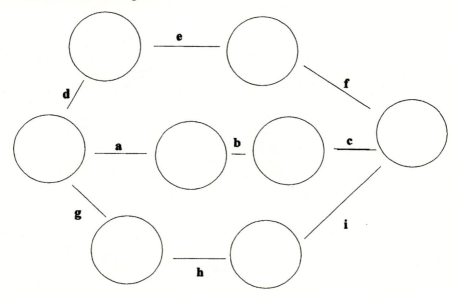

Figure 16.3
Worksheet: Project Action Plans

Action Steps	By	Schedule (by time reporting period)			
		1	2	3	4
1.					
2.					
3.					

Resources	By	$ Cost	Comments
		Budget	
A.			
B.			
C.			

my action plan. As an example, this major client wanted to introduce a new product and was looking for various concepts to present to their new-product development team. What they had in mind was preparation of concept sketches that they could review. Instead, I put our design team to work and not only created sketches, we also developed prototype models of various products. When I presented this to the client, they were ecstatic. It certainly did cost more money to create the models but for me the cost was nominal as I work with a network of freelance consultants who enjoy using their creativity. One of the concepts was so intriguing to them they started calling it by our company name and from there the rest is history. The lesson I would like people to take away is for you to consider your client needs and how you can do them one step better. Surprising them creates a lasting impression and loyalty to your organization. Obviously not all new-product concepts will be a success. However, in the mean time we continue to write orders for our traditional products that we supply the company. Supplying the sizzle works.

Development Issues: Try to look at new-product development from the eyes of your clients and what the barriers are that they need to overcome internally. Examine how you can supply surprising service to them at little cost to you. It is not important for you to get the credit for product development but it is important for you to make your contact within the organization the hero.

Action Tips:

- Look at your client's internal bureaucracy and determine where you can supply surprising service.
- Establish a publications budget for sales professionals and encourage them to subscribe to and regularly read business journals, publications, or technical trade journals.
- Assign a leader or experienced champion to each team to manage the process.

DOES YOUR ORGANIZATION SPONSOR PROGRAMS FOR DEVELOPING NEW PRODUCTS, SERVICES, AND MANAGING PROJECTS?

Where should you start in your quest to help sales professionals develop new products, develop new services, and manage projects? Consult the following checklist of developmental strategies to build competence in this area, then use the sample plan to help build the competence of your sales professionals in enhancing ongoing client and stakeholder informational processes.

- ☐ Offer a new-product development fundamentals course.
- ☐ Review competitor offerings and compare them to your offerings.
- ☐ Conduct a formalized benchmarking analysis of products and services.
- ☐ Ask sales professionals to visit local retail establishments, trade shows, or conferences and bring back creative ideas for your organization to consider for new products and discussion at future sales meetings.
- ☐ Conduct new-product focus groups with clients as well as independent audiences.
- ☐ Ask your legal counsel to conduct an orientation session focused on trademarks, copyright, and protecting your innovations and intellectual capital.
- ☐ Ask your legal counsel to conduct an orientation session on confidentiality agreements, secrecy agreements, and new-product development contracts.

A Sample Program Outline to Guide Developing New Products and Services and Managing Projects

Title: Knowledge of Products and Services

Competency Dimension: Developing new products and services and managing projects

Learning Objectives:

- Communicate insights related to new products and services.
- Demonstrate ability to develop innovative solutions for new business.
- Conduct planning session focused on creative new-product development.

- Describe business reasons for effectively managing projects.
- Demonstrate the use of an effective project-management approach to achieve specific business objectives.

Potential Content Topics:

- Innovative problem solving
- Creativity and innovation
- Breakthrough thinking
- Managing new-product development
- Business ethics
- Project management
- Resource management
- Strategic management
- Sales professional and the law
- Business networking

Afterword

The sections in this book provide an overview of the sales process and a framework to guide the creation or revitalization of a sales-development program. The ideas presented and examples shared are relevant for larger organizations as well as small businesses. The questions in each chapter were designed to allow organizations to examine their current sales training structure and identify opportunities for change and potential improvement. The Competency Development Framework presented is grounded in research and the authors' observations and combined experiences over the past twenty-plus years in business, industry, and higher education.

A comprehensive sales development program can play a significant role in the effectiveness and retention of high-performing sales professionals. As sales managers, small business owners and others responsible for sales staff reflect on the contents of this book, it is important to remember that the purpose of the book was not, as many sales books do, to provide a selling system that individual sales professionals could adopt and theoretically become high performers. Rather, we examined the comprehensive roles of sales professionals in business organizations and addressed in a broad manner the core competencies required to perform in a sales position and provided the essential elements of a sales-development program.

The ideas and issues presented in Part I examined the need for a sales-development program and reviewed the planning and preparation required to successfully create that in-house capability. As we discussed, any type of change initiative must receive top-level support to have a chance for long-term success. The Competency Development Framework provided in Parts II, III, and IV identified a core set of competencies that can be used by sales organizations to create their own customized competency framework that reflects the nuances of the industry or service sector that they compete in. The resources provided throughout the book were included for readers to develop their own toolbox for coaching and training sales professionals. Organizations that rely on a team of sales professionals as their primary source of sales revenue must recognize the need to train and develop that group on an ongoing basis.

Sales are the lifeblood of most businesses, and without them, they will be out of business. Building in-house sales training and development programs for your sales professionals is critical to you and your organization's success.

Customized Job Profile: Client Manager

The customized job profile for a client manager in Table A.1 is provided as an example of a tool that can be used to facilitate the identification, confirmation, and documentation of position-specific competencies and associated skills, tasks, attitudes, and behavioral descriptors.

Table A.1
Skills, Tasks, Attitudes, and Behavioral Descriptors

Competency Dimension		A	B	C	D
Interpersonal selling skills and self-development	1	Makes effective presentations to individuals and groups	Listens and effectively identifies client needs	Demonstrates effective phone skills, planning and call script	Shares information with coworkers and managers
Client communications	2	Maintains regular and ongoing contact	Responds to requests and follows-up	Maintains client database	Provides product and service updates to clients
Negotiation and influence skills	3	Negotiates contracts for win-wins	Closes sales	Maintains positive relationships and uses power appropriately	Understands body language and controls emotions
Resolving sales and interpersonal conflicts	4	Able to resolve conflict and cope with change	Collects data and facts	Addresses customer complaints	Arbitrates and facilitates disputes
Establishing ongoing informational processes	5	Understands importance of collecting and sharing client feedback	Completes required sales call and other client tracking forms	Completes billing and order information	Understands expense account forms and completes properly
Identifying and communicating product features and benefits	6	Understands difference between features and benefits	Takes time to learn about product changes	Knowledgeable of product or service capabilities	Analyzes client information and identifies needs

Table A.1 (*continued*)

E	F	G	H	I
Accepts job ambiguity and is flexible	Sensitive to cultural differences	Communicates effectively one-on-one	Pursues self-development opportunities	
Interfaces with nonclient stakeholders	Ethical and honest in all interactions with clients	Understands and utilizes WEB effectively	Writes professional letters and proposals	
Plans for negotiation and remains objective	Understands structured negotiation	Works effectively in project teams	Makes reasonable requests of coworkers	
Understands conflict resolution process	Appreciates different perspectives and cultural differences	Recognizes when to collaborate or amend expectations	Understands how to get to root of causes of conflict	Works to maintain relationships even after failed conflict resolution
Provides appropriate product and service evaluation information	Understands how the organization's products or services are created	Understands importance of communicating product changes to clients	Understands budgeting and pricing processes	
Aware of potential and frequent product problems	Maintains frequently asked questions file	Overcomes objections objectively	Understands value-added selling	

Competency Dimension		A	B	C	D
Establishing and maintaining a competitive analysis process	7	Identifies and maintains file on top competitors	Maintains product comparison of top competitors	Scans for new competitors and collects and shares information	Collects information on economic performance of competitors
Linking sales and market strategies	8	Understands overall market strategy and business direction	Understands impact of personal performance on overall strategy	Reads company news releases and product updates	Understands organizational and business unit goals
Forecasting, planning, prospecting for clients	9	Monitors regional, national, and international economic environment and trends	Develops accurate sales projections based on data	Analyzes potential clients for financial viability and potential	Monitors regional business information for start-ups and new ventures
Managing calls, time, and sales territory	10	Arranges sales calls and focuses time on proper clients	Develops geographical knowledge of territory	Uses personal planner to track time and effort	Manages multiple priorities
Providing service and managing client relationships	11	Handles all client inquiries and complaints in a positive manner	Knows about important deadlines and how to meet them	Checks on deliveries and tracks schedules	Reviews newspapers and other publications for client information
Developing new products, services and managing projects	12	Communicates client requests for new or modified products or services	Participates in new product development teams	Serves as team leader when appropriate	Manages meetings effectively

Table A.1 (*continued*)

E	F	G	H	I
Reads industry magazines and journals to identify trends and changes	Understands basic marketing and market research concepts	Is ethical in all behaviors and actions		
Understands impact of advertising campaigns and publicity	Communicates value of organization beyond product	Recognizes importance of brand image	Aware of market channels and segments	Works to appropriately position organization in the marketplace
Regularly calls potential new clients	Aware of profitability of products sold	Maintains key prospect file		
Secures new appointments and follows-up on all leads	Schedules regular appointments with existing clients	Uses e-mail, phone, the Web, and video conferencing effectively	Understands breakeven analysis	Monitors, budgets, and keeps client statistics
Develops and maintains multiple contracts with clients	Displays computer and technology literacy	Manages stress and changing business relationships	Displays professional image in dress, grooming, and demeanor	
Maintains high ethical standards	Understands and applies project management concepts	Understands and follows relevant laws		

A Written Questionnaire to Assess Sales Training Needs

The following sales training needs self-assessment is provided as an example of a tool that can be used to facilitate the identification and confirmation of organization-specific training needs. As in the sales process the identification of client (in this case sales professional's) needs is essential in the creation of a sales training program. A sales training program must be driven by client needs. It is essential that the sales professionals participating in the program have ownership in the program content and design.

SELF-ASSESSMENT: SALES PROFESSIONALS' EDUCATION, TRAINING, AND DEVELOPMENT NEEDS

This is a survey about your education, training, and development needs. The results will be used to assist with training and educational planning for your organization. Please do not put your name on this survey. Thank you.

Instructions

Read each item carefully. Circle the number that best fits (1) how important you think it is to performing your job, and (2) whether you have a need for development and training in this area. The lowest rating is 1; the highest rating is 5.

On the last pages of this survey you will be given the opportunity to provide specific information about your job. This information will enable your sales executives to more accurately assess the needs of the group and make recommendations for development. Thank you for completing this survey.

	Importance	Development Need
1. Enhancing Interpersonal Selling Skills and Self-Development—Consults and responds appropriately to the needs, feelings, capabilities, and interests of clients and coworkers; supports organizational values, diversity plans, and vision; provides internal and external feedback; closes sales and provides follow-up; realistically assesses own strengths, weaknesses, and impact on others, and invests in self-development.	1 2 3 4 5	1 2 3 4 5
2. Managing Client Communications—Listens to clients and others; makes clear and effective oral presentations to groups; manages telephone and e-mail communication; develops appropriate proposals; communicates effectively in writing; plans and executes appropriate follow-up.	1 2 3 4 5	1 2 3 4 5
3. Enhancing Negotiation and Influencing Skills—Networks with and provides information to clients, key groups, and individuals; appropriately uses negotiation, persuasion, and influencing skills to achieve objectives.	1 2 3 4 5	1 2 3 4 5
4. Resolving Sales and Interpersonal Conflicts and Coping with Change—Anticipates and seeks to resolve possible confrontations, disagreements, and complaints in a constructive manner; manages conflicts with other sales staff, operational people, and stakeholders in a constructive manner; copes effectively with sales pressures.	1 2 3 4 5	1 2 3 4 5
5. Establishing Ongoing Client and Stakeholder Informational Processes—Creates ongoing process to keep clients and stakeholders informed; communicates organizational methods and procedures; introduces range of products and services and resources available to support the selling process.	1 2 3 4 5	1 2 3 4 5
6. Identifying and Communicating Product Features and Benefits—Demonstrates technical understanding of product features and benefits as well as limitations; able to understand client needs, to communicate value of products and services and to respond appropriately to clients.	1 2 3 4 5	1 2 3 4 5

	Importance	Development Need
7. Establishing and Maintaining a Competitive Analysis Process—Stays informed of industry trends; captures and maintains competitor information; understands impact and uses of different sources and types of information; uses information in decision making.	1 2 3 4 5	1 2 3 4 5
8. Linking Sales and Market Strategies—Stays informed of market trends; links market strategies and activities to sales and promotion; understands relationship between sales, marketing, and business results.	1 2 3 4 5	1 2 3 4 5
9. Managing Calls, Time, and Sales Territory—Works persistently toward goals; organizes, plans, schedules, and sets priorities for sales calls to clients; manages own time and travel efficiently.	1 2 3 4 5	1 2 3 4 5
10. Providing Service and Managing Client Relationships—Actively seeks internal and external client input; ensures client needs are met; continuously seeks to improve quality of services, products, and processes; provides follow-up in a professional manner.	1 2 3 4 5	1 2 3 4 5
11. Developing New Products, Services, and Managing Projects—Develops insights and innovative solutions for developing new business; fosters creativity and new-product development among others; coordinates and manages projects to achieve objectives.	1 2 3 4 5	1 2 3 4 5

Written Comments

Please provide your honest opinions to the following questions. Please do not provide names. We are interested in the issue and how you handled it. Please use the back inside cover for additional writing space.

12. Describe the most difficult challenge you have faced in a sales related situation. What happened? Where? Why?

13. In your opinion, how should such a challenge be met, solved, or avoided?

14. Could education or training help meet, solve, or avoid the challenge you experienced? If so, what do you recommend?

15. What are the most recent sales-related education or training programs you have taken and how have they contributed to your organization's success?

16. Describe the typical challenges you face on a daily basis in sales related situations. What happens? Where? Why?

17. In your opinion, how should such challenges be met, solved, or avoided?

18. Could education or training help meet, solve, or avoid the challenges you experience? If so what do you recommend?

Other Comments

19. Please make any additional comments below that might be used to assist with sales related training and educational planning for your organization.

Consolidation of Action Tips from Critical Situations

The following action tips are summarized from the critical situations contained in each chapter. They are included as a reference guide.

PART I: ESSENTIALS OF CREATING IN-HOUSE SALES TRAINING AND DEVELOPMENT PROGRAMS

Chapter 1:
Defining Sales Staff Roles and Functions

- Document and communicate your organization's sales vision, mission, and goals.
- Clarify and document the roles, responsibilities, and expectations of sales professionals.
- Ask your sales staff what policies and procedures get in the way of serving your customers and clients, and prioritize.
- Review or flowchart business processes that are causing problems; then consider streamlining.
- Hold regular training sessions with your sales staff, conducted by appropriate members of your support functions; that is, accounting and finance operations to discuss policies and define requirements.
- Document and communicate key methods and procedures. Planned training efforts can be a significant part of a retention strategy. Sales professionals are not a plentiful commodity.

- Consider that planned training efforts can be a cheap investment compared to fines, lawsuits, or loss of a major client.
- Take steps to manage changing roles and functions. Change is a necessity and should be managed. Staff turnover can provide an opportunity to facilitate warranted restructuring of roles and responsibilities.
- Ask your sales staff to describe how they currently manage their time. Ask them how much their time is worth in dollars per hour.

Chapter 2:
Identifying Staff Training Needs and Designing Curricula

- Conduct a needs and gap analysis. Ask yourself what skills and knowledge would the ideal sales professional have for a particular position. Compare the desired skills and knowledge to the current skills and knowledge of incumbent sales professionals to determine their needs and performance gaps.
- Identify selected training and development actions that close the performance gaps.
- Segment sales professionals into logical groups to initiate planned development efforts such as new salespeople, telesales, customer service, and so on.
- Set goals and objectives for the selected group(s).
- Assemble exemplary performers from each group to brainstorm critical job-related activities and actions needed to achieve desired performance.
- Document critical skills and tasks needed to achieve goals.
- Establish programs for your critical performance areas. Consider a cross-training or job-rotation initiative plan.
- Consider developing a succession plan for key leadership positions.
- Ask your sales professionals what help or support is needed for them to do a better job of meeting client needs. Organize a representative team to formulate recommended actions.
- Pilot recommendations on a small scale to gain insight and obtain wider scale buy-in.
- Ask your sales staff what the most critical sales situation is they have experienced in their career; then analyze for training needs.
- Ask your sales staff what are the typical challenges they face on a daily basis; then analyze for training needs.
- Ask your sales group what type of learning style they prefer and would best suit their needs. Consider offering multiple training delivery options: classroom, self-paced audio, on-line, and so forth.

Chapter 3:
Planning Learning and Development Opportunities

- Establish a development plan format for sales professionals to input and submit annually. Provide an individual development plan template for your sales professionals to input and track.
- Ask sales professionals to identify education and training opportunities or other learning resources they believe might help them improve their performance.

- Consider weekly "customer service in review" sessions.
- Ask your sales professionals each week what they have done that was exemplary and what they learned.
- Take an inventory of your sales team's technology needs before implementing on-line learning activities.
- Ask your on-line learning provider if the company has a twenty-four-hour help desk, and check out their reputation.
- Consider assigning seasoned sales professionals to provide on-the-job training to new salespeople. Select those who have the skills and patience to explain the tricks of the trade.
- Expose new sales professionals to a variety of your exemplary performers and highlight what it is about those professionals that make them exemplary and potentially good role models.
- Ask your sales professionals who they believe would make good sales mentors or sounding boards. Assemble a list of possible mentors and ask if they would serve in that capacity.
- Match mentors with mentees. Consider how you will reward mentors.
- Proactively identify potential education and training providers in your industry and area and create a database of learning resources.

Chapter 4: Leading and Evaluating an In-House Sales Training and Development Program

- Align performance management and reward structure with organizational goals and objectives.
- Establish a sales scorecard to communicate results.
- Document the exemplary practices of your sales professionals.
- Create a resource guide or instructional manual for your sales professionals.
- Assign one staff member as the communication link and repository for ongoing updates.

PART II: KNOWLEDGE OF SELF

Chapter 5:
Enhancing Interpersonal Selling Skills and Self-Development

- Have all of your sales professionals complete an interpersonal-styles inventory to make them aware of their preferences and others.
- Commission a psychologist to conduct periodic sessions on rejection and stress management. Train and assign coaches to help with daily rejection.
- Offer free assistance and counseling to your sales professionals as they will undoubtedly hit a slump at various times throughout the year.
- Remember, as a sales executive, you are ultimately responsible for providing a safe and positive work environment.

- Ask sales professionals to prepare scripts of typical calls and review them at sales team meetings. Record and document those scripts that are deemed the best.
- Develop a laminated card listing successful selling phrases and tips for your sales organization.
- Develop a listing of successful closing techniques and document them.
- Make sure that your call or presentation ends on a strong, positive note.
- Make a list of frequently asked questions from clients for formalized sales presentations and ask your sales professionals for their input and suggestions.
- Prepare for unsolicited and/or unwanted questions during formal sales presentations.
- Develop a list of responses for your sales professionals to consider using, such as "I'll be happy to address that issue after I'm done"; or, "I'll be happy to discuss that issue with you in private after I'm done."

Chapter 6: Managing Client Communications

- Brainstorm with your sales team how to streamline and maximize client communication. Good communicators make much better sales professionals.
- Establish a communications matrix: clients versus communication methods, and frequency of communication. Ask each sales professional to complete and update an individual matrix plan annually.
- Stress to sales professionals the need to write concise and grammatically correct e-mails.
- Develop an annual action plan for trade shows.
- Prepare a press kit checklist.
- Reinforce to sales professionals the need to ask open-ended questions to uncover client needs, and to ask specific questions if they want a specific answer. Have sales professionals develop a list of common questions to ask clients that will help them get the right answers.
- Ask sales professionals to practice using examples or illustrations, especially striking ones, to enhance their message.
- Consider preparing a set of customizable visuals to communicate desired sales messages.
- Have your sales professionals identify their top ten clients or prospects and ask your sales professionals to observe and document what they see in their clients or prospects' offices or places of work.
- Based on identified client interests, ask your sales professionals to brainstorm a list of inexpensive mementos that might be given to clients with similar interests such as golf balls, pens, notepads, mouse pads, and so forth.
- Use sales professionals that are most skilled at communicating as role models.
- During informal settings or social events, always have your business cards and a pencil with you for networking purposes.
- Establish a process to follow-up and cultivate potential business relationships. Send contacts inexpensive mementos with your name and number on them to remind

them who you are, such as pens, or a post-it note with your company name, logo, and pertinent information printed on them.

Chapter 7: Enhancing Negotiating and Influencing Skills

- Take a supply-chain management course and profile your various clients according to wants and needs.
- Outline the value-added benefits that your base product or service might offer that costs you very little to include.
- Encourage sales professionals to practice listening skills to "read" client needs and identify appropriate negotiation and influencing strategies.
- Teach sales professionals not to concede points without receiving something in return.
- Determine your strategy according to the type of negotiation.
- Don't talk price until all of the other details are taken care of or the situation is understood.
- Share only necessary information. Listen more than you talk.
- Have sales professionals set realistic sales objectives and abandon unrealistic ones.
- Encourage sales professionals to be flexible and patient. It is a sign of strength, not of weakness.
- Encourage sales professionals to study famed negotiators and share insights with you and other members of your team.

Chapter 8: Resolving Sales and Interpersonal Conflicts and Coping with Change

- During stressful situations, it is a good idea to count to ten before responding to potential conflict situations and accommodate minor requests.
- Wait until the next day to respond to negative or critical e-mails.
- Write short, concise e-mails. Saying too much can often times make a potential conflict situation worse.
- Ask your sales professionals to make a list of examples of typical conflicts they experience on a daily basis. Discuss how to avoid and plan for them.
- Ask your sales professionals to describe the biggest or most critical conflict they have experienced in their sales career, how they handled it, and what they would do differently. Take time to debrief and document.
- Remind sales professionals that in hostile conflict situations they have to sometimes think of themselves as actors, not get defensive, and play the role of client advocate. They are being paid to keep clients, not lose them.
- Ask your sales professionals to share how they spot conflict warning signals and appropriate actions for avoiding.
- Encourage your sales professionals to ask themselves why they experience conflict or resistance from clients or other stakeholders. Reinforce that we should never assume we know what people think—ask them.

- Identify those in your sales organization who manage and cope with conflict and stress in a constructive manner and use them as role models.
- Reinforce that resolving interpersonal conflicts and coping with change and stress is part of every sales professional's job. Ask them to keep in mind that technology is changing more today than it has in the history of mankind.

PART III: KNOWLEDGE OF PRODUCTS AND SERVICES

Chapter 9: Establishing Ongoing Client and Stakeholder Informational Processes

- Establish FAQs for your products and services.
- Establish guidelines to ensure everyone in your sales organization is treated equally, fairly, and with respect.
- Ask your organization's department heads to prepare and conduct an educational segment for your sales professionals to highlight the products, services, and value-added of their department or work unit.
- Consider conducting, at least annually, a short course or symposium focused on your products and services and invite selected clients and new employees to attend.
- Communicate to clients or coworkers based on their experience or educational backgrounds.
- Prohibit sales professionals from talking negatively about other units in your organization (sales versus production).

Chapter 10: Identifying and Communicating Product Features and Benefits

- Develop a list of questions relating to the features and benefits of your products that can serve as a lead-in for new sales professionals during sales calls.
- Develop a family of specification sheets outlining features and benefits.
- Create a client-needs assessment questionnaire based or anchored to the features and benefits of your products and services.
- Reinforce to sales professionals that product literature is secondary to face-to-face communication and should be integrated as show-and-tell to support a sales call.
- Explain to sales professionals that they should distribute each piece of literature individually to clients and provide the client a brief description, rather than handing over a packet of information that may never be opened and viewed.

Chapter 11: Establishing and Maintaining a Competitive Analysis Process

- Determine what competitive information you need and want and then develop a database template or format for your sales professionals to use.
- Establish a minilibrary of competitor information and assign one person to be responsible for maintaining it. Consider establishing a database repository for competitor information and designate a single point of contact.

- Ask sales professionals to select specific market areas, and be responsible for monitoring trends and keeping your team informed.
- Inform all sales professionals and staff about the necessity and legality of keeping private information confidential.
- Make a checklist of what specifically your organization considers trade secrets and review it with your staff. Conversely, ask them to be on the lookout for similar information about competitors.
- Conduct simple market research with clients by developing a series of specific open questions that encourage clients to separate their true needs from wants.
- Consider questions to separate how important delivery and price are to the client; these might include "What happens in your organization if delivery is delayed for some reason?" or, "If you could take a whole truckload, we could give you a better price, is this attractive to you?" Doing this will separate how important delivery and how important price are to the client.
- Develop a checklist of action steps to guide new-product development that includes market research.
- Have your sales professionals conduct simple market research on selected products or services to demonstrate understanding and stress importance.

Chapter 12: Linking Sales and Marketing Strategies

- Document and communicate marketing strategies.
- Ask sales professionals to align their sales goals and promotional plans with market strategies.
- Develop a family image and guidelines for all sales and promotional materials that fit with your overarching market strategies.
- Establish specific marketing metrics and a reporting scorecard.
- Visit state and federal trade offices. They can be valuable sources of business development help.
- Ask sales professionals to review and analyze market distribution channels to uncover linkages and sources of sales and marketing information.

PART IV: KNOWLEDGE OF CLIENTS AND BUSINESS

Chapter 13: Forecasting, Planning, and Prospecting for Clients

- Ask each sales professional to develop and maintain a listing of prospects and to prioritize the list. Review each listing on at least a monthly basis.
- Think about your promotional items and use them as an incentive to collect information, not just as a giveaway.
- Ask clients for referrals.
- Use trade shows as prospecting opportunities to target large organizations.
- Purchase or obtain trade show directories in advance and prioritize planned prospecting efforts.

- Establish a formalized reporting structure that can be easily consolidated and reviewed by you and other sales managers on a weekly and monthly basis.
- Search and network for trustworthy agents in various parts of the world of interest to you and your organization.
- Conduct an annual symposium to orient, update, and train not only your sales professionals but also your sales agents as well.

Chapter 14: Managing Calls, Time, and Sales Territory

- Research telemarketing and call-management systems to increase prospecting effectiveness.
- Benchmark your prospecting and call-management activities with others in your industry.
- Establish templates and databases for collecting and consolidating prospect and client information.
- Provide all sales professionals with "To-Do List" pads and ask them to prioritize demands on their time as well as track how they spend their time.
- Prioritize clients according to sales potential. Plan frequency and types of ongoing contact.
- Ask sales professionals to create an annual travel planning calendar to encourage thoughtful travel planning and appropriate frequency of face-to-face client interactions.
- Ask sales professionals to create a listing of tasks that are not time-effective for them to do and can be delegated.
- Establish an annual communications calendar to manage client relationships with multiple communication methods.
- Establish a newsletter for dissemination several times a year incorporating dissemination of product information to be sent at the same mailing.
- Establish a list of client problems or opportunities for improvement that your products or services can help solve.
- Consider asking sales professionals to take turns facilitating sales meetings in order to give them practice conducting formal meetings and facilitating team activities. Ask them to prepare agendas for meetings and provide summary reports to your sales organization and clients.
- Ask exemplary salespeople to share their effective best practices and serve as mentors.
- Implement metrics that encourage add-on sales and capturing of referral information.

Chapter 15: Providing Service and Managing Client Relationships

- Create customized job profiles of critical jobs and processes within your organization. Create an orientation curriculum for each major job process or category that can be communicated to new sales professionals and clients.
- Establish a routine process for obtaining input from clients and other stakeholders relating to the performance of your sales professionals.
- Treat lack of client input as a warning sign.

- Provide all sales professionals with professionally printed "Thank you" cards and ask that they set aside time to write several each week.
- Ask past clients why they stopped using your products or services.
- Brainstorm what tickets (sporting events, cultural events, and so on) might be good mechanisms to build customer relationships and allegiance.
- Treat others the way you want to be treated. Make good on all promises.
- Reinforce with sales professionals that they may only get one chance to make a favorable first impression.

Chapter 16: Developing New Products and Services and Managing Projects

- Encourage sales professionals to develop friendships within client organizations that serve as listening portals.
- Follow a formalized project-management process and establish templates in your organization to aid your sales professionals. Assign a leader or experienced champion to each project team to manage the process.
- Conduct brainstorming sessions with your sales professionals for innovative ideas to repackage your products into multiple formats targeted at new markets.
- Conduct focus groups with your clients and external constituents to give you an honest impression of your products and services and ideas for repositioning them in new markets.
- Ask your clients for feedback before investing a lot in new-product development. Look at your client's internal bureaucracy and determine where you can supply surprising service.
- Set challenging but realistic new product development goals and deadlines.
- Consider the strengths of each of your sales professionals and assign them to selected new-product development projects. Document the scope and desired outcome of individual projects.
- Ask your legal counsel to conduct a miniseminar related to ethical standards, trade secrets, trademarks, patents, and so on. Document the questions your sales professionals ask and responses given.
- Remind sales professionals it is sometimes better to walk away from situations they are not comfortable with. Also, remind them that your organization can't do everything. However explain the importance of not burning bridges and to try and leave the door open for future discussions if situations change.
- Establish a publications budget for sales professionals and encourage them to subscribe and routinely read business journals, publications, or technical trade journals.

References

Alessandra, T., & Barrera, R. (1993). *Collaborative selling: How to gain the competitive advantage in sales*. New York: John Wiley & Sons.

Anderson, P. (1989). Refresher sales training. *Training* (suppl.), 19–22.

A. Fresina & Associates. (1988). *Sales training in America: A benchmarking report on sales training and development practices in 235 companies in seven major industries*. Palatine, IL: Executive KnowledgeWorks.

Asherman, I., & Asherman, S. (Eds.). (1992). *The sales management sourcebook*. Amherst, MA: Human Resource Development Press.

Atkinson, W. (1989). A new approach to sales training. *Training, 26* (3), 57–60.

Baker, J. (1990). How video and film can improve your sales training presentations. In R. Craig & L. Kelly (Eds.), *Sales training handbook: A guide to developing sales performance* (pp. 469–491). Englewood Cliffs, NJ: Prentice Hall.

Basarab, D. (1991). Evaluation of sales training on the bottom line. *Performance and Instruction, 30* (6), 7–12.

Bell, C. (1990). Consulting with external sales trainers: A four-phase process. In R. Craig & L. Kelly (Eds.), *Sales training handbook: A guide to developing sales performance* (pp. 630–649). Englewood Cliffs, NJ: Prentice Hall.

Bersani, M. (1999). A revolution in sales training. *Technical Training, 10* (3), 25–27.

Blake, R., & McKee, R. (1994). *Solution selling: The gridscience approach*. Houston: Gulf.

Boyan, L., & Enright, R. (1992). *High-performance sales training: 64 interactive projects*. New York: Amacom.

Bragg, A. (1989). Prove that you produce sales. *Sales and Marketing Management, 14* (1), 54–59.

Burgas, N. (1989). Going global: What it means to the sales training community. *Sales and Marketing Training, 3* (3), 13–24.

Callahan, M. (Ed.). (1986). Train your sales people for success. *Info-Line*, Stock No. 248603. Alexandria, VA: American Society for Training and Development.

Campbell, T. (1998). Beating sales force technophobia. *Sales and Marketing Management, 150* (13), 68–72.

Cataldo, P., & Cooper, D. (1990). Computer-based and interactive video training technology. In R. Craig & L. Kelly (Eds.), *Sales training handbook: A guide to developing sales performance* (pp. 492–510). Englewood Cliffs, NJ: Prentice Hall.

Cespedes, F., Doyle, S., & Freedman, R. (1989). Teamwork for today's selling. *Harvard Business Review, 67* (2), 44–58.

Christeson, E. (1992). The trainer's role in sales automation. *Training and Development, 46* (12), 67–70.

Coker, D., Del Gazio, E., Murray, K., & Edwards, S. (2000). *High performance sales organizations: Achieving competitive advantage in the global marketplace* (2d ed.). New York: McGraw-Hill.

Corcoran, K., Corcoran, J., Petersen, L., Baitch, D., & Terharr, M. (2000). *High performance sales organizations: Achieving competitive advantage in the global marketplace*. Chicago, IL: Irwin Professional Books.

Costa, J. (1989). Game shows in corporate America: Where business training and pleasure do mix. *Sales and Marketing Training, 3* (4), 16–18.

Cottrell, Dorothy, Davis, L., Detrick, P., & Raymond, M. (1992). Sales training and the Saturn difference. *Training and Development, 46* (12), 38–43.

Craig, R., & Kelly, L. (Eds.). (1989). *The sales training handbook: A guide to developing sales performance*. Englewood Cliffs, NJ: Prentice Hall.

Currie, T. (1990). Practical guidelines for measuring what trainees learn. In R. Craig & L. Kelly (Eds.), *Sales training handbook: A guide to developing sales performance* (pp. 533–547). Englewood Cliffs, NJ: Prentice Hall.

David Michael's stamp is a team effort. (2000). *Beverage Industry, 91* (2), 43.

Del Gazio, E., & Fox, D. (1990). Sources of sales training information. In R. Craig & L. Kelly (Eds.), *Sales training handbook: A guide to developing sales performance* (pp. 583–606). Englewood Cliffs, NJ: Prentice Hall.

Dubois, D., & Rothwell, W. (2000). *The competency toolkit.* 2 vols. Amherst, MA: Human Resource Development Press.

Eady, P. (1988). Sales training—done all wrong. *ABA Banking Journal, 80* (11), 64, 66.

Eline, L. (1997). IBT's place in the sun. *Technical Training, 8* (6), 12–17.

Erffmeyer, R., Russ, K., & Hair, J. (1991). Needs assessment and evaluation in sales-training programs. *Journal of Personal Selling and Sales Management, 11* (1), 17–30.

Erffmeyer, R., Russ, K., & Hair, J. (1992). Traditional and high-tech sales training methods. *Industrial Marketing Management, 21* (2), 125–131.

Evered, J. (1988). Measuring sales training effectiveness. *Sales and Marketing Training, 2* (1), 9–18.

Evered, J. (1990). Developing professional selling skills: The role of the sales trainer. In R. Craig & L. Kelly (Eds.), *Sales training handbook: A guide to developing sales performance* (pp. 3–26). Englewood Cliffs, NJ: Prentice Hall.

Faloon, K. (2000). Adding value. *Supply House Times, 43* (10), 47–48.

Falvey, J. (1988). Do-it-yourself sales training. *Sales and Marketing Management, 140* (4), 77–78.

Falvey, J. (1990). The top ten sales training myths. *Small Business Report, 15* (3), 68–77.

Ferguson, D. (1998). Laying track while the locomotive is rolling: GEIS sales training goes cyber. *Training Directors' Forum Newsletter, 14* (4), 1–3.

Ferrar, P. (1991). Open learning for business success at Bradford & Bingley Building Society. *International Journal of Bank Marketing, 9* (4), 17–19.

Fickel, L. (1998). MicroAge's Internet-based training program. *CIO Magazine, 7*, 2.

Force, C. (1990). Sales training: Hot dogs, peanuts, and interactive video? *Instruction Delivery Systems, 4* (4), 8–12.

Foshay, R. (1988). Evaluating student evaluations: Getting the complete picture. *Sales and Marketing Training, 2* (1), 34–36.

Fox, D. (1992). The fear factor: Why traditional sales training doesn't always work. *Sales and Marketing Management, 144* (2), 60–64.

Games trainers play. (1990). *Sales and Marketing Training, 4* (4), 12–13.

Grant, A., & Schlesinger, L. (1995). Realize your customers' full profit potential. *Harvard Business Review, 73* (5), 59–72.

Greer, M., & McClure, J. (1996). Sales training at resporonics. In *In action: designing training programs*. Alexandria, VA: American Society for Training and Development.

Hahne, C., Lefton, R., & Buzzotta, V. (1990). Measuring training results: Behavioral change and performance improvement. In R. Craig & L. Kelly (Eds.), *Sales training handbook: A guide to developing sales performance* (pp. 548–582). Englewood Cliffs, NJ: Prentice Hall.

Hahne, C., & Schultze, D. (1996). Sales training. In R. Craig (Ed.), *The ASTD training and development handbook: A guide to human resource development* (pp. 864–888). New York: McGraw-Hill.

Harris, E. (2000). Best at sales training. *Sales and Marketing Management, 152* (7), 68.

Harris, E. (2001). Stars in the making. *Sales and Marketing Management, 153* (3), 58–61.

Herr, J. (1992). Sales training—is it the problem . . . or . . . the solution? *Supervision, 53* (9), 7–8.

Hessan, D., & Keiser, T. (1990). The big picture: How to create a theme for your sales training program. In R. Craig & L. Kelly (Eds.), *Sales training handbook: A guide to developing sales performance* (pp. 177–192). Englewood Cliffs, NJ: Prentice Hall.

Higgins, R. (Ed.). (1993). *The sales manager's guide to training and developing your team*. Homewood, IL: Richard D. Irwin.

Honeycutt, E., Harris, C., & Castleberry, S. (1987). Sales training: A status report. *Training and Development Journal, 41* (5), 42–45.

Honeycutt, E., & Stevenson, T. (1989). Evaluating sales training programs. *Industrial Marketing Management, 18* (3), 215–222.

How Xerox Document University keeps the company's sales force on the cutting edge of e-business. (1999). *The New Corporate University Review, 7* (5), 6–7.

Huckaba, R. (1999). Picking up the sales training ball. *Life Association News, 94* (12), 152.

Husted, S. (1990). Sales and marketing education: Programs offered by colleges and universities. In R. Craig & L. Kelly (Eds.), *Sales training handbook: A guide to developing sales performance* (pp. 607–629). Englewood Cliffs, NJ: Prentice Hall.

Immel, R. (1990). Determining sales training needs. In R. Craig & L. Kelly (Eds.), *Sales training handbook: A guide to developing sales performance* (pp. 154–176). Englewood Cliffs, NJ: Prentice Hall.

Jolles, R. (1998). *Customer centered selling: Eight steps to success from the world's best sales force.* New York: The Free Press.

Kaeter, M. (1998). Case study: Creating one team from two. *Potentials in Marketing, 31* (2), 13.

Kahn, R. (1997). 21st century training. *Sales and Marketing Management, 149* (6), 81–88.

Keenan, W. (1990). Are you overspending on training? *Sales and Marketing Management, 142* (1), 56–60.

Kerr, M., & Burzynski, B. (1988). Missing the target: Sales training in America. *Training and Development Journal, 42* (7), 68–70.

Kersen, I. (1990). The learning environment and its impact on your sales training. In R. Craig & L. Kelly (Eds.), *Sales training handbook: A guide to developing sales performance* (pp. 217–241). Englewood Cliffs, NJ: Prentice Hall.

Kerwin, K. (1994, April 18). This is not your father's sales training. *Business Week*, pp. 28a–28d.

Kinney, C. (1990). The manager's role in sales training. In R. Craig & L. Kelly (Eds.), *Sales training handbook: A guide to developing sales performance* (pp. 27–41). Englewood Cliffs, NJ: Prentice Hall.

Kodiyalam, S., Segal, R., & Pathak, D. (1988). Anatomy of today's sales training programs. *Medical Marketing & Media, 23* (3), 8–16.

Koslow, L. (1996). *Business abroad.* Houston, TX: Gulf.

Kotler, G. (1990). Self-study and self-development, flexibility, and learner initiative for your sales training system. In R. Craig & L. Kelly (Eds.), *Sales training handbook: A guide to developing sales performance* (pp. 306–335). Englewood Cliffs, NJ: Prentice Hall.

Kurzrock, W. (1990). Developing and writing successful sales training programs. In R. Craig & L. Kelly (Eds.), *Sales training handbook: A guide to developing sales performance* (pp. 193–213). Englewood Cliffs, NJ: Prentice Hall.

Lafferty, J., & Range, T. (1990). Gaming and simulation in sales training. In R. Craig & L. Kelly (Eds.), *Sales training handbook: A guide to developing sales performance* (pp. 422–438). Englewood Cliffs, NJ: Prentice Hall.

Law, W. (1990). Sales training management: How to develop performance leaders. In R. Craig & L. Kelly (Eds.), *Sales training handbook: A guide to developing sales performance* (pp. 42–67). Englewood Cliffs, NJ: Prentice Hall.

Leigh, T. (1987). Cognitive selling scripts and sales training. *Journal of Personal Selling and Sales Training, 7* (2), 39–48.

Lindheim, E. (1994). Just-in-time training development—DocuTech Production Publisher sales training program (part 2). *Performance & Instruction, 33* (2), 8–12.

Marx, G. (1990). Administering sales training. In R. Craig & L. Kelly (Eds.), *Sales training handbook: A guide to developing sales performance* (pp. 242–269). Englewood Cliffs, NJ: Prentice Hall.

Magee, J. (2001). *The sales training handbook: 52 quick, easy to lead mini-seminars.* New York: McGraw-Hill.

Martin, W., & Collins, B. (1991). Sales technology applications: Interactive video technology in sales training: A case study. *Journal of Personal Selling and Sales Management, 11* (3), 61–66.

Marchetti, M. (1996). Classes drive speedy growth. *Sales and Marketing Management, 148* (11), 33–34.

Mason, J. (1992). No train, no gain. *Sales and Marketing Manager Canada, 33* (4), 7–11.

McClung, K. (1990). Performance systems design: How to develop an instructional system in eight steps. In R. Craig & L. Kelly (Eds.), *Sales training handbook: A guide to developing sales performance* (pp. 125–152). Englewood Cliffs, NJ: Prentice Hall.

McCullough, R. (1990). When and how to use packaged sales training programs. In R. Craig & L. Kelly (Eds.), *Sales training handbook: A guide to developing sales performance* (pp. 650–671). Englewood Cliffs, NJ: Prentice Hall.

McGurer, D. (1990). Staffing for sales training: How to improve your selection techniques and predict performance. In R. Craig & L. Kelly (Eds.), *Sales training handbook: A guide to developing sales performance* (pp. 68–89). Englewood Cliffs, NJ: Prentice Hall.

McLaughlin, I. (1982). *Successful sales training: How to build a program that works.* Boston: CBI.

McMaster, M. (2001). Is your training a waste of money? *Sales and Marketing Management, 153* (1), 40–48.

McNerney, D. (1994). Texas Instruments opens its Virtual University. *HRFocus, 71* (1), 14–15.

Mendosa, R. (1995). Is there a payoff? *Sales and Marketing Management, 147* (6), 64.

Moses, A. (1992). Sales training: pluses & minuses. *Sales and Marketing Management in Canada, 33* (1), 19–20.

Moxley, J. (1993). Delivery of pharmaceutical sales training. *Journal of Interactive Instruction Development, 5* (3), 22–26.

Newman, T. (1990). The case method: Teaching sales managers to make better decisions. In R. Craig & L. Kelly (Eds.), *Sales training handbook: A guide to developing sales performance* (pp. 403–421). Englewood Cliffs, NJ: Prentice Hall.

Parker, R., Pettijohn, C., & Carner, W. (1993). Survey of bank sales training practice. *Human Resource Development Quarterly, 4* (2), 171–183.

Parry, S. (1990). Using role playing for sales training. In R. Craig & L. Kelly (Eds.), *Sales training handbook: A guide to developing sales performance* (pp. 364–402). Englewood Cliffs, NJ: Prentice Hall.

Peterson, R. (1990). What makes sales training programs successful? *Training and Development Journal, 44* (8), 59–64.

Peterson, R. (1992). Selling the sales training. *American Salesman, 37* (9), 9–11.

Pike, R. (1990). Lecture method and classroom: The most frequent method in sales training. In R. Craig & L. Kelly (Eds.), *Sales training handbook: A guide to developing sales performance* (pp. 336–363). Englewood Cliffs, NJ: Prentice Hall.

Quinn, J. (1990). Professional networking for sales training. In R. Craig & L. Kelly (Eds.), *Sales training handbook: A guide to developing sales performance* (pp. 707–718). Englewood Cliffs, NJ: Prentice Hall.

Rackham, N. (1997). ROI for sales training. In J. Phillips (Ed.), *In action: Measuring return on investment*, vol. 2. Alexandria, VA: American Society for Training and Development.

Rapp, J. (1990). Training pays off big for Reynolds Metals. *Sales and Marketing Training, 4* (2), 8–10.

Rasmusson, E. (1998). After the merger: Learning to be a team. *Sales and Marketing Management, 150* (12), 93.

Rasmusson, E. (1999). Getting plugged in: The 5 steps to successful sales force automation. *Sales and Marketing Management, 151* (3), 35–40.

Recchio, J. (1989). How to create a newsletter which addresses and reinforces skills. *Sales and Marketing Training, 3* (4), 22–23.

Retooling sales training for the e-biz world: A four step plan. (1999). *The New Corporate University Review, 7* (5), 1–5.

Richman, T. (1991). Sales training: An in-house sales school. *Inc, 13* (5), 85–86.

Robinson, L. (1987). Role playing as a sales training tool. *Harvard Business Review, 65* (3), 34–35.

Rogers, R. (1994). Distance learning: It played well in Peoria. *Training, 31* (11), 51–54.

Rojas, A. (1988). Evaluation of sales training impact: A case study using the organizational elements model. *Performance Improvement Quarterly, 1* (2), 71–84.

Rosen, J. (1998a). Building a sales training program. *Corporate University Review, 6* (4), 44–47.

Rosen, J. (1998b). Planning a sales training program. *Corporate University Review, 6* (3), 70–73.

Rosen, J. (1998c). The sales training program life cycle. *Corporate University Review, 6* (6). 55–57.

Rothwell, W., Donahue, W., & Park, J. (2001). *A survey about sales training programs* (unpublished survey results). University Park, PA: Pennsylvania State University.

Rothwell, W., Hohne, C., & King, S. (2000). *Human performance improvement: Building practitioner competence*. Woburn, MA: Butterworth-Heinemann.

Rothwell, W., & Kazanas, H. (1994). *Improving on-the-job training*. San Francisco: Jossey-Bass.

Rothwell, W., & Kazanas, H. (1998). *Mastering the instructional design process: A systematic approach* (2d ed.). San Francisco: Jossey-Bass.

Rothwell, W., & Lindholm, J. (1999). Competency identification, modelling and assessment in the USA. *International Journal of Training and Development, 3* (2), 90–105.

Rothwell, W., Sanders, E., & Soper, J. (1999). *ASTD models for workplace learning and performance: Roles, competencies, outputs*. Alexandria, VA: American Society for Training and Development.

Rothwell, W., & Sredl, H. (2000). *The ASTD reference guide to workplace learning and performance*. 2 vols. (3d ed.). Amherst, MA: Human Resource Development Press.

Rottenberger, K. (1990). Sales training enters the space age. *Sales and Marketing Management, 142* (12), 46–50.

Russ, K., Heir, J., Erffmeyer, R., & Easterling, D. (1989). Usage and perceived effectiveness of high-tech approaches to sales training. *Journal of Personal Selling and Sales Management, 9* (1), 46–54.

Sales managers as trainers: More find it accelerates learning curves. (1995). *Training Directors' Forum Newsletter, 11* (8), 5.

Sales training basics. (1993). *Info-Line*. Alexandria, VA: American Society for Training and Development.

Sales training: Keeping ahead of the pack. (1987). *Industrial Distribution, 76* (6), 34–37.

Sales training: Programs for the next generation. (1989). *Sales and Marketing Training, 3* (1), 6–8.

Sales training resources in print. (1992). Alexandria, VA: American Society for Training and Development.

Salisbury, F. (1998). *Sales training* (2d ed.). London: Gower.

Schrage, C., & Jedlicka, A. (1999). Training in transition economies. *Training and Development, 53* (6), 38–41. Available at: http://www.astd.org/members/td_magazine/mem_td_previous_issues.html.

Schrello, D. (1990). Public seminars as a sales training resource. In R. Craig & L. Kelly (Eds.), *Sales training handbook: A guide to developing sales performance* (pp. 672–706). Englewood Cliffs, NJ: Prentice Hall.

Schriver, R., & Giles, S. (1998). Web-based regulatory training. *Technical Training, 9* (3), 36. Available at: http://www.astd.org/members/ezine/tt_index.html.

Segall, L. (1986). Turning order-takers into salesmen. *Training and Development, 40* (1), 72–73.

Singer, W., & Lees, J. (1994). Just-in-time training development—DocuTech Production Publisher sales training program (part 1). *Performance & Instruction, 33* (1), 7–11.

Smith, H. (1990). How to improve your sales meetings. In R. Craig & L. Kelly (Eds.), *Sales training handbook: A guide to developing sales performance* (pp. 512–525). Englewood Cliffs, NJ: Prentice Hall.

Sohmer, S. (2000). Emerging as a global sales success. *Sales and Marketing Management, 152* (5), 124–125.

Spikes, W. (1990). How adults learn: Instructional guidelines for sales training. In R. Craig & L. Kelly (Eds.), *Sales training handbook: A guide to developing sales performance* (pp. 107–124). Englewood Cliffs, NJ: Prentice Hall.

Stamps, D. (1997). Training for a new sales game. *Training, 34* (7), 46–52.

Stolz, P., Majors, R., & Soares, E. (1994). *Sales training: The complete guide.* New York: Amacom.

Technology, 'virtual' instructors help train far-flung salesforce. (1994). *Training Directors' Forum Newsletter, 10* (9), 4.

Urbanski, A. (1987). American abroad: Iveco's man in Yugoslavia. *Sales and Marketing Management, 138* (8), 76–78.

Vaccaro, J. (1991). Planning and conducting a sales training program: A sales manager's challenge. *Journal of Professional Services Marketing, 7* (2), 87–97.

Ward, N., & Wolfson, K. (1990). Coaching and on-the-job sales training. In R. Craig & L. Kelly (Eds.), *Sales training handbook: A guide to developing sales performance* (pp. 273–305). Englewood Cliffs, NJ: Prentice Hall.

Web sales training speeds new reps to work at Electric Lightwave. (1999). *Training Directors' Forum Newsletter, 15* (4), 4.

Weiler, T., & Tuffli, C. (2000). Getting beyond pay in managing "the deal" with your sales force. *Compensation and Benefits Review, 32* (1), 53–60.

Wenschlag, R. (1990). Preparing sales trainers. In R. Craig & L. Kelly (Eds.), *Sales training handbook: A guide to developing sales performance* (pp. 90–104). Englewood Cliffs, NJ: Prentice Hall.

Whitcup, J. (1992). How to choose a sales training vendor. *Sales and Marketing Management, 144* (8), 106–107.

Wills, R. (1990). Effective audio visual media in sales training. In R. Craig & L. Kelly (Eds.), *Sales training handbook: A guide to developing sales performance* (pp. 439–468). Englewood Cliffs, NJ: Prentice Hall.

Zoltners, A., Sinha, P., & Zoltners, G. (2001). *The complete guide to accelerating sales force performance*. New York: Amacom.

Index

ABOUT THE AUTHORS

William J. Rothwell is Professor of Human Resource Development in the Department of Adult Education, Instructional Systems and Workforce Education and Development in the College of Education at Penn State University. Previously he was assistant vice president and management development director for the Franklin Life Insurance Company and training director for the Illinois office of auditor general. He is also president of Rothwell & Associates, a private consulting firm. He is the author of, among other books, *Building In-House Leadership and Management Development Programs* (with H. Kazanas, Quorum Books, 1999).

Wesley E. Donahue is Director of Penn State Management Development Programs and Services, a self-supporting provider of education and training services to business and industry clients around the world. Before joining Penn State, he was regional sales vice president for Mar-Kay Plastics in Kansas City, Missouri; co-founder and executive vice president of Leffler Systems of New Jersey, a manufacturing company; and manager of technology for a Fortune 500 company. He also co-owned and operated a retail business for ten years.

John E. Park is Associate Director of Penn State Management Development Programs and Services with special interests in sales, marketing, and strategic planning. Prior to joining Penn State, he was assistant vice president of Glenn Insurances Inc. in New Jersey; senior casualty underwriter with Commercial Union Insurance, Mechanicsburg, Pensylvania; and commercial underwriter with Pennsylvania National Insurance in Pittsburgh. He has also been involved in all facets of a family business for over twenty-five years.